TWENTIETH CENTURY VIEWS

The aim of this series is to present the best in contemporary critical opinion on major authors, providing a twentieth century perspective on their changing status in an era of profound revaluation.

Maynard Mack, *Series Editor*
Yale University

JAMES FENIMORE COOPER

JAMES FENIMORE COOPER

A COLLECTION OF CRITICAL ESSAYS

Edited by:
Wayne Fields

Prentice-Hall, Inc. *Englewood Cliffs, N.J.*

Library of Congress Cataloging in Publication Data
Main entry under title:

COOPER, A COLLECTION OF CRITICAL ESSAYS.

(Twentieth century views) (A Spectrum Book)
Bibliography: p.
1. Cooper, James Fenimore, 1789-1851—Criticism and
interpretation—Addresses, essays, lectures. I. Fields,
Wayne.
PS1438.C6   813'.2   79-12869
ISBN 0-13-509943-9 case
ISBN 0-13-509935-8 pbk.

PS
1438
J3
1979

Editorial/production supervision by Betty Neville
Cover design by Stanley Wyatte
Manufacturing buyer: Cathie Lenard

10 9 8 7 6 5 4 3 2 1

PRENTICE-HALL INTERNATIONAL, INC. *(London)*
PRENTICE-HALL OF AUSTRALIA PTY. LIMITED *(Sydney)*
PRENTICE-HALL OF CANADA, LTD. *(Toronto)*
PRENTICE-HALL OF INDIA PRIVATE LIMITED *(New Delhi)*
PRENTICE-HALL OF JAPAN, INC. *(Tokyo)*
PRENTICE-HALL OF SOUTHEAST ASIA PTE. LTD. *(Singapore)*
WHITEHALL BOOKS LIMITED *(Wellington, New Zealand)*

Contents

Introduction
by Wayne Fields 1

James Fenimore Cooper: Critic
by Vernon Louis Parrington 13

Fenimore Cooper or The Ruins of Time
by Yvor Winters 16

Fenimore Cooper's Leatherstocking Novels
by D. H. Lawrence 37

Natty Bumppo and Chingachgook
by Leslie A. Fiedler 53

Cooper's *The Pioneers:*
Origins and Structure
by Thomas Philbrick 58

From the Ruins of History:
The Last of the Mohicans
by Terence Martin 80

Beyond Definition:
A Reading of *The Prairie*
by Wayne Fields 93

Love and Sexuality in *The Pathfinder*
by Annette Kolodny 112

Moral and Physical Action in *The Deerslayer*
by Marius Bewley 117

The Unstable Element
by Kay Seymour House 129

vii

Light and Shadow in *The Bravo*
  by Donald A. Ringe   145

Satanstoe: The Case for Permanence
  by H. Daniel Peck   153

"The American Democrat"
  by John P. McWilliams, Jr.   167

The Later Landscapes
  by Blake Nevius   181

Chronology of Important Dates   *191*
Notes on the Editor and Contributors   *194*
Selected Bibliography   *196*

JAMES FENIMORE COOPER

Introduction

by Wayne Fields

When American children are still quite young, many of them become familiar with James Fenimore Cooper's name and face from the card game "Authors." As they grow older, they hear of a character called Leatherstocking and, perhaps, gain a vague sense of his adventures from comic books and television productions. Rarely are they expected, however, as their parents and grandparents were, to read a Cooper novel, an experience no longer thought necessary to an understanding of the American past. True, one or two of Cooper's characters have become part of our popular culture and are familiar (like Daniel Boone and Davy Crockett) as frontier caricatures, but few Americans of any age actually read a Cooper novel—not even one of the Leatherstocking tales.

The irony that a writer dead for more than 125 years should have a face and name better known than any of his literary works suggests the curious position Cooper holds in twentieth-century America and the ambivalence with which even literary critics regard his work. Modern readers are attracted by Cooper's tales of wilderness adventure but are also put off by his language and manner. In our day we favor a leaner, more disciplined prose and expect novels to be more compatible with our everyday experience. Thus we are torn between an attraction to the world Cooper explores in his romances and an aversion to a fiction that seems so antique and unreal. The cost of this ambivalence is an inability to see that Cooper wrote, along with some decidedly inferior works, several of rare beauty. For the student of America, the cost is even greater, since Cooper struggled to understand his country and his countrymen with a persistence and a profundity unequaled by any other American novelist. He attempted much, and if those of us coming to his writings in the closing decades of the twentieth century are to understand the significance of his efforts, we must recognize the concerns, both literary and social, that he attempted to conjoin.

I

In February 1852, five months after Cooper's death, a commemorative service was held in New York's Metropolitan Hall. Appropriately, it was Daniel Webster who had the first and last words. Twenty-seven years earlier at Bunker Hill Webster had called a new generation to the demanding task of nurturing a republic. By 1852 that generation was at last laying down its burden, and so, at Metropolitan Hall, he hailed Cooper—even as, eight months later, his own eulogists would hail him—as one who had dutifully accepted the charge. "Mr. Fenimore Cooper," he declared,

> showed the power, imbued with deep principle, of amusing, and to a great extent enlightening the rising generation, without any injury to their morals or any solicitation of depraved passions. This is his great praise; and what is more honorable, and what is more likely to endure, than the fame that is secured by writings of this tendency—full of amusement and information, founded on our own American habits, on our own American scenery, and therefore likely to go on improving the generations which are to succeed us, and in transmitting the original American character from his generation to the generations which should succeed him?[1]

Even though it comes from one who Cooper himself had insisted was "not a great man—merely a man of great peculiarities," Webster's tribute is an appropriate link between two men who, though profoundly separated by politics, were the giants of those literary genres so important in the decades before the Civil War—oratory and romance. After independence, America's cultural spokesmen, anxious to discover what being American might mean, disdained any birthright derived from modern Europe and insisted instead that the United States was the natural successor to the ancient republics of Greece and Rome. The family resemblance, however, was not immediately evident—especially from across the Atlantic—and had to be made manifest in more ways than naming towns

[1]Fletcher Webster, ed., *The Writings and Speeches of Daniel Webster* (Boston: Little, Brown and Company, 1903), p. 502.

Rome, Syracuse, and Utica. The architecture of neoclassical Washington, D. C. was to dramatize the new country's aspirations, but their highest expression had to be literary. In the old world, republican politics had produced the orations of Cicero and republican art the *Aeneid:* in the new, republican politics and art must produce American versions of these masterpieces—this, at least, was the claim of literary nationalists writing in such journals as *The Monthly Anthology* and *The North American Review.* Webster and Cooper were what they got. There were, of course, other orators, but none of Webster's preeminence; and although it is true that Cooper's novels are not in any formal sense epics like the *Aeneid,* still, as William Gilmore Simms (himself a writer of romances) said, "The modern Romance is the substitute which the people of the present day offer for the ancient epic." Certainly the romance assumes the same vast scope and, at least in America, shares with that older genre the power to provide a people with both past and purpose.

Webster's tribute to the dead novelist suggests a similarity between them more significant than their parallel careers as republican men of letters: They were both representative, often self-consciously so, of the second American generation. Webster praised Cooper for binding those who had been with those who were to be, for "transmitting the original American character...to the generations which should succeed him." If the task of the founding fathers had been to create, that of their children was to preserve and protect, to be the good stewards who could pass on the vineyard, grown even more productive, to subsequent generations. Hence both men interpreted and commemorated the work of the first generation— Webster at places like Plymouth and Bunker Hill, Cooper in such works as *The Spy, The Pioneers* and *The Pilot*—and both warned against the seductive powers of innovation and excess. Both men also understood that their work must be at once aesthetic and political. Consequently, Webster was as concerned with the literary quality of his orations as he was with the political arguments they advanced, and Cooper as much with the social themes that run through his works as with the stories they tell. Both men struggled, too, with the classic American conflict between conservative and liberal principles as they tried to define what liberated people must conserve if there is to be any value in their freedom. But whereas Webster made union the all-important end of that conserving work, depicting it as a great and steady light before which all other issues would subside, Cooper explored the shadows. Although he championed consolidation, he offered no single beacon; his America was to be served by the smaller beams of reason and taste. A Jacksonian democrat who feared a tyranny of the majority, he disdained the oversimplification to which democratic politics are so prone without disdaining the political struggles of a democracy.

II

Robert E. Spiller has observed of Cooper:

> He was the second generation of pioneering stock in the region which he knew; the fifth generation in America; but he was not himself a pioneer. His mind and his ambitions looked downward into the soil and eastward to the older homes of culture. The son of a pioneer, he was himself rather the builder and critic of civilizations.[2]

As Webster observes in Cooper a conjunction of high moral principle with entertainment, so Spiller notes in him an equal sensitivity to the promise and beauty of a virgin land and to the taste and cultivation of established societies. This too reflects the vantage point of a second or middle generation. Midway between wilderness and cultivation, there is the responsibility not simply to exploit the former in the service of the latter but to preserve that which can elevate and inform subsequent generations. To be civilized and still to be "American" is to have the best of both worlds, the one that has passed and the one that is yet to be. But these dual roles are not so easily reconciled. At once novelist and moralizer, patriot and critic, Cooper either could not or would not practice the diplomacy (or artistry) that submerges the moralizer in the novelist and the critic in the patriot. No matter how completely he thought he' had combined these roles (the true artist is necessarily moral even as the genuine patriot is his country's most persistent critic), his countrymen have rarely found them to be compatible.

During Cooper's lifetime his most troublesome detractors concentrated on the conflict between patriot and critic. When in 1826 he sailed for Europe, it was a triumphal departure. The author of five novels in six years, he was at that moment more honored in

[2]Robert E. Spiller, *Fenimore Cooper: Critic of His Times* (New York: Minton, Balch, and Company, 1931), p. 3.

America than he would ever be again. Charles King, editor of the *New York American* and, later, president of Columbia University, offered the farewell toast as New York's elite gathered for a testimonial dinner:

> To the author of *The Spy* and *The Pioneers* we are indebted, not only for much individual gratification, but for much and enduring national renown. It had been said again and again, and repeated until it had almost acquired the weight of a demonstration, that under our system of government, and in a state of society where there is so much equality of condition and of employment—where there are no hereditary statesmen, nor richly endowed scholarships to patronize or to force the growth of literature; where all are engaged in pursuits of necessary industry, and idlers are unknown—it had been said, that the flowers of fancy, and the inspirations of genius, could find no aliment. It was conceded that we might have good lawyers, skillful physicians, ingenious artists, because all these were called for by the everyday wants of a growing and prosperous country; but the regions of fancy, the domains of fiction and of invention, were, it was contended, shut out from our approach.[3]

Cooper left America having played the role assigned by literary nationalists: He had become an ornament to his society, living proof that the finer arts can prosper in a republic more noted for its devotion to the practical ones. He had, said King, looked upon America "with a poet's fancy and a painter's eye" and, in so doing, had dispelled the "inculcated notion that on our soil 'fancy sickens and genius dies.'" Honored as a poet, Cooper departed without any indication that he was, or should be, a critic of the society he was leaving behind.

Seven years in Europe do little for any American's reputation, but Cooper suffered more than most. During those years the social criticism that had in fact always been a part of Cooper's fiction became much more obvious. *Notions of the Americans*, although a flattering presentation of America, is a statement of political opinion, and the nationalistic bias of the work did not conceal the fact that its opinions differed from those popular in Jacksonsonian America. But it was the novels, especially the European trilogy, that made his countrymen aware of Cooper's desire to be more than an ornament. "Naturally," Professor Spiller observes, "his shift from action to inquiry was not popular with the American public. The complaint

[3]Quoted in Spiller, Ibid., pp. 92-93.

was twofold: first, that he had no business to write problem novels of any sort; second, that any sort of criticism of America...was indefensible."[4] Reviews of *The Bravo* led Cooper into an embittered battle with the press that was as much concerned with defining the limits of the fourth estate as with vindicating the novelist. So disillusioned was he that less than one year after his return to America he wrote *A Letter to His Countrymen* and announced his intention to "lay aside" his pen. He did not, however, stop writing, although for a while he concentrated on satire and nonfiction. By 1837, his battle with the newspapers and his conflict with residents of Cooperstown over public use of family land in the Three Mile Point controversy had taken him into the courts and, in 1838, into another novel—or, more precisely, into two more novels, *Home As Found* and *Homeward Bound.*

Though he continued to write at a phenomenal rate for the remainder of his life, at the time of his death the public controversy and the precedent-setting libel cases had upstaged all else. Shortly after Cooper's funeral, Francis Parkman noted "the outcries, not unprovoked, which of late have been raised against him;" and William Cullen Bryant remarked at the New York Commemorative service that in the end, Cooper seemed to have served literature and America best through his litigation: "He put a hook into the nose of this huge monster [the press], wallowing in his inky pool and bespattering the passers-by; he dragged him to the land and made him tractable."

III

Cooper at first fared little better in the more rarefied air of late nineteenth- and early twentieth-century criticism, and for decades was ignored by scholars. But so great was his influence on European perceptions of America and, though we were a long time admitting it, upon our own self-perceptions, that he could not be totally ignored. The most serious critics, however, remained aloof, dismissing him as a ghost from our culture's infancy whose novels were now appropriate only for children cutting their literary teeth. They felt more comfortable pretending that America's literature began with that decade in which appeared the brightest creations of Hawthorne,

[4]Ibid., p. 222.

Melville, Thoreau, and Whitman, a decade that conveniently opened with Cooper's death. For the most part, the twentieth-century view of Cooper harks back to an article published five years before the century began: Mark Twain's "Fenimore Cooper's Literary Offenses." Twain insists, among other things, that in the "space of two thirds of a page" in *Deerslayer,* "Cooper has scored 114 offenses against literary art out of a possible 115. It breaks the record." The talk of Cooper's characters, he argues, is the only thing less probable than the stories in which those characters find themselves.

All of this was worth saying, and it tells us a great deal both about the direction in which Twain and his contemporaries were moving and about their need to free themselves from their literary predecessors. But what Twain's critique does not tell us is how the writings of Cooper work on their own terms. In his attack on *The Deerslayer* we see little more of that novel than we see of European architecture and art in *Innocents Abroad.* What we see is the distance between those works and the no-nonsense American angle of vision embodied in the persona of Mark Twain. Both the humor and the judgment come from displacing Cooper's work and showing its incongruity when seen through Twain's own highly tinted spectacles.

Joseph Conrad, who dismissed the "Literary Offenses" as the work of "that dismal bajazzo," offered intelligent praise of Cooper's fictions but did not significantly divert the drift of critical opinion. Twain's attack was effective because it was outrageous, and it required an equally outrageous defense to counteract, in some measure, its effect. This defense D. H. Lawrence supplied in *Studies in Classic American Literature,* published in 1923, where he hails the Leatherstocking series as the great mythic creation of American literature, singling out *The Deerslayer* as "loveliest" of all. Twain, incensed by the improbabilities of that novel and the inaccuracies of its language, had declared,

> I may be mistaken, but it does seem to me that *Deerslayer* is not a work of art in any sense; it does seem to me that it is destitute of every detail that goes to the making of a work of art; in truth, it seems to me that *Deerslayer* is just simply a literary *delirium tremens.*

Lawrence, without challenging any of the realists' criteria for rejecting the text, ignores Twain's complaints and observes instead, "It is a gem of a book. Or a bit of perfect paste. And myself, I like a bit of perfect paste in a perfect setting, so long as I am not fooled by pretence of reality." Echoing an observation which Parkman had thought a telling complaint, he continues,

> Of course it never rains: it is never cold and muddy and dreary: no one has wet feet or toothache: no one ever feels filthy, when they can't wash for a week. God knows what the women would really have looked like, for they fled through the wilds without soap, comb, or towel. They breakfasted off a chunk of meat, or nothing, lunched the same, and supped the same.
>
> Yet at every moment they are elegant, perfect ladies, in correct toilet.
>
> Which isn't quite fair. You need only go camping for a week, and you'll see.

And then Lawrence adds a line which Twain would never admit to understanding: "But it is a myth, not a realistic tale. Read it as a lovely myth. Lake Glimmerglass."

"Life is life and art is art," observes Conrad at the end of his discussion of Cooper's sea fiction, "and truth is hard to find in either." But of Cooper he insists, "The truth is within him." For Twain "truth" meant representing talk and the world as they "really" are, and he attacked Cooper for being false in both regards. But Lawrence, who declared the Leatherstocking tales "lovely half-lies"— lovely because they are half-lies—put aside "impatience at the unreality" and viewed the novels "as presentations of a deep subjective desire, real in their way, and almost prophetic." Conrad's sense of the truth in Cooper does not ignore the failings Twain observed ("His [Cooper's] method may be often faulty, but his art is genuine") nor does it fail to note the mythic power so important in Lawrence's essay; yet it claims for Cooper a combination of reality with "inspired vision." "The road to legitimate realism," Conrad insisted, "is through poetical feeling, and he possesses that—only it is expressed in the leisurely manner of his time."

A conflict that had been political was displaced by one that was predominantly aesthetic. The early controversy testifies to Cooper's involvement with those questions that were poignantly "real" in his own age, and the social critic, at least the kind that criticizes a particular society, must to some degree be acknowledged a realist. And yet, as the most recent controversy suggests, the artist who works on the broad canvas that we see in novels like *The Prairie, The Deerslayer,* and *The Sea Lions* is moving toward an aesthetic vision that is more universal than Twain's notion of realism tolerates. It is this vision that Lawrence identifies as mythic. If Twain spoke for one of our biases as modern readers, Lawrence spoke for another.

There is no single critical road to Cooper, not just because he wrote more than thirty novels, but because our responses to his work —both positive and negative—are too complicated for any one explanation. The potential richness of Cooper criticism results, in part, from the fact that his work is not guided by an elaborate theory of fiction. A mixture of the naive and the sophisticated, the novels do not embody an abstract definition of art; rather, they are stories in which the struggle to entertain and to inform tests the very limits of both literary pleasure and social criticism.

In the twenties and thirties critics slowly began to rediscover Cooper, though they tended to see him exclusively in terms of either one or the other of those roles which, according to Webster, had been conjoined in the novels. If Lawrence saw the entertainer, Vernon Parrington, in *Main Currents in American Thought,* saw the moralist. And Robert Spiller, the person who perhaps did most to initiate modern Cooper scholarship, accurately entitled his book-length study *Fenimore Cooper: Critic of His Times.* Published in 1931, it provided the first comprehensive—and still today a most perceptive—analysis of Cooper's social criticism.

For other critics the emphasis has been on the mythopoetic writer praised by Lawrence. Drawn primarily to the Leatherstocking tales and the Littlepage novels, they have concentrated on Cooper the romancer. Such scholars as Richard Chase and Joel Porte, in studies of that fictional hybrid the romance, have greatly added to our understanding of Cooper's aesthetic ties to the novelists of the American renaissance, ties that had previously been ignored. Yet another landmark in Cooper criticism is Henry Nash Smith's *The Virgin Land* (a work that any student of American literature must read in its entirety), in which he discusses Leatherstocking as part of a larger pattern of national myth and, for the first time, considers Cooper's place in popular culture rather than in the more elitist realm of literary history.

Depending upon whether they pursue the social critic or the myth maker, most scholars tended to concentrate either on the "white" novels or on the Indian tales. Gradually, however, Cooper criticism has moved toward a more inclusive view, an effort greatly aided by James Grossman's distinguished work, *James Fenimore Cooper: A Biographical and Critical Study.* Kay House has examined in great detail the American types who inhabit Cooper's novels, and Thomas Philbrick, in addition to his other contributions to Cooper criticism, has reasserted the significance of the sea fiction. Howard Mumford Jones, James F. Beard, Donald Ringe, and Blake Nevius have elaborated the ties between Cooper and nineteenth-century landscape painters and have added greatly to our understanding of the novelist's literary techniques. In recent years a number of younger scholars have continued the effort to explore and describe both the diversity and the continuity of Cooper's work. Their scholarship has benefited enormously, of course, from what must stand as the most valuable contribution to Cooper studies, Beard's masterful edition of *The Letters and Journals of James Fenimore Cooper.*

IV

In *Notions of the Americans* Cooper voices the perennial complaint of American novelists, a complaint repeated later in the century by both Hawthorne and James: There is in America a poverty of materials with which the artist can work.

> There is scarcely an ore which contributed to the wealth of the author, that is found, here, in veins rich as in Europe. There are no annals for the historian; no follies (beyond the most vulgar and commonplace) for the satirist; no manners for the dramatist; no obscure fictions for the writer of romance; no gross and hardy offenses against decorum for the moralist; nor any of the rich auxiliaries of poetry.

Yet Cooper managed more than thirty novels, most of which are almost excessively American (even in the eighteenth-century Venice of *The Bravo* he speaks to his countrymen, warning them of the danger of oligarchical power in a republic), reenacting with patriotic fevor the eras of settlement and revolution and shaping a new world vision that superseded all the previous mythologies. He remade the past as no other American had, remolding the views that Europeans had received from the first voyages of discovery, and so great was his success that no one in Europe or America, whatever their regard for Cooper as an artist, could ever again interpret the United States without confronting him.

Convinced that this country denied him the conventional materials for serious literature, Cooper spent his career discovering new subject matter. Howard Mumford Jones, in listing the possibilities that Cooper identified, says:

> He was the first novelist of the sea. He was the first effective novelist of the frontier. He was the first historian of the American navy, and still one of the best. He was the first American novelist to conceive of novels in series. He was the first of our writers to make the succession of generations in a single family the theme of fiction, which he did at least three times. ... He was the first American novelist to make the morbidity of the New England conscience the theme of major fiction, which he did in *Lionel Lincoln* and again in *The Wept of Wish-ton-Wish*. He wrote the first full-dress social utopia in American fiction in *The Crater*, preceding it by the anti-utopia of *The Monikins*. He was the first American to write the international novel, and the first in fiction to treat the Tories sympathetically. ...[5]

To this should be added that he was first in those two genres which are now such favorites in popular literature, the western and the spy story. If this impressive list seems more predictable when qualified by Professor Jones's comment that Cooper was also the first professional man of letters in American literature, it nevertheless suggests the adventuresome spirit with which Cooper attacked the business of writing and the incredible persistence with which he engaged America.

It is precisely because Cooper explored so many literary possibilities that most of the essays collected here concentrate on a single text—this in spite of a tendency in literary criticism either to treat recurring themes or to offer all-encompassing generalizations. As a result, many of the works important to the social historian, like the Home novels, are not discussed. Missing, too, is any study of *The Spy*, the novel that first gained an audience for Cooper. Perhaps even more regrettable than these omissions is the absence of commentary on works of special literary merit whose very titles are unfamiliar to modern readers: books like *Oak Openings* and *The Sea Lions*. Despite this, essays gathered here suggest the breadth of

[5]Howard Mumford Jones, "Prose and Pictures: James Fenimore Cooper," *Tulane Studies in English*, III (1952), 136-37.

the literature and the variety of critical approaches it sustains. They remind us, too, that whatever the prejudice against him, Cooper is an artist worth confronting, even if the confrontation will not necessarily lead to any simple reconciliation of all the themes and forces with which he deals.

The man Webster praised for conjoining amusement and information, the man who attempted to bridge the gap between virgin land and cultivated society and who supported Jackson while he defended natural aristocracy, is full of uneasy alliances if not contradictions. Criticized as incapable of creating believable characters, he created in Leatherstocking one of the most enduring figures in fiction. As a social thinker he tried to fuse the real with the ideal. He honored the genteel and yet, even in the salons of Europe, spun stories of adventure—adventures on the sea, adventures in the wilderness that had been and in the wilderness that, farther west, still remained. All these tensions, even the contradictions, should be familiar to us, for they are quint-essentially American. Cooper was, after all, the son of a man who cleared an estate from the New York wilderness and then imported European trees to line his drive. And so, as Americans, are we all.

James Fenimore Cooper: Critic

by Vernon Louis Parrington

Fenimore Cooper is one of the puzzling figures of his generation. In his substantial character was embodied what may well
appear no more than a bundle of contradictions. Romancer and
social critic, feudal-minded yet espousing a republican faith, he
pretty much baffled his own generation in its testy attempts to
understand him, as he has pretty much baffled later times. No
other major writer, unless it be Whitman, has been so misunder-
stood, and no other offers a knottier problem to the student of
American letters. The stubborn clay of his nature was molded to a
pattern unlike that of his fellows, and the difference was long ac-
counted to him as a grave shortcoming. His outspoken individualism was a constant irritant to a sensitive majority, and his aloof-
ness from the common enthusiasms was reckoned no better than
treason to his native land. The right of the individual to question
the herd pronouncements was a right not acknowledged by the
herd, and the more it tried to silence Cooper's tongue the more
caustic and loquacious it became. He refused to be silenced though
it should come to open warfare. His later years in consequence were
rendered unhappy by a thousand petty vexations, and his creative
work was brought only this side of shipwreck.

How and why so great a misadventure befell him are questions of
prime importance to which little attention has been given. That his
tacklessness was at fault is commonly believed—his tacklessness and
a certain pugnacious virtue that would inculcate righteousness by

"James Fenimore Cooper: Critic." Excerpted from Vernon Louis Parrington, *The
Romantic Revolution in America* Main Currents in American Thought, vol. II.
(New York: Harcourt Brace and World), pp. 214-16 and p. 229. Copyright, 1927, by
Harcourt Brace Jovanovich, Inc.; renewed, 1955, by Vernon L. Parrington, Jr.,
Louise P. Tucker, Elizabeth P. Tucker. Reprinted by permission of the publishers.

means of a broken head. But such an explanation, true enough so far as it goes, does not go far enough. The trouble lay deeper than that; it lay in the mind of Cooper himself, in the doubts and uncertainties that dwelt side by side with stubborn dogmatisms, troubling his speculations and perplexing his plainest counsels. And that trouble must be traced to an underlying conflict between the man and his age, between the ideal and the real, between high loyalties and petty fact. Fenimore Cooper was the barometer of a gusty generation, sensitive to every storm on the far horizon. No other observer of that changing generation suffered so keenly in mind and conscience from the loosening of ancient ties, and none labored so hard to keep his countrymen to the strait path of an old-fashioned rectitude. His busy life covered the middle years of the great shift from an aristocratic order to a capitalistic order, and this revolutionary change provided him ample materials for brooding speculation. At every turn in the road fresh doubts assailed him. The perplexities and dogmatisms that clutter so many of his later pages, playing havoc with his romantic art, are a testimony to the confusions of a generation in the midst of epic changes. As honest a man as ever spoke his mind frankly, he endeavored to reconcile the irreconcilable, and establish sure standards amid the wreck of all standards. He could not drift. He must discover some working agreement between the old America and the new, between the reputed excellencies of the traditional aristocratic order, and the reputed justice of the democratic ideal. But unfortunately for this difficult business he was temperamentally ill-equipped. He was always at war with himself. His loyalties and his conscience ran at cross-purposes. His mind was packed with prejudices as an egg with meat. He was too partisan to compromise, and too honest to be content with the shoddy. His instinctive romanticisms were always being buffeted by fact, and his troubled mind in consequence was forever constructing laborious defense-mechanisms.

For those deep confusions that marred his later work and brought such bitter misunderstanding upon him, his heritage was much to blame. A romantic at heart, he was out of sympathy with the dominant romanticisms of his generation. Certain hold-overs from the past held him back from hearty participation in the present. He loved the world that was falling into decay too much to put away its virtues with its smallclothes; he would preserve what was excellent in the old to enrich and dignify what was excellent in the new; he would have the young democracy learn the decorum of a staid aristocracy. It is this fond lingering between worlds that sets Cooper apart from his fellows. He was an English squire of the old school turned republican, who did not quite like the company he found himself in. He was equally puzzled at the bumptious leveling of the coonskin democracy, and the exploitative spirit of Wall Street Whiggery. But though he railed at the newfangled ways with the testiness of a squire, he was too confirmed a republican, too deeply concerned that the great venture in republicanism should demonstrate its wisdom, to overlook its shortcomings. He would have it be so true to its ideal that the world would acknowledge its excellence. He could not circumscribe his duties to election-day hurrahs; he must ferret out treason in the market place; he must be faithful in counsel though he utter unwelcome truths. It was the very faithfulness of Cooper to his conception of an ideal republic that brought him into collision with his fellows and filled his later days with bitterness. ...

Like Hugh Henry Brackenridge before him, Cooper was a democrat who criticized the ways of a reputed democracy because of his love for an ideal republic. Too few of his kind have arisen in America; too few who dare to speak their minds unterrified by public opinion. An individualist of the old English breed, he could not be intimidated or coerced in the matter of his rights by any clamor, whether of newspapers or mobs. He had his shortcomings in plenty, both as romancer and critic. Testy, opinionated, tactless, forever lugging in disagreeable truths by the ears, he said many wise things so blunderingly as to make truth doubly offensive, and he hewed at his art so awkwardly as well-nigh to destroy the beauty of his romance. Yet the more intimately one comes to know him, the more one comes to respect his honest, manly nature that loved justice and decency more than popularity. His daily life became a long warfare with his fellows, who exacted of him a great price for his idealism; but later generations should love him none the less for the battles he fought. That America has been so tardy in coming to know him as a man and a democrat, as well as a romancer, is a reflection upon its critical acumen.

Fenimore Cooper or The Ruins of Time

by Yvor Winters

"From this point the northern side of the bay is a confused mass of villages, villas, ruins, palaces, and vines,
until we reach its extremity; a low promontory, like its opposite neighbor. A small island comes next, a sort of natural sentinel; then the coast sweeps northward into another
and smaller bay, rich to satiety with relics of the past,
terminating at a point some miles farther seaward, with a
high, reddish, sandy bluff, which almost claims to be a
mountain."

— WING-AND-WING

Since the publication of Robert Spiller's admirable work on
Cooper,[1] his importance as a social critic has been generally recognized; his literary virtues have had in the past their distinguished
admirers, though today his reputation as a literary artist is very
much in eclipse. Of these virtues Mr. Spiller, who has done more for
him than has any other critic of our period, says relatively little, and
it may be profitable to attempt a redefinition of them in part in the
light of Mr. Spiller's examination of the social theories.

Cooper believed in democratic government; and, as an aggres-
sively patriotic American, he was capable, among the enemies of
democratic theory, of going to considerable length in its defense;
but he distrusted the common and uneducated man—that is, he
feared irrational mob action; he feared that the idea of democracy
might easily be degraded into the dogma that whatever a majority

[1]*Fenimore Cooper, Critic of His Times,* by Robert E. Spiller; Minton Balch and
Co., 1931.

decides is right. Such a degradation would result naturally in the immediate subversion of law and of civilization; and it would open the way for all kinds of illegal individual action, which might in turn lead to the acquisition by a few uneducated and unscrupulous men of great power, either by way of finance or by way of demagoguery— that is, he saw that it might be only a short step from irrational democracy to unscrupulous oligarchy. In such works as *The Redskins, Home as Found,* and *The Ways of the Hour*—extremely bad novels, all of them, but extremely acute criticism of his period and of ours—he portrays and more particularly he comments directly upon the incipient symptoms of the disease which he intensely feared, even though he did not and could scarcely have been expected to foresee the rapidity and extent of its development. In *The Bravo,* in so far as the book is to be regarded merely as a social novel, he depicts the evils of oligarchy; within a decade of his death, the oligarchy of which he had discerned the first symptoms was developing with astonishing rapidity, and within two decades of his death it had as regards practical results rendered the legal government very largely null, and the nation was adrift in the administration of U. S. Grant.

The nature of this development he understood well enough; with characteristically heavy but accurate irony, he described it in the pages of his neglected satirical allegory, *The Monikins,* a work which contains much of his ablest prose: "I found...that the wisest and best of the species, or, what is much the same thing, the most responsible, uniformly maintain that he who has the largest stake in society is, in the nature of things, the most qualified to administer its affairs. By a stake in society is meant, agreeable to universal convention, a multiplication of those interests which occupy us in our daily concerns—or what is vulgarly called property. This principle works by exciting us to do right through those heavy investments of our own which would inevitably suffer were we to do wrong. The proposition is now clear, nor can the premises readily be mistaken. Happiness is the aim of society; and property, or a vested interest in society, is the best pledge of our disinterestedness and justice, and the best qualification for its proper control. It follows as a legitimate corollary, that a multiplication of those interests will increase the stake, and render us more and more worthy of the trust by elevating us as near as may be to the pure and ethereal condition of the angels." This may fairly be taken as a prophecy of the approach, if not of the imminence, of celestial luminaries of the quality of Vanderbilt, Sage, Drew, and Gould.

As a check to the social danger, he envisaged two defenses, both of which were more or less in effect at the time of his writing and both of which crumbled at the first impact of the enemy in the actual event: abstract principle, as embodied in law, especially in the courts; and the extension into other parts of the country, and the perpetuation, of an hereditary landed aristocracy such as that of New York—of a class wealthy enough to enjoy leisure for study and for self-cultivation, yet not wealthy enough, and too cultivated to desire, to obtain inordinate power for its own sake. This aristocracy should serve as a guide, a model, and a stabilizing force; it was the class of which his American Gentleman was the type. In the Littlepage trilogy he made his most ambitious and successful effort to portray this aristocracy as it had existed in New York and to define its social function.

In connection with this check to the danger, he seems to have been guilty of certain errors. He failed to see that because of technological and industrial growth and because of the westward expansion which was receiving only at the time of his death the rapid acceleration which was to effect in three decades the greatest migration in the annals, whether written or reconstructed, of man, a new financial oligarchy was bound to arise so rapidly as to render his landed aristocracy negligible and casually to feed upon and absorb it. Further, he apparently believed it possible to establish in actual social institutions a close relationship between worth and ability on the one hand, and, on the other hand, wealth, family, and political influence, whereas all history indicates this to be impossible. At the end of his life, he still preferred democratic government to any other, but he had little hope for democracy. Spiller quotes the following passage from a posthumous fragment:[2] "Nevertheless the community will live on, suffer, and be deluded; it may even fancy itself almost within reach of perfection, but it will live on to be disappointed. There is no such thing on earth—and the only real question for the American statesman is, to measure the results of different defective systems for the government of the human race. We are far from saying that our own, with all its flagrant and obvious defects, will be the worst, more especially when considered solely in connection with whole numbers; though we cannot deny, nor do we wish to conceal,

[2]Ibid., pages 315-6.

the bitterness of the wrongs that are so frequently inflicted by the many on the few. This is, perhaps, the worst species of tyranny. He who suffers under the arbitrary power of a single despot, or by the selfish exactions of a privileged few, is certain to be sustained by the sympathies of the masses. But he who is crushed by the masses themselves must look beyond the limits of his earthly being for consolation and support. The wrongs committed by democracies are of the most cruel character; and though wanting in that apparent violence and sternness that mark the course of law in the hands of narrower governments, for it has no need of this severity, they carry with them in their course all the feelings that render injustice and oppression intolerable."

Of these wrongs he himself had suffered more than the common portion. Out of love for his country and the desire to perpetuate her institutions, he had criticized such of her vices as appeared to imperil her life, and he had been met with hatred. His criticism being unanswerable, and the hatred therefore intense, he had been libelled in the press, and though for fifteen years he had won suit after suit in the courts and had silenced his detractors, the press had won the sympathy of the multitude and Cooper had lost his public. He had defined for posterity the dangers which threatened; and he had established in legal precedent that was to endure until late in the century the laws of libel and the public rights of the private gentleman; but he knew at the end that he could not stay or turn the enchanneled torrent of human stupidity, which, when eventually we regard it behind us, we know as history. His concern was primarily for public morality; it was the concern of the statesman, or of the historian, first, and of the artist but secondarily; this concern was already obsolescent in America, and Henry Adams found it a generation after Cooper's death to be obsolete. Its disappearance, no less than the disappearance of the theological dogmas supporting private morality, contributed in some measure to the later difficulties of Henry James.

II

The Littlepage novels—*Satanstoe*, *The Chainbearer*, and *The Redskins*— were written to illustrate a thesis: the justice of the property-rights of the landed proprietors. But underlying this is a more general thesis: the social function of an aristocracy, a concept based on the old but dying social organization of New York. To illustrate this thesis, he was forced to contrast the virtues of the aristocracy with the defects of the vulgar; that this contrast represented not his own complete view of the two social classes thus roughly divided but an arbitrary isolation of qualities in each class for purposes of expository effectiveness, we may see readily enough in his other novels: in his novels of adventure, his favorite characters are drawn from the lower classes, and in *The Bravo,* another thesis novel, this one written to exhibit the dangers of oligarchy, his heroic figures are drawn from the lower classes and his corrupt from the upper.

Like most novelists of class-struggle, he separated his characters pretty sharply into the more or less Calvinistical categories of the socially saved and the socially damned. The only American novel of class-struggle of any importance, and so far as my reading extends, to surpass this formula, is *The Octopus,* by Frank Norris; a novel in which the social struggle sets in motion and complicates certain dramas of private morality, so that we get a novel of a very impressive kind in spite of the illiteracy of two thirds of the writing, and in spite of the plunge into Emersonian mysticism at the close, in which the author endeavors to cancel the drama that he has constructed. Since Cooper is dealing primarily with manners and not with morals—that is, with society as such, and not with the salvation of the soul—his figures must of necessity be offered as representative social types and not as moral abstractions like the figures in Hawthorne.

They are types of manners, and not types of morality; they are thus closer to the surface of life, to the daily reality which we perceive superficially about us; and we are tempted—or more truly, we are forced—to regard them as human beings primarily, not as dramatized ideas. But as human beings they are unduly simplified, and in their purity of type inheres a certain quality, very slight in a few cases, very great in a few, and moderately obvious in most, of priggishness or of unreality. Furthermore, the dichotomy of Good and Evil in Hawthorne is essentially so serious that the extreme concentration upon it which is implicit in allegorical simplification appears justified. The corresponding concepts in the field of manners, however,—the Genteel and the Vulgar—appear at a considerable remove from the spiritual seriousness of the Good and the

Evil; we can demonstrate certain imperfect relationships between the two pairs of concepts easily enough in a rational fashion, but the second pair is derivative and therefore inferior, and it is bound to be felt as inferior when perceived in action; so that a concentration by Cooper upon the second pair of abstractions comparable, though far less intense, to the concentration upon the first pair by Hawthorne, is certain in itself to create in some degree an atmosphere of priggishness. The vigor with which Cooper realizes at least a few characters and patterns of action, and the sense with which he leaves us when the books have long been read and laid away, of a rich and varied way of life, are sufficient evidence of the reality of his genius, for these ends are achieved in the face of obstacles.

This effect of priggishness is sure to be intensified in an era like our own, in which the concept of a traditional aristocracy is obsolete and even as an historical phenomenon is seldom understood. For the modern American who has let himself be seduced by any of the absolute categories of our own period—more especially, in this case, of the radical labor movement, since these categories are diametrically opposed to those of Cooper—an understanding of Cooper, and I mean an understanding of Cooper merely as an artist portraying in some measure a life which he knew, may prove difficult or even impossible. Cooper's dichotomy of the Genteel and the Vulgar may appear to correspond precisely to the later dichotomy of the Parasitic and the Productive, the emphasis having been shifted from intrinsic qualities to what is conceived as material effectiveness. For any modern American, an act of sympathetic historical imagination is necessary to understand Cooper; for the American whose perceptions are governed by a scheme as simple as Cooper's, but the exact reverse of it, this act will presumably be impossible.

Because of the simplification, the central figures of the Littlepage novels—the Littlepages and their respective loves—were doomed to be uninteresting, even if Cooper had not had an unqualified penchant for conventional sentimental romance as the structural principle in plot. The secondary figures, even when employed more or less obviously for illustrative purposes, are frequently more successful. The best single creation of the Littlepage novels—a creation rivalling Natty Bumppo—is Jason Newcome, the devious and moralizing New Englander. In *Satanstoe,* the secondary and tragic love affair of Guert Ten Eyck and of Mary

Wallace is moving and suggests complexity and fullness of character not found in any other love story in Cooper. Guert, Mary Wallace, the loping dominie, Andries Coejemans, and in a smaller measure the somewhat melodramatic but still effective Aaron Thousandacres, are memorable creations.

In the first two novels, especially, of the Littlepage trilogy, Cooper endeavored to underline certain aspects of New York society which he believed deserving of preservation and extension; and in the third of the series, *The Redskins,* he sought primarily to demonstrate the opposing evil, the evil of confusing the whim of the mob with the principle of democracy, a subject with which he dealt in other late novels: in *The Crater,* in *Home as Found,* and especially in *The Ways of the Hour,* a novel in which is portrayed in a manner of the greatest accuracy so far as the social phenomena are concerned, though profoundly unsatisfactory as art, the way in which criminal justice may be subverted by unrestrained popular meddling. In *The Redskins, Home as Found,* and *The Ways of the Hour* Cooper is nearly at his worst as a novelist—his worst, absolutely considered, is the initial effort, *Precaution,* and its nearest rival, perhaps, is *Mercedes of Castille*—for in these three works, he is not displaying a way of life, but is demonstrating assorted vices and his tendency to overemphasis becomes so extreme as to destroy both plot and character. The criticism offered in these books, however, is both just and penetrating, and the reader with taste and patience can cull from them if he so desires a collection of epigrams as sound, as biting, and as numerous as he is likely to find in any other three volumes in English. *The Monikins,* a satirical allegory on the subject of various social systems, though tiresome in the main, offers the same fragmentary rewards, and perhaps in a larger measure, in addition to the remarkable summary of the life and death of the elder Goldencalf, with which the work begins.

The Monikins has commonly been regarded as one of the worst of Cooper's efforts, and even those who have found it in one manner or another interesting have objected to the narrator's account of his pedigree and of his childhood, but there is something horrible in the account, which, brief and fragmentary as the passage may be, is unrivalled in its particular fashion in English prose. "I have generally considered myself on a level with the most ancient gentlemen of Europe, on the score of descent," says the narrator, "few families being more clearly traced into the mist of time than that of which I am a member. My descent from my father is undeniably established by the parish register as well as by the will of that person himself, and I believe no man could more directly prove the truth of the whole career of his family than it is in my power to show that of my ancestor up to the hour when he was found, in the second year of his age, crying with cold and hunger in the parish of St. Giles, in the city of Westminster, and in the United Kingdom of Great Britain." In the same tone of precise and unwavering respect, the career of the elder Goldencalf, financial and domestic, and fearful in its intense inhumanity, is carried to its close: "The difficult breathing, haggard countenance, and broken utterance of my father struck me with awe. This was the first death-bed by which I had ever stood; and the admonishing picture of time passing into eternity was indelibly stamped on my memory. It was not only a death-bed scene, but it was a family death-bed scene. I know not how it was, but I thought my ancestor looked more like the Goldencalfs than I had ever seen him look before." Thomas Goldencalf is literally on the brink of eternity throughout the short narrative; for, as his son, the supposed narrator, informs us, he rose directly and with no antecedents from the obscurity of time, and his life was reduced so purely to a single passion, one might say to a single perception, that he existed but as a silhouette upon the void and sank as directly into the void as he had arisen from it. The cold and formal irony of the prose achieves at times a metaphysical violence which puts one in mind of Pope.

The Bravo, one of the most important of the novels of social criticism, suffers in certain respects by comparison with the first two novels of the Littlepage trilogy: no single Italian character is realized with the same effect of intimacy as that achieved in the best American characters, although no major character, perhaps, is quite so simplified as are the representatives of the Littlepage family itself, for the conception of *The Bravo* does not enforce such simplification. The protagonist is a more or less normal man, endeavoring to maintain his integrity in a struggle with a variety of hidden evils. He is essentially active and individual, and not a social type, although the subtleties of his surface are not rendered with any such perception as that displayed in the creation of Jason Newcome and of Guert Ten Eyck. The manner in which the aristocrats themselves are corrupted by their fears of each other—the subtle inter-relation and inter-propagation among such vices as avarice, desire for power, and fear—offers a moral portrait worthy of Hawthorne.

The stylistic tone of *The Bravo* is of the slightly sentimental variety at the time regarded as indispensable to historical romance; this is no doubt a defect, but the tone is at least consistently maintained, so that once one has become familiar with it, one can in a measure forget it, and can appreciate subtleties of perception much as in any other style. The fifteenth chapter, for example, describing the murder of Antonio, is very impressive as one comes to it in the actual narrative, but is much less impressive if one reads it in isolation. Coming to it from the beginning of the story, one is not only familiar with the style, but one is acutely aware of the symbolic value of the moonlit water, and of fragments of action discernible upon it, in this narrative of secret and evasive evil. In isolation the passage appears to display something of the over-wrought affectation of Poe; in its context, the tone is supported, as it is never supported in Poe, by a comprehensible theme, so that the details, melodramatic, perhaps, if read alone, are sustained by a genuinely dramatic significance. The two companion pieces of *The Bravo, The Heidenmauer* and *The Headsman,* are less remarkable, though *The Heidenmauer* contains a fairly memorable character in the Abbot of Limburg.

III

In the Leatherstocking Series, as in the other novels of American history and of frontier adventure, and as in the sea stories (except *The Crater),* we have nothing whatever to do with social criticism, or at least nothing of importance. One of the Leatherstocking Series, however, *The Pioneers,* the fourth in the series but the first to be written, should be mentioned in connection with *Satanstoe* and *The Chainbearer* as one of Cooper's three most interesting novels of manners; like the first two Littlepage novels, it is a portrait of life on the frontier, but in a considerable measure of the semi-aristocratic frontiersman. These three works should be regarded as a prelude to such works by Mrs. Wharton as the four novelettes of the Old New York Series and *The Age of Innocence;* in spite of great defects they have great vigor, and as regards the portrayal of their particular place and period they have no rivals and must always remain as a part of our historical literature if as nothing more.

The inferiority of plot in Cooper to the incidental is tacitly recognized by him in the fact that the one figure who unifies all five of the Leatherstocking novels is a secondary figure in all of them; in each novel he is the practical abettor of the loves of the pair about whom the conventional plot is constructed, although in *The Pathfinder* he appears for a time as a rival in love to his friend.

These novels are familiar to every reader, and comment upon them may appear superfluous; nevertheless, familiarity appears to have bred in this case a good deal of contempt, and certain things, perhaps, need to be stated briefly.

It is the isolated adventures of Natty, and the continuity of his character, that bring the novels to life; although there are other excellent characterizations, especially of the residents of the frontier village of *The Pioneers,* and of the Indians Mahtoree and Hardheart, and of the emigrant family of *The Prairie.* And here we begin to encounter some of the strange paradoxes of Cooper's achievement; for if Natty is his greatest single achievement—and great he is, a great national myth, with a life over and above the life of the books in which he appears, a reality surpassing that even of an historical figure such as Daniel Boone—yet only two of these novels, *The Pioneers* and conceivably *The Prairie,* could rank among Cooper's half dozen best individual novels. Furthermore, the best single passage of prose in Cooper is probably the seventh chapter of *The Deerslayer,* a book which displays few other serious merits, and which even as a story purely of adventure is far inferior in plot and in movement to half a dozen other stories by Cooper. The next best prose in the series, and perhaps in Cooper, though this is doubtful, is probably to be found in the first and last chapters of *The Prairie,* heavily dramatic as they may conceivably be. The best single plot of adventure in Cooper is beyond a doubt that of *The Last of the Mohicans,* but the style in this work is so consistently florid and redundant that in spite of the action, in spite of the magnificent timing of many scenes, in spite of a certain amount of fairly respectable characterization, the book nowhere rises to a level of seriousness. It is curious that the tone of conventional romance which vitiates a great part of his effort should have accumulated so unfortunately here, for there are passages in other books in the series which are not only beautiful but beautiful in a restrained and classical fashion, and which display great richness of moral substance.

The seventh chapter of *The Deerslayer,* or more properly its first incident, Natty's encounter with the Indian whom he is forced to kill, is probably as great an achievement of its length as one will find in American fiction outside of Melville. The prose is plain and factual, yet by rendering with a kind of bare precision the drifting of the canoes, the motion of the water, and the caution with which Natty views the edge of the forest, Cooper communicates with a power that has rarely been equalled the tremendous and impersonal quiet of the virgin American wilderness: "The air, for wind it could scarcely be called, was still light, it is true, but it had increased a little in the course of the night, and as the canoes were mere feathers on the water, they had drifted twice the expected distance; and, what was still more dangerous, had approached so near the base of the mountain that here rose precipitously from the eastern shore as to render the carols of the birds plainly audible. This was not the wòrst. The third canoe had taken the same direction, and was slowly drifting toward a point where it must inevitably touch, unless turned aside by a shift of wind or human hands. In other respects nothing presented itself to attract attention or to awaken alarm."

One of the canoes goes aground, and Natty must rescue it, in spite of the danger to himself, in order to insure the safety of his friends. "If anyone had been lying in wait for the arrival of the waif, he must be seen, and the utmost caution in approaching the shore became indispensable; if no one was in ambush, hurry was unnecessary. The point being nearly diagonally opposite the Indian encampment, he hoped the last, though the former was not only possible but probable; for the savages were prompt in adopting all the expedients of their particular modes of warfare, and quite likely had many scouts searching the shores for crafts to carry them off to the castle. As a glance at the lake from any height or projection would expose the smallest object on its surface, there was little hope that either of the canoes could pass unseen; and Indian sagacity needed no instruction to tell which way a boat or a log would drift when the direction of the wind was known. As Deerslayer drew nearer and nearer to the land, the stroke of his paddle grew slower, his eye became more watchful, and his ears and nostrils almost dilated with the effort to detect any lurking danger. 'Twas a trying moment for a novice, nor was there the encouragement which even the timid sometimes feel when conscious of being observed and commended. He was entirely alone, thrown on his own resources, and was cheered by no friendly eye, emboldened by no encouraging voice. Notwithstanding all these circumstances, the most experienced veteran in forest warfare could not have behaved better. Equally free from recklessness and hesitation, his advance was marked by a sort of philosophical prudence that appeared to render him superior to all motives but those which were best calculated to effect his purpose. Such was the commencement of a career in forest exploits that afterward rendered this man, in his way, and under the limits of his habits and opportunities, as renowned as many a hero whose name has adorned the pages of works more celebrated than legends simple as ours can ever become." The explicit comment of the historian at the close of this passage is one of the greatest triumphs of Cooper's rhetoric; the quietness of the prose and of the scene is not impaired, but the prose suddenly takes on a quality of universality and of grandeur such as to prepare one for the metaphysical quality of the action shortly to follow.

The Indian in ambush fires and misses, attacks, and then, being outwitted by Deerslayer but allowed to escape, retreats to cover; Deerslayer is quickly on shore and behind a tree. Then commences the series of hesitations on the part of Deerslayer to kill this man, hesitations which arouse the wonder and then the contempt of the Indian. Deerslayer has never killed a man, yet he has embarked upon the career of a professional scout, and this Indian is his enemy. His wonder, his hesitation, the infallibility of his instincts and muscular reactions, the immense passivity of the morning wilderness, give the scene something of the tenderness and wonder of idyllic first love. But this is first death, and not first love; and the act must be committed in solitude and with deliberation. Deerslayer's consciousness of the significance of the act which he momentarily withholds, and the pure spiritual isolation of the consciousness, the quiet clarity with which the whole is rendered, constitute, surely, one of the most remarkable passages in our literature.

After some maneuvering, Deerslayer persuades the Indian to give up the canoes without bloodshed, or he believes that he persuades him, and then, after a momentary suspicion of treachery, he pushes off from shore: "This distrust, however, seemed to be altogether uncalled for, and, as if ashamed to have entertained it, the young man averted his look, and stepped carelessly up to his boat. Here he began to push the canoe from the shore, and to make his other preparations for departing. He might have been thus employed a minute, when, happening to turn his face toward the land, his quick and certain eye told him at a glance, the imminent jeopardy in which his life was placed. The black, ferocious eyes of the savage were glancing on him, like those of the crouching tiger, through a small opening in the bushes, and the muzzle of his rifle seemed already to be opening in a line with his own body.

"Then, indeed, the long practice of Deerslayer as a hunter did him good service. Accustomed to fire with the deer on the bound, and often when the precise position of the animal's body had in a manner to be guessed at, he used the same expedients here. To cock and poise his rifle were the acts of a single moment and a single motion; then, aiming almost without sighting, he fired into the bushes where he knew a body ought to be in order to sustain the appalling countenance which alone was visible. There was not time to raise the piece any higher or to take a more deliberate aim. So rapid were his movements that both parties discharged their pieces at the same instant, the concussions mingling in one report. The mountains, indeed, gave back but a single echo. Deerslayer dropped his piece, and stood, with head erect, steady as one of the pines in the calm of a June morning, watching the result, while the savage gave the yell that has become historical for its appalling influence, leaped through the bushes, and came bounding across the open ground, flourishing a tomahawk. Still Deerslayer moved not, but stood with his unloaded rifle fallen against his shoulders, while, with a hunter's habits, his hands were mechanically feeling for the powder-horn and charger. When about forty feet from his enemy, the savage hurled his keen weapon; but it was with an eye so vacant, and a hand so unsteady and feeble, that the young man caught it as it was flying past him. At that instant the Indian staggered and fell his whole length on the ground." We have thus the instantaneous coincidence of intuition and determinant action, and the quick rush and ebbing of life, as symbolized by the ease with which the hatchet falls into the hand of Deerslayer; and thereafter a brief passage in which the Indian dies in Deerslayer's arms at the edge of the lake, a passage in which the quiet of the morning is reestablished. One should mention also Deerslayer's perception of the opening of the rifle muzzle, a fine detail, by means of which his perception of the Indian's aim is communicated.

The skill of this backwoodsman, and the skill as well as other characteristics attributed by Cooper to the Indians, are frequently derided, but probably with small justice. In any environment certain particular skills will be generally developed, which are foreign to other environments, and the skills required in the wilderness are now far away from us and of their nature we can have but very small understanding. Yet the feats performed in Cooper's novels with the canoe are of no greater moment than the feats performed daily on our highways with much more dangerous engines, sometimes disastrously, often with success; they are as nothing compared to the daily feats of the army flyer. We should remember, moreover, that if any particular way of life long exists, or even if any particular exercise is long practiced with assiduity, there will inevitably arise, once or twice or occasionally more often in a generation, an individual of a skill such as far to surpass the powers of credible description. The boxer of genius, or even the billiard-player of genius, may perform feats which if recounted in detail would seem far less plausible than the most extraordinary feats of Leatherstocking.

Furthermore, as to feats of woodmanship, the historic feats of the partisan leader, Rogers, as described by the meticulous Parkman in *Montcalm and Wolfe,* surpass anything imagined by Cooper. And Parkman, who objects to Cooper's treatment of Indian character, especially in regard to the capacity delineated for heroic action and for love at a higher level than that of physical passion, yet recounts in *The Conspiracy of Pontiac* the case of a young Indian who followed his white mistress back to the edge of the settlements when she had been captured by a marauding band of whites, in order to be with her as long as possible and to hunt for her; and his account of Pontiac himself establishes that remarkable Ottawa not only as a man of genius but as thoroughly capable of heroic action. Our historic knowledge of Tecumseh, of King Philip, of Massassoit, of the humane and heroic Canonchet, should justify Cooper beyond all question at least as regards the general outlines of his characterization. That such characters were exceptional among the Indians goes without saying, but they would have been exceptional anywhere; and that there were aspects of Indian life on which Cooper seldom dwells is equally certain, but it is also true that the houses of Shakespeare's London were in general, drafty, smoky, dirty, infected with disease, and full of vermin, and Shakespeare is not in general blamed for dealing primarily with the spiritual problems of such men as Macbeth and Coriolanus.

Anyone who will take the trouble to acquaint himself with the works of Parkman—and anyone who will not is to be commiserated in general and distrusted in particular as a commentator on certain aspects of American literature and history—or anyone who will read a dozen odd journals of life in the wilderness, will scarcely, I imagine, object very seriously to this aspect of Cooper on purely factual grounds. Cooper errs not in the plausibility of his facts, but in relying so heavily for the maintenance of interest on so limited a range of facts, and frequently in the sentimental and inflated redundancy with which the facts are rendered; and so far as the Indians are concerned, this redundancy is not without its verisimilitude, whatever we may think of its absolute merits as style, for the eloquence of the Indians in their more formal and heroic moments, as we find it recorded by those who knew them intimately and in their primitive condition, is not as remote from the redundant passages of Cooper as one might at first glance suppose.

This particular defect of style damages white and Indian character about equally, so far as its effect on the modern reader is concerned—and indeed, though the Indian, historically considered, may actually have employed a roughly similar style on certain occasions, one may reasonably protest that in the interests of true eloquence he should not have done so—but in some of the novels, in which the style is not pushed to the appalling limits reached in *The Last of the Mohicans,* one becomes, as I have said in discussing *The Bravo,* more or less accustomed to it, and forgets it. This is largely true of *The Wept of Wish-ton-Wish,* a novel containing three of Cooper's best Indian Characters, all of them based on historic Indians: Uncas, the Pequot or Mohegan, who betrayed his chieftain, Sassacus, sold himself to the English, and helped in the destruction of his own people, first in the Pequot War, and later, as an old man, in King Philip's War; Philip, or Metacom, the Wampanoag; and Canonchet, the Narraganset. One of the better scenes in Cooper, in spite of the sentimental rhetoric is that in which Uncas, who feels himself to be judged a traitor by his captive Canonchet, whose father, Miantonomo, he had murdered years before, endeavors to break the moral character of Canonchet by subtle spiritual torture before murdering him. The conception of Canonchet's white wife, who recovers only at the moment before death her memory of childhood and her childish fear of the forest and of the Indian as the symbols of darkness and of evil, is a conception which deserved a more successful rendering, but which is rendered with sufficient success to merit more appreciation than it has received.[3] This novel is notable also for certain passages of historical exposition, especially in the earlier chapters; passages in which Cooper appears as one of the last representatives of the great tradition of formal historical narrative, of which Hume, Gibbon, and Macaulay are the masters. The passages are brief and scattered; they show the tradition in a state of decay, and corroded by sentiment; but they are still in the great tradition, and as prose they probably surpass most passages of comparable length to be found in Prescott or even in Parkman; they are a moving, if melancholy, spectacle.

One other novel of frontier adventure, *The Oak Openings,* deserves particular attention, if only because of its extraordinary difference from the other novels on similar subjects. As a story of simple adventure, it is one of Cooper's best; as a portrait of the Indian in his more familiar and less heroic moments, it is both convincing and amusing and has no parallel in Cooper or elsewhere in our literature. The scenes in which the assembled chieftains discuss the anthropological theories of the errant clergyman and conclude that the Indians are not descended from the lost tribes of Israel are especially admirable. "I am a Pottawattamie," says Crowsfeather. "My brothers know that tribe. It is not a tribe of Jews, but a tribe of Injins. It is a great tribe. It never was *lost.* It *cannot* be lost. No tribe better knows all the paths, and all the best routes to every point where it wishes to go. It is foolish to say you can lose a Pottawattamie. A duck would be as likely to lose itself as a Pottawattamie. I do not speak for the Ottawas; I speak for the Pottawattamies.... We are not lost; we are not Jews. I have done."

IV

In addition to the novels which I have mentioned and a few others of similar nature, there remain a somewhat miscellaneous lot of novels superficially of a class in that they are all novels of adven-

---

[3]Parkman recounts in *Pontiac,* Chapter XXVIII, an historical incident closely though incompletely resembling this.

ture and all save two, *The Spy* and *Lionel Lincoln,* of adventure at sea.

The Spy, a very early and fairly popular work, is a second rate novel of adventure, as are also *Homeward Bound, The Pilot,* and *The Two Admirals. The Red Rover,* a sea story, is probably the best tale of adventure, questions of style aside, to be found in Cooper except for *The Last of the Mohicans,* but like *The Last of the Mohicans* it has few other merits. *Afloat and Ashore,* and its sequel, *Miles Wallingford,* combine fair sea-adventure, one of the best incidents being based on an actual occurrence recounted by Irving in his *Astoria,* with a fairly pleasant and moderately sentimental portrait of early New York manners. *Jack Tier* is a novel of sentimental adventure at sea which is chiefly remarkable for the portrait of the extraordinary figure from whom the book takes its title; among the sea stories, it has something of the casual charm displayed by *The Oak Openings* among the novels of the wilderness. *The Sea Lions,* though diffuse and full of irrelevancies, offers a portrait of Yankee avarice in a struggle with death in the antarctic circle, which deserved a more careful treatment.

Three other stories—*Lionel Lincoln, Wing-and-Wing,* and especially *The Water-Witch*—are remarkable for their rhetorical experiments, and display Cooper in a capacity in which he has never been seriously studied or even regarded.

In *Lionel Lincoln,* the character in connection with whom the experimental rhetoric is most often successful, is Polwarth, a British officer stationed in Boston, a gentleman by birth and courageous by nature, but stout, overfond of eating, and somewhat talkative. Polwarth must beyond any question be the prototype of W. G. Simms' Porgy, and though Cooper makes less use of Polwarth than Simms makes of his southerner, Cooper's portrait is in some ways the more effective. Polwarth speaks a species of semi-Elizabethan prose which is not without its wit and its poetry, and of which the very affectation has a real stylistic charm. The following passage, taken from the ninth chapter, is descriptive of the removal of the British troops from Boston the night before the battle of Lexington:

"Polwarth had established himself by the side of Lionel, much to the ease of his limbs, and as they moved slowly into the light, all those misgivings which had so naturally accompanied his musings on the difficulties of a partisan irruption, vanished before the loveliness of the time, and possibly before the quietude of the action.

"'There are moments when I could fancy the life of a sailor,' he said, leaning indolently back, and playing with one hand in the water. 'This pulling about in boats is easy work, and must be capital assistance for a heavy digestion, inasmuch as it furnishes air with as little violent exercise as may be. Your marine should lead a merry life of it!'

"'They are said to murmur at the clashing of their duties with those of the sea-officers,' said Lionel; 'and I have often heard them complain of a want of room to make use of their legs.'

"'Humph!' ejaculated Polwarth; 'the leg is a part of a man for which I see less actual necessity than for any other portion of his frame. I often think there has been a sad mistake in the formation of the animal; as, for instance, one can be a very good waterman, as you see, without legs—a good fiddler, a first-rate tailor, a lawyer, a doctor, a parson, a very tolerable cook, and in short, anything but a dancing-master. I see no use in a leg unless it be to have the gout— at any rate, a leg of twelve inches is as good as one a mile long, and the saving might be appropriated to the nobler parts of the animal; such as the brain and the stomach.'

"'You forget the officer of light-infantry,' said Lionel, laughing.

"'You might give him a couple of inches more; though as everything in this wicked world is excellent only by comparison, it would amount to the same thing, and on my system a man would be just as fit for the light-infantry without, as with legs; and he would get rid of a good deal of troublesome manoeuvering, especially of this new exercise. It would then become a delightful service, Leo; for it may be said to monopolize all the poetry of military life, as you may see. Neither the imagination nor the body can require more than we enjoy at this moment, and of what use, I would ask, are our legs? if anything, they are incumbrances in this boat. Here we have a soft moon, and softer seats—smooth water, and a stimulating air—on one side fine country, which, though but faintly seen, is known to be fertile and rich to abundance; and on the other a picturesque town, stored with condiments of every climate—even those rascally privates look mellowed by the moonbeams, with their scarlet coats and glittering arms! ... Where now are your companies of the lines; your artillery and dragoons; your engineers and staff! nightcapped and snoring to a man, while we enjoy here the very dessert of existence— I wish I could hear a nightingale!'"

This is obviously less excellent than Falstaff, but on the other hand it does not really endeavor to compete with Falstaff, and, having a minor excellence of its own, should survive the comparison. I should like to insist that here, as in other scattered passages of Cooper, there is a prose possessing at once an authentic poetic perception and a rhetorical procedure both ingenious and controlled; that these scattered passages are frequently of sufficient length to be impressive; that among them there is considerable variety as regards the kind of prose employed; and that they display a stylist superior to any other in America—and I do not except Hawthorne—before Melville, one who in some respects foreshadows Melville, and one who can still be examined with pleasure and with profit.

In *Wing-and-Wing,* Cooper writes a story of his favorite type of sailing vessel, a light and elusive fugitive from authority; and he places the vessel in the marine setting which of all he regarded as the most beautiful and the most ethereal, the Mediterranean. The plot, as in nearly all of his tales of adventure, is one of pursuit and flight, but in these conditions the pursuit and flight acquire an air of illusion which at a few moments, especially in the discussion of solipsistic philosophy which takes place between the vice-governor of Elba and his podesta while halfway down the ship's ladder of a British cruiser, all but evaporates into madness.

Wing-and-Wing, though occasionally amusing or even beautiful, is less certain of its intention than the earlier novel of a somewhat similar kind, *The Water-Witch.* The action of *The Water-Witch* is extremely unreal, and the unreality, not to say the impossibility of much of it, would be preposterous did Cooper not utilize this very quality. It has the plot, entrances, exits, abductions, and mysteries of a comic opera; and the style is adjusted to the plot in a manner at once brilliant and meticulous. Plot and character alike have the unreality, but the consistency within themselves, of the plot and character, let us say, of *Volpone;* and Cooper endeavors to achieve a style not dissimilar, so far as the limits of prose permit, to the style of Jonson's dramatic verse. This novel, though imperfect artistically, is imperfect in minor ways; questions of scope aside, it is probably Cooper's ablest piece of work, as it is certainly one of the most brilliant, if scarcely one of the most profound, masterpieces of American prose.

The numerous quotations from Shakespeare employed in this work give a clue to the Elizabethan models for the prose; and if they did not, there would be clues sufficiently obvious scattered throughout the prose itself. The following commentary, for example is spoken by the incredible Thomas Tiller: "'Every craft has its allotted time, like a mortal,' continued the inexplicable mariner of the India-shawl. 'If she is to die a sudden death, there is your beam-end and stern-way, which takes her into the grave without funeral service or parish prayers; your dropsy is being water-logged; gout and rheumatism kill like a broken back and loose joints; indigestion is a shifting cargo, with guns adrift; the gallows is a bottomry-bond, with lawyers' fees; while fire, drowning, death by religious melancholy, and suicide, are a careless gunner, sunken rocks, false lights, and a lubberly captain.'"

The best prose, however, is to be found where the imitation of rhetorical forms is not so close, but where the intention of schematization is equally marked. The two most successful characters, from the point of view of one who seeks this particular quality, are the loquacious Dutch Alderman, Van Beverout, and his taciturn and aristocratic young friend, Oloff Van Staats, the Patroon of Kinderhook, the former as a commentator on the action and on life at large, and the latter as one providing much food for comment. To the reader who does not find a certain pleasure in the texture of the prose in which the meditations of the Alderman are couched, the Alderman must needs be very tiresome; but his reveries and his commercial imagery possess a hard and clear, if somewhat baroque and elaborate, beauty, which, though it does not lend itself convincingly to brief quotation, is fairly impressive in the text.

The essential difficulty in connection with these rhetorical excursions resides simply in the fact that the subject is never adequate to permit the extraction from the rhetoric its full possibilities, so that we have a species of lyricism, which, though real enough, is frequently all but verbal or even syntactical; we have something approaching pure rhetoric. Cooper conceived a comic-opera plot to provide the motive for his poetry; in *Moby Dick,* on the other hand, the plot is the plot of an epic, and not only are the possibilities of the rhetoric exhausted, but the rhetoric has greater possibilities.

V

If we except *The Water-Witch,* a minor but original masterpiece, not flawless, perhaps, but still a unit, we find Cooper to be essentially a man of fragments; it is likely that the best part of him is in the fragments, moreover, and not in *The Water-Witch.* He embodies a social ideal that in his own lifetime was so far gone in decay that his defense of it cost him his reputation, and that it may scarcely be said to have survived him to the extent of two decades. He displays at his best a rhetorical grandeur of a kind cognate with his social ideals, but habitual rather than understood, and commonly collapsing for lack of support from his action; that is, he displays a great traditional moral sense corroded by the formulary romantic sentiment of his own period, and apparently with no realization that the two are incompatible. On a few occasions he displays great vigor of conception, as in the creation of such plots as *The Sea Lions* and *The Wept of Wish-ton-Wish,* as in the creation of such characters as Leatherstocking and Jason Newcome, as in the residual feeling of intimacy with which he leaves one, from perhaps a half-dozen of novels, with life in frontier and provincial New York. This is a vigor which has little to do with rhetoric, or at least has to do with it but seldom, and which frequently survives a great deal of bad rhetoric: the figure of Leatherstocking emerges from the debris of the five novels in which he was created, independent, authentic, and unforgettable. For the American who desires a polite education in his own literature, the five novels of the Leatherstocking series are indispensable, as are the first two Littlepage novels, *The Bravo, and The Water-Witch.* For the American who desires an education historical as well as literary, and richly literary instead of superficially, the entire work should be exhumed. It is a mass of fragments, no doubt; but the fragments are those of a civilization.

Fenimore Cooper's Leatherstocking Novels

by D. H. Lawrence

In his Leatherstocking books, Fenimore is off on another track. He is no longer concerned with social white Americans that buzz with pins through them, buzz loudly against every mortal thing except the pin itself. The pin of the Great Ideal. One gets irritated with Cooper because he never for once snarls at the Great Ideal Pin which transfixes him. No, indeed. Rather he tries to push it through the very heart of the Continent. But I have loved the Leatherstocking books so dearly. Wish-fulfilment!

Anyhow, one is not supposed to take LOVE seriously, in these books. Eve Effingham, impaled on the social pin, conscious all the time of her own ego and of nothing else, suddenly fluttering in throes of love: no, it makes me sick. LOVE is never LOVE until it has a pin pushed through it and becomes an IDEAL. The ego, turning on a pin, is wildly IN LOVE, always. Because that's the thing to be.

Cooper was a GENTLEMAN, in the worst sense of the word. In the Nineteenth Century sense of the word. A correct, clock-work man.

Not altogether, of course.

The great national Grouch was grinding inside him. Probably he called it COSMIC URGE. Americans usually do: in capital letters.

Best stick to National Grouch. The great American grouch.

Cooper had it, gentleman that he was. That is why he flitted round Europe so uneasily. Of course, in Europe he could be, and was, a gentleman to his heart's content.

"In short," he says in one of his letters, "we were at table two counts, one monsignore, an English Lord, an Ambassador, and my humble self."

Were we really!

How nice it must have been to know that one self, at least, was humble.

And he felt the democratic American tomahawk wheeling over his uncomfortable scalp all the time.

The great American grouch.

Two monsters loomed on Cooper's horizon.

Mrs. Cooper	My Work
My Work	My Wife
My Wife	My Work
	The Dear Children
	My Work!!!

There you have the essential keyboard of Cooper's soul.

If there is one thing that annoys me more than a business man and his Business, it is an artist, a writer, painter, musician, and My Work. When an artist says My Work, the flesh goes tired on my bones. When he says My Wife, I want to hit him.

Cooper grizzled about his work. Oh, heaven, he cared so much whether it was good or bad, and what the French thought, and what Mr. Snippy Knowall said, and how Mrs. Cooper took it. The pin, the pin!

But he was truly an artist: then an American: then a gentleman.

And the grouch grouched inside him, through all.

They seem to have been specially fertile in imagining themselves "under the wigwam," do these Americans, just when their knees were comfortably under the mahogany, in Paris, along with the knees of

4 Counts

2 Cardinals

1 Milord

5 Cocottes

1 Humble Self

You bet, though, that when the cocottes were being raffled off, Fenimore went home to his WIFE.

Wish Fulfilment		*Actuality*
THE WIGWAM	*vs.*	MY HOTEL
CHINGACHGOOK	*vs.*	MY WIFE
NATTY BUMPPO	*vs.*	MY HUMBLE SELF

Fenimore, lying in his Louis Quatorze hotel in Paris, passionately musing about Natty Bumppo and the pathless forest, and mixing his imagination with the Cupids and Butterflies on the painted ceiling, while Mrs. Cooper was struggling with her latest gown in the next room, and the déjeuner was with the Countess at eleven. ...

Men live by lies.

In actuality, Fenimore loved the genteel continent of Europe, and waited gasping for the newspapers to praise his WORK.

In another actuality he loved the tomahawking continent of America, and imagined himself Natty Bumppo.

His actual desire was to be: *Monsieur Fenimore Cooper, le grand écrivain américain.*

His innermost wish was to be: Natty Bumppo.

Now Natty and Fenimore, arm-in-arm, are an odd couple.

You can see Fenimore: blue coat, silver buttons, silver-and-diamond buckle shoes, ruffles.

You see Natty Bumppo: a grizzled, uncouth old renegade, with gaps in his old teeth and a drop on the end of his nose.

But Natty was Fenimore's great wish: his wish-fulfilment.

"It was a matter of course," says Mrs. Cooper, "that he should dwell on the better traits of the picture rather than on the coarser and more revolting, though more common points. Like West, he could see Apollo in the young Mohawk."

The coarser and more revolting, though more common points.

You see now why he depended so absolutely on MY WIFE. She had to look things in the face for him. The coarser and more revolting, and certainly more common points, she had to see.

He himself did so love seeing pretty-pretty, with the thrill of a red scalp now and then.

Fenimore, in his imagination, wanted to be Natty Bumppo, who,

I am sure, belched after he had eaten his dinner. At the same time Mr. Cooper was nothing if not a gentleman. So he decided to stay in France and have it all his own way.

In France, Natty would not belch after eating, and Chingachgook could be all the Apollo he liked.

As if ever any Indian was like Apollo. The Indians, with their curious female quality, their archaic figures, with high shoulders and deep, archaic waists, like a sort of woman! And their natural devilishness, their natural insidiousness.

But men see what they want to see: especially if they look from a long distance, across the ocean, for example.

Yet, the Leatherstocking books are lovely. Lovely half-lies.

They form a sort of American Odyssey, with Natty Bumppo for Odysseus.

Only, in the original Odyssey, there is plenty of devil, Circes and swine and all. And Ithacus is devil enough to outwit the devils. But Natty is a saint with a gun, and the Indians are gentlemen through and through, though they may take an occasional scalp.

There are five Leatherstocking novels: a *decrescendo* of reality, and a crescendo of beauty.

1. *Pioneers:* A raw frontier-village on Lake Champlain, at the end of the eighteenth century. Must be a picture of Cooper's home, as he knew it when a boy. A very lovely book. Natty Bumppo an old man, an old hunter half civilized.

2. *The Last of the Mohicans:* A historical fight between the British and the French, with Indians on both sides, at a Fort by Lake Champlain. Romantic flight of the British general's two daughters, conducted by the scout, Natty, who is in the prime of life; romantic death of the last of the Delawares.

3. *The Prairie:* A wagon of some huge, sinister Kentuckians trekking west into the unbroken prairie. Prairie Indians, and Natty, an old, old man; he dies seated on a chair on the Rocky Mountains, looking east.

4. *The Pathfinder:* The Great Lakes, Natty, a man of about thirty-five, makes an abortive proposal to a bouncing damsel, daughter of the Sergeant at the Fort.

5. *Deerslayer:* Natty and Hurry Harry, both quite young, are hunting in the virgin wild. They meet two white women. Lake Champlain again.

These are the five Leatherstocking books: Natty Bumppo being Leatherstocking, Pathfinder, Deerslayer, according to his ages.

Now let me put aside my impatience at the unreality of this vision, and accept it as a wish-fulfilment vision, a kind of yearning myth. Because it seems to me that the things in Cooper that make one so savage, when one compares them with actuality, are perhaps, when one considers them as presentations of a deep subjective desire, real in their way, and almost prophetic.

The passionate love for America, for the soil of America, for example. As I say, it is perhaps easier to love America passionately, when you look at it through the wrong end of the telescope, across all the Atlantic water, as Cooper did so often, than when you are right there. When you are actually in America, America hurts, because it has a powerful disintegrative influence upon the white psyche. It is full of grinning, unappeased aboriginal demons, too, ghosts, and it persecutes the white men, like some Eumenides, until the white men give up their absolute whiteness. America is tense with latent violence and resistance. The very common sense of white Americans has a tinge of helplessness in it, and deep fear of what might be if they were not common-sensical.

Yet one day the demons of America must be placated, the ghosts must be appeased, the Spirit of Place atoned for. Then the true passionate love for American Soil will appear. As yet, there is too much menace in the landscape.

But probably, one day America will be as beautiful in actuality as it is in Cooper. Not yet, however. When the factories have fallen down again.

And again, this perpetual blood-brother theme of the Leatherstocking novels, Natty and Chingachgook, the Great Serpent. At present it is a sheer myth. The Red Man and the White Man are not blood-brothers: even when they are most friendly. When they are most friendly, it is as a rule the one betraying his race-spirit to the other. In the white man—rather high-brow—who "loves" the Indian, one feels the white man betraying his own race. There is something unproud, underhand in it. Renegade. The same with the Americanised Indian who believes absolutely in the white mode. It is a betrayal. Renegade again.

In the actual flesh, it seems to me the white man and the red man cause a feeling of oppression, the one to the other, no matter what the good will. The red life flows in a different direction from the white life. You can't make two streams that flow in opposite directions meet and mingle soothingly.

Certainly, if Cooper had had to spend his whole life in the backwoods, side by side with a Noble Red Brother, he would have screamed with the oppression of suffocation. He had to have Mrs. Cooper, a straight strong pillar of society, to hang on to. And he had to have the culture of France to turn back to, or he would just have been stifled. The Noble Red Brother would have smothered him and driven him mad.

So that the Natty and Chingachgook myth must remain a myth. It is a wish-fulfilment, an evasion of actuality. As we have said before, the folds of the Great Serpent would have been heavy, very heavy, too heavy, on any white man. Unless the white man were a true renegade, hating himself and his own race-spirit, as sometimes happens.

It seems there can be no fusion in the flesh. But the spirit can change. The white man's spirit can never become as the red man's spirit. It doesn't want to. But it can cease to be the opposite and the negative of the red man's spirit. It can open out a new great area of consciousness, in which there is room for the red spirit too.

To open out a new wide area of consciousness means to slough the old consciousness. The old consciousness has become a tight-fitting prison to us, in which we are going rotten.

You can't have a new, easy skin before you have sloughed the old, tight skin.

You can't.

And you just can't, so you may as well leave off pretending.

Now the essential history of the people of the United States seems to me just this: At the Renaisance the old consciousness was becoming a little tight. Europe sloughed her last skin, and started a new, final phase.

But some Europeans recoiled from the last final phase. They wouldn't enter the *cul de sac* of post-Renaissance, "liberal" Europe. They came to America.

They came to America for two reasons:

1. To slough the old European consciousness completely.

2. To grow a new skin underneath, a new form. This second is a hidden process.

The two processes go on, of course, simultaneously. The slow forming of the new skin underneath is the slow sloughing of the old skin. And sometimes this immortal serpent feels very happy, feeling a new golden glow of a strangely-patterned skin envelop him: and sometimes he feels very sick, as if his very entrails were being torn out of him, as he wrenches once more at his old skin, to get out of it.

Out! Out! he cries, in all kinds of euphemisms.

He's got to have his new skin on him before ever he can get out.

And he's got to get out before his new skin can ever be his own skin.

So there he is, a torn, divided monster.

The true American, who writhes and writhes like a snake that is long in sloughing.

Sometimes snakes can't slough. They can't burst their old skin. Then they go sick and die inside the old skin, and nobody ever sees the new pattern.

It needs a real desperate recklessness to burst your old skin at last. You simply don't care what happens to you, if you rip yourself in two, so long as you do get out.

It also needs a real belief in the new skin. Otherwise you are likely never to make the effort. Then you gradually sicken and go rotten and die in the old skin.

Now Fenimore stayed very safe inside the old skin: a gentleman, almost a European, as proper as proper can be. And, safe inside the old skin, he *imagined* the gorgeous American pattern of a new skin.

He hated democracy. So he evaded it, and had a nice dream of something beyond democracy. But he belonged to democracy all the while.

Evasion! — Yet even that doesn't make the dream worthless.

Democracy in America was never the same as Liberty in Europe. In Europe Liberty was a great life-throb. But in America Democracy was always something anti-life. The greatest democrats, like Abraham Lincoln, had always a sacrificial, self-murdering note in their voices. American Democracy was a form of self-murder, always. Or of murdering somebody else.

Necessarily. It was a *pis aller*. It was the *pis aller* to European Liberty. It was a cruel form of sloughing. Men murdered themselves into this democracy. Democracy is the utter hardening of the old skin, the old form, the old psyche. It hardens till it is tight and fixed and inorganic. Then it *must* burst, like a chrysalis shell. And out must come the soft grub, or the soft damp butterfly of the American-at-last.

America has gone the *pis aller* of her democracy. Now she must slough even that, chiefly that, indeed.

What did Cooper dream beyond democracy? Why, in his immortal friendship of Chingachgook and Natty Bumppo he dreamed the nucleus of a new society. That is, he dreamed a new human relationship. A stark, stripped human relationship of two men, deeper than the deeps of sex. Deeper than property, deeper than fatherhood, deeper than marriage, deeper than love. So deep that it is loveless. The stark, loveless, wordless unison of two men who have come to the bottom of themselves. This is the new nucleus of a new society, the clue to a new world-epoch. It asks for a great and cruel sloughing first of all. Then it finds a great release into a new world, a new moral, a new landscape.

Natty and the Great Serpent are neither equals nor unequals. Each obeys the other when the moment arrives. And each is stark and dumb in the other's presence, starkly himself, without illusion created. Each is just the crude pillar of a man, the crude living column of his own manhood. And each knows the godhead of this crude column of manhood. A new relationship.

The Leatherstocking novels create the myth of this new relation. And they go backwards, from old age to golden youth. That is the true myth of America. She starts old, old, wrinkled and writhing in an old skin. And there is a gradual sloughing of the old skin, towards a new youth. It is the myth of America.

You start with actuality. *Pioneers* is no doubt Cooperstown, when Cooperstown was in the stage of inception: a village of one wild street of log cabins under the forest hills by Lake Champlain: a village of crude, wild frontiersmen, reacting against civilization.

Towards this frontier-village in the winter time, a negro slave drives a sledge through the mountains, over deep snow. In the sledge sits a fair damsel, Miss Temple, with her handsome pioneer father, Judge Temple. They hear a shot in the trees. It is the old hunter and backwoodsman, Natty Bumppo, long and lean and uncouth, with a long rifle and gaps in his teeth.

Judge Temple is "squire" of the village, and he has a ridiculous, commodious "hall" for his residence. It is still the old English form.

Miss Temple is a pattern young lady, like Eve Effingham: in fact, she gets a young and very genteel but impoverished Effingham for a husband. The old world holding its own on the edge of the wild. A bit tiresomely too, with rather more prunes and prisms than one can digest. Too romantic.

Against the "hall" and the gentry, the real frontiers-folk, the rebels. The two groups meet at the village inn, and at the frozen church, and at the Christmas sports, and on the ice of the lake, and at the great pigeon shoot. It is a beautiful, resplendent picture of life. Fenimore puts in only the glamour.

Perhaps my taste is childish, but these scenes in *Pioneers* seem to me marvellously beautiful. The raw village street, with woodfires blinking through the unglazed windowchinks, on a winter's night. The inn, with the rough woodsman and the drunken Indian John; the church, with the snowy congregation crowding to the fire. Then the lavish abundance of Christmas cheer, and turkey-shooting in the snow. Spring coming, forests all green, maple-sugar taken from the trees: and clouds of pigeons flying from the south, myriads of pigeons, shot in heaps; and night-fishing on the teeming, virgin lake; and deer-hunting.

Pictures! Some of the loveliest, most glamorous pictures in all literature.

Alas, without the cruel iron of reality. It is all real enough. Except that one realizes that Fenimore was writing from a safe distance, where he would idealize and have his wish-fulfilment.

Because, when one comes to America, one finds that there is always a certain slightly devilish resistance in the American landscape, and a certain slightly bitter resistance in the white man's heart. Hawthorne gives this. But Cooper glosses it over.

The American landscape has never been at one with the white man. Never. And white men have probably never felt so bitter anywhere, as here in America, where the very landscape, in its very beauty, seems a bit devilish and grinning, opposed to us.

Cooper, however, glosses over this resistance, which in actuality can never quite be glossed over. He *wants* the landscape to be at one with him. So he goes away to Europe and sees it as such. It is a sort of vision.

And, nevertheless, the oneing will surely take place—some day. The myth is the story of Natty. The old, lean hunter and backwoodsman lives with his friend, the grey-haired Indian John, an old Delaware chief, in a hut within reach of the village. The Delaware is christianized and bears the Christian name of John. He is tribeless and lost. He humiliates his grey hairs in drunkenness, and dies, thankful to be dead, in a forest fire, passing back to the fire whence he derived.

And this is Chingachgook, the splendid Great Serpent of the later novels.

No doubt Cooper, as a boy, knew both Natty and the Indian John. No doubt they fired his imagination even then. When he is a man, crystallized in society and sheltering behind the safe pillar of Mrs. Cooper, these two old fellows become a myth to his soul. He traces himself to a new youth in them.

As for the story: Judge Temple has just been instrumental in passing the wise game laws. But Natty has lived by his gun all his life in the wild woods, and simply childishly cannot understand how he can be poaching on the Judge's land among the pine trees. He shoots a deer in the close season. The Judge is all sympathy, but the law *must* be enforced. Bewildered Natty, an old man of seventy, is put in stocks and in prison. They release him as soon as possible. But the thing was done.

The letter killeth.

Natty's last connexion with his own race is broken. John, the Indian, is dead. The old hunter disappears, lonely and severed, into the forest, away, away from his race.

In the new epoch that is coming, there will be no letter of the Law.

Chronologically, *The Last of the Mohicans* follows *Pioneers*. But in the myth, *The Prairie* comes next.

Cooper of course knew his own America. He travelled west and saw the prairies, and camped with the Indians of the prairie.

The Prairie, like *Pioneers*, bears a good deal the stamp of actuality. It is a strange, splendid book, full of sense of doom. The figures of the great Kentuckian men, with their wolf-women, loom colossal on the vast prairie, as they camp with their wagons. These are different pioneers from Judge Temple. Lurid, brutal, tinged with the sinisterness of crime; these are the gaunt white men who push west, push on and on against the natural opposition of the continent. On towards a doom. Great wings of vengeful doom seem spread over the west, grim against the intruder. You feel them again in Frank Norris' novel, *The Octopus*. While in the West of

Bret Harte there is a very devil in the air, and beneath him are sentimental self-conscious people being wicked and goody by evasion.

In *The Prairie* there is a shadow of violence and dark cruelty flickering in the air. It is the aboriginal demon hovering over the core of the continent. It hovers still, and the dread is still there.

Into such a prairie enters the huge figure of Ishmael, ponderous, pariah-like Ishmael and his huge sons and his were-wolf wife. With their wagons they roll on from the frontiers of Kentucky, like Cyclops into the savage wilderness. Day after day they seem to force their way into oblivion. But their force of penetration ebbs. They are brought to a stop. They recoil in the throes of murder and entrench themselves in isolation on a hillock in the midst of the prairie. There they hold out like demi-gods against the elements and the subtle Indian.

The pioneering brute invasion of the West, crime-tinged!

And into this setting, as a sort of minister of peace, enters the old, old hunter Natty, and his suave, horse-riding Sioux Indians. But he seems like a shadow.

The hills rise softly west, to the Rockies. There seems a new peace: or is it only suspense, abstraction, waiting? Is it only a sort of beyond?

Natty lives in these hills, in a village of the suave, horse-riding Sioux. They revere him as an old wise father.

In these hills he dies, sitting in his chair and looking far east, to the forest and great sweet waters, whence he came. He dies gently, in physical peace with the land and the Indians. He is an old, old man.

Cooper could see no further than the foothills where Natty died, beyond the prairie.

The other novels bring us back east.

The Last of the Mohicans is divided between real historical narrative and true "romance." For myself, I prefer the romance. It has a myth meaning, whereas the narrative is chiefly record.

For the first time we get actual women: the dark, handsome Cora and her frail sister, the White Lily. The good old division, the dark sensual woman and the clinging, submissive little blonde, who is so "pure."

These sisters are fugitives through the forest, under the protection of a Major Heyward, a young American officer and Englishman. He is just a "white" man, very good and brave and generous, etc., but limited, most definitely *borné*. He would probably love Cora, if he dared, but he finds it safer to adore the clinging White Lily of a younger sister.

This trio is escorted by Natty, now Leatherstocking, a hunter and scout in the prime of life, accompanied by his inseparable friend Chingachgook, and the Delaware's beautiful son—Adonis rather than Apollo—Uncas, The last of the Mohicans.

There is also a "wicked" Indian, Magua, handsome and injured incarnation of evil.

Cora is the scarlet flower of womanhood, fierce, passionate off-spring of some mysterious union between the British officer and a Creole woman in the West Indies. Cora loves Uncas, Uncas loves Cora. But Magua also desires Cora, violently desires her. A lurid little circle of sensual fire. So Fenimore kills them all off, Cora, Uncas, and Magua, and leaves the White Lily to carry on the race. She will breed plenty of white children to Major Heyward. These tiresome "lilies that fester," of our day.

Evidently Cooper—or the artist in him—has decided that there can be no blood-mixing of the two races, white and red. He kills 'em off.

Beyond all this heart-beating stand the figures of Natty and Ching-achgook: the two childless, womanless men, of opposite races. They are the abiding thing. Each of them is alone, and final in his race. And they stand side by side, stark, abstract, beyond emotion, yet eternally together. All the other loves seem frivolous. This is the new great thing, the clue, the inception of a new humanity.

And Natty, what sort of a white man is he? Why, he is a man with a gun. He is a killer, a slayer. Patient and gentle as he is, he is a slayer. Self-effacing, self-forgetting, still he is a killer.

Twice, in the book, he brings an enemy down hurtling in death through the air, downwards. Once it is the beautiful, wicked Magua—shot from a height, and hurtling down ghastly through space, into death.

This is Natty, the white forerunner. A killer. As in *Deerslayer*, he shoots the bird that flies in the high, high sky, so that the bird falls out of the invisible into the visible, dead, he symbolizes himself. He will bring the bird of the spirit out of the high air. He is the stoic American killer of the old great life. But he kills, as he says, only to live.

Pathfinder takes us to the Great Lakes, and the glamour and beauty of sailing the great sweet waters. Natty is now called Pathfinder. He is about thirty-five years old, and he falls in love. The damsel is Mabel Dunham, daughter of Sergeant Dunham of the Fort garrison. She is blonde and in all things admirable. No doubt Mrs. Cooper was very much like Mabel.

And Pathfinder doesn't marry her. She won't have him. She wisely prefers a more comfortable Jasper. So Natty goes off to grouch, and to end by thanking his stars. When he had got right clear, and sat by the campfire with Chingachgook, in the forest, didn't he just thank his stars! A lucky escape!

Men of an uncertain age are liable to these infatuations. They aren't always lucky enough to be rejected.

Whatever would poor Mabel have done, had she been Mrs. Bumppo?

Natty had no business marrying. His mission was elsewhere.

The most fascinating Leatherstocking book is the last, *Deerslayer*. Natty is now a fresh youth, called Deerslayer. But the kind of silent prim youth who is never quite young, but reserves himself for different things.

It is a gem of a book. Or a bit of perfect paste. And myself, I like a bit of perfect paste in a perfect setting, so long as I am not fooled by pretence of reality. And the setting of Deerslayer *could* not be more exquisite. Lake Champlain again.

Of course it never rains: it is never cold and muddy and dreary: no one has wet feet or toothache: no one ever feels filthy, when they can't wash for a week. God knows what the women would really have looked like, for they fled through the wilds without soap, comb, or towel. They breakfasted off a chunk of meat, or nothing, lunched the same, and supped the same.

Yet at every moment they are elegant, perfect ladies, in correct toilet.

Which isn't quite fair. You need only go camping for a week, and you'll see.

But it is a myth, not a realistic tale. Read it as a lovely myth. Lake Glimmerglass.

Deerslayer, the youth with the long rifle, is found in the woods with a big, handsome, blonde-bearded backwoodsman called Hurry Harry. Deerslayer seems to have been born under a hemlock tree out of a pine-cone: a young man of the woods. He is silent, simple, philosophic, moralistic, and an unerring shot. His simplicity is the simplicity of age rather than of youth. He is race-old. All his re-actions and impulses are fixed, static. Almost he is sexless, so race-old. Yet intelligent, hardy, dauntless.

Hurry Harry is a big blusterer, just the opposite of Deerslayer. Deerslayer keeps the centre of his own consciousness steady and unperturbed. Hurry Harry is one of those floundering people who bluster from one emotion to another, very self-conscious, without any centre to them.

These two young men are making their way to a lovely, smallish lake, Lake Glimmerglass. On this water the Hutter family has es-tablished itself. Old Hutter, it is suggested, has a criminal, coarse, bucaneering past, and is a sort of fugitive from justice. But he is a good enough father to his two grown-up girls. The family lives in a log hut "castle," built on piles in the water, and the old man has also constructed an "ark," a sort of house-boat, in which he can take his daughters when he goes on his rounds to trap the beaver.

The two girls are the inevitable dark and light. Judith, dark, fear-less, passionate, a little lurid with sin, is the scarlet-and-black blos-som. Hetty, the younger, blonde, frail and innocent, is the white lily again. But alas, the lily has begun to fester. She is slightly imbecile.

The two hunters arrive at the lake among the woods just as war has been declared. The Hutters are unaware of the fact. And hostile Indians are on the lake already. So, the story of thrills and perils.

Thomas Hardy's inevitable division of women into dark and fair, sinful and innocent, sensual and pure, is Cooper's division too. It is indicative of the desire in the man. He wants sensuality and sin, and he wants purity and "innocence." If the innocence goes a little rotten, slightly imbecile, bad luck!

Hurry Harry, of course, like a handsome impetuous meat-fly, at once wants Judith, the lurid poppy-blossom. Judith rejects him with scorn.

Judith, the sensual woman, at once wants the quiet, reserved, un-mastered Deerslayer. She wants to master him. And Deerslayer is half tempted, but never more than half. He is not going to be mas-tered. A philosophic old soul, he does not give much for the tempta-tions of sex. Probably he dies virgin.

And he is right of it. Rather than be dragged into a false heat of deliberate sensuality, he will remain alone. His soul is alone, for ever alone. So he will preserve his integrity, and remain alone in the flesh. It is a stoicism which is honest and fearless, and from which Deerslayer never lapses, except when, approaching middle age, he proposes to the buxom Mabel.

He lets his consciousness penetrate in loneliness into the new continent. His contacts are not human. He wrestles with the spirits of the forest and the American wild, as a hermit wrestles with God and Satan. His one meeting is with Chingachgook, and this meeting is silent, reserved, across an unpassable distance.

Hetty, the White Lily, being imbecile, although full of vaporous religion and the dear, good God, "who governs all things by his providence," is hopelessly infatuated with Hurry Harry. Being innocence gone imbecile, like Dostoevsky's Idiot, she longs to give herself to the handsome meat-fly. Of course he doesn't want her.

And so nothing happens: in that direction. Deerslayer goes off to meet Chingachgook, and help him woo an Indian maid. Vicarious.

It is the miserable story of the collapse of the white psyche. The white man's mind and soul are divided between these two things: innocence and lust, the Spirit and Sensuality. Sensuality always carries a stigma, and is therefore more deeply desired, or lusted after. But spirituality alone gives the sense of uplift, exaltation, and "winged life," with the inevitable reaction into sin and spite. So the white man is divided against himself. He plays off one side of himself against the other side, till it is really a tale told by an idiot, and nauseating.

Against this, one is forced to admire the stark, enduring figure of Deerslayer. He is neither spiritual nor sensual. He is a moralizer, but he always tries to moralize from actual experience, not from theory. He says: "Hurt nothing unless you're forced to." Yet he gets his deepest thrill of gratification, perhaps, when he puts a bullet through the heart of a beautiful buck, as it stoops to drink at the lake. Or when he brings the invisible bird fluttering down in death, out of the high blue. "Hurt nothing unless you're forced to." And yet he lives by death, by killing the wild things of the air and earth.

It's not good enough.

But you have there the myth of the essential white America. All the other stuff, the love, the democracy, the floundering into lust, is a sort of by-play. The essential American soul is hard, isolate, stoic, and a killer. It has never yet melted.

Of course, the soul often breaks down into disintegration, and you have lurid sin and Judith, imbecile innocence lusting, in Hetty, and bluster, bragging, and self-conscious strength, in Harry. But there are the disintegration products.

What true myth concerns itself with is not the disintegration product. True myth concerns itself centrally with the onward adventure of the integral soul. And this, for America, is Deerslayer. A man who turns his back on white society. A man who keeps his moral integrity hard and intact. An isolate, almost selfless, stoic, enduring man, who lives by death, by killing, but who is pure white.

This is the very intrinsic-most American. He is at the core of all the other flux and fluff. And when *this* man breaks from his static isolation, and makes a new move, then look out, something will be happening.

Natty Bumppo and Chingachgook

by Leslie A. Fiedler

Two mythic figures have detached themselves from the texts of Cooper's books and have entered the free domain of our dreams: Natty Bumppo, the hunter and enemy of cities; and Chingachgook, nature's nobleman and Vanishing American. But these two between them postulate a third myth, an archetypal relationship which also haunts the American psyche: two lonely men, one dark-skinned, one white, bend together over a carefully guarded fire in the virgin heart of the American wilderness; they have forsaken all others for the sake of the austere, almost inarticulate, but unquestioned love which binds them to each other and to the world of nature which they have preferred to civilization. To understand these figures and their relationship, we must first understand the order of the genesis of their myth: the sequence of the novels in which they appear, both as Cooper wrote them and in terms of the dates of their actions.

Though *The Pioneers* appeared in 1823, it is set in 1793, when Natty is over seventy; and though *The Deerslayer,* the last of the novels to be published, came out in 1841, the events it describes belong to the years between 1740 and 1745, when Natty is not yet twenty-five. Between the first and last written of the Leatherstocking Tales, the protagonist grows backward in time from old age to youth, from experience to innocence, from a world which Cooper could still, though barely, remember (in 1793, he would have been four years old) to an era before his father was born, a completely imaginary past. But Natty also moves through time from a moment when the United States had won its independence and had established a Constitution to a period when its separate existence had not yet been imagined.

But it is not quite as simple as all that; for if, on the one hand, Cooper between 1823 and 1840 re-imagined Leatherstocking from an "old and helpless man" to a youth not yet initiated into a career of killing, on the other hand, by 1827 he had also moved him *forward* some ten years, converting him from a pathetic-comic oldster with one tooth, haunting the margins of the settlements he despises— to a magnificent old patriarch who has come to die in ultimate loneliness in the ultimate West. After *The Pioneers,* that is to say, there are two separate pairs of books: one pair, *The Last of the Mohicans* and *The Prairie,* appearing in 1826 and 1827, the other, *The Pathfinder* and *The Deerslayer,* being published in 1840 and 1841. In the first book of each pair, Natty is placed in middle life (in *The Last of the Mohicans,* he is just the age of his author at the moment of writing the book); then he is either pushed forward into a mythical old age, or back to a legendary youth. In each of the later books of the pairs, he stands on the verge of a critical transition: in *The Deerslayer,* he is initiated into manhood; in *The Prairie,* inducted through death into whatever lies beyond. Each romance celebrates, as it were, a *rite de passage.*

In both cases, Natty is transfigured by a confrontation with death; in one, with that of his first victim, in the other, with his own. But in both, he is mythicized, transformed from the mundane reality of *The Pioneers* to another order of being. In that first novel, he is an old outcast, by turns noble and absurd, the kind of peripheral character who in a play by Shakespeare would have talked in prose. In Cooper, he talks by fits and starts a semi-comic American dialect which sets him off from the gentle characters who talk like an English novel for ladies. Natty is an ambiguous type at this stage, a kind of cross between Huck Finn and his Pap, alternately fleeing and defying the law for dubious reasons, and in the end, "lighting out for the Territory." Attending him and reinforcing his meanings is Old John Mohegan (the *first* last of the Mohicans), an Indian as old as he or older, who has been converted both to the white man's religion and the white man's firewater. Twin symbols of dispossession, of all that cannot survive the inevitable and desirable (providential, says pious Mr. Cooper) march of civilization, they are not only doomed, but degraded. Yet the one is capable of setting out once more to pursue the retreating West, and the other of destroying himself in a symbolic holocaust. In that flight and from those ashes, they are reborn, stripped by youth or age of their accidental comic attributes (the dripping nose, the rags, the lone tooth-stump) until they are revealed in all their mythic purity: the Christian Nobel Savage and the pagan Nobel Savage, confronting each other across the "ideal boundary," the fleeting historical moment at which, both harried by the civilization that will ultimately destroy them, they meet. In the end, one is a little paganized, the other a little Christianized—their respective nobilities both augmented in the process.

Natty is an oddly elusive character, almost anonymous. He apparently shuns his baptismal name and is finally buried under a mere initial. Almost as if he were an Indian, he earns not inherits his name, and is known variously as Deerslayer, Hawkeye, Pathfinder, Long Rifle, Leatherstocking, the Trapper. He is overtly pious, meek, chaste (of course!), sententious—often a bore, a Protestant Noble Savage, worshiping in the Universalist Church of the Woods; and yet he is also a dangerous symbol of Cooper's secret protest against the gentle tyranny of home and woman. A white man, who knows the "gifts" of his color and will not take a scalp or be rude to a lady, a man without caste, who knows his place and recognizes all officers and gentlemen as his superiors, he is still a law unto himself: judge and executioner, the man with the gun, the killer—however reluctant. He is the prototype of all pioneers, trappers, cowboys, and other innocently destructive children of nature, which is to say, of the Westerner, quick on the draw and immune to guilt.

In some ways, Leatherstocking seems a Faust in buckskins. Faustian man, however, knows even as he acts that he is damned; that his enterprise is ambiguous at the very least, and that he must pay in suffering for the freedom he demands. Though he defines himself by denying the Calvinist or Catholic theology of his world, the Faustian man needs that theology to create the tensions of his life; he is a blasphemer, and blasphemy is the sign of the secret though tormented believer. The Westerner, on the other hand, knows that what he does is blessed; that God and nature are one; that man, even in solitude, is good. Faust without sin is Natty Bumppo.

And the Devil who is his companion, when genteel Christianity has denied the ultimate reality of the demonic, is Chingachgook,

the Great Serpent, as he is called by one to whom the Serpent is no
longer the eternal Adversary. The Indian represents to Cooper
whatever in the American psyche has been starved to death, whatever genteel Anglo-Saxondom has most ferociously repressed, whatever he himself had stifled to be worthy of his wife and daughters;
but the Indian also stands for himself, which is to say, for a people
dispossessed in the name of a God they do not know and whose
claims they will not grant. The charge of General Lewis Cass and
other literal-minded critics of Cooper that his Indians have "no
living prototypes in our forest," that they are "of the school of Mr.
Heckewelder and not of the school of nature," is quite beside the
point, though no more than Cooper deserves for his own insistence
on the historical truth of his "narratives."

Cooper tells precisely the same sort of truth about the Indian that
Mrs. Stowe was to tell about the Negro; in each it is guilt that speaks,
the guilt of a whole community. Cooper's own boyhood was passed
after the last Indian inruptions into his part of the world were over,
after the Anglo-Saxons had triumphed not only over the savages but
over their allies, the French, too—dark aliens who had once unleashed the primitive terror. Yet when he was a child, the night-
mare of the red uprising still haunted his home town, and at one
point the militia was organized to stand off a raid that never ma-
terialized. It is a little like the Southerners' uneasy dream of the
black insurrection, almost as much a wish as a fear. To exorcise that
self-punishing bad dream, Cooper returns, through the long story it
took him nearly twenty years to tell, to the good dream which is its
complement and antidote: the dream of primeval innocence and the
companionship of red man and white. Ironically enough, he situates
that dream in a time when the Indian menace was still real, had not
yet been transformed from a daylight threat to a nighttime shadow
troubling the *yengsees'* sleep.

Though the Leatherstocking romances are, first of all, entertain-
ments, they are also propitiatory offerings. There is in all of them,
at one point or another, a reflection of Cooper's quarrel with himself (with the "Indian" deep within him): the sound of an inner
voice explaining, justifying, endlessly hashing over the appropriation of the land, on which Cooper's own wealth and status so directly
depended. His first means of coming to terms with his guilt-feelings
is by identifying himself with the injured party, dissociating himself from the exploiters. In reading his romances, the American boy

becomes for a little while the Indian, the trapper; and returning later to his memories or to the books themselves, finds it easy to think of himself as somehow really expropriated and dispossessed, driven from the Great Good Place of the wilderness by pressures of maturity and conformism...

Cooper's *The Pioneers:*
Origins and Structure

by Thomas Philbrick

It was characteristic of Cooper's cross-grained talent that many of the major new departures of his literary career were provoked or directed by his dissatisfaction with what he considered the failings and evasions of other writers and by his intensely competitive desire to demonstrate what they might have done. If his famous contempt for a certain British novel of manners led him to try to write a better book in *Precaution,* if his sense of the inadequacies of the nautical portions of Scott's *The Pirate* induced him to invent the sea novel in *The Pilot* (1824), we may expect to find some similar stimulus at work in the composition of *The Pioneers.* Cooper's critical remarks on *The Sketch Book* and *Bracebridge Hall* and, more important, several rather striking parallels between Irving's books and *The Pioneers* in general design and in specific detail suggest that Irving furnished just such a stimulus.[1] In the three pieces describ-

"Cooper's *The Pioneers:* Origins and Structure" by Thomas Philbrick. Reprinted by permission of the Modern Language Association of America from *Publications of the Modern Language Association,* 79 (December 1964), pp. 583-93. Copyright 1964 by The Modern Language Association of America. The opening pages of the essay, which provide a more complete literary background for *The Pioneers,* have been omitted here.

[1]In his admirably full discussion of *The Pioneers* in *Fenimore Cooper: Sa Vie et son oeuvre: La Jeunesse (1789-1826)* (Aix-en-Provence, 1938), Marcel Clavel rejects the notion that Cooper's novel owes anything whatsoever to Irving's Bracebridge sketches on the ground that *Bracebridge Hall* was published (May 1822) several months after *The Pioneers* was first conceived (pp. 353-354). M. Clavel overlooks the fact that the Bracebridge materials in *The Sketch Book* had appeared some two years before *Bracebridge Hall* itself; moreover, being unaware of Cooper's probable authorship of the review of *Bracebridge Hall* in the May issue of the *Repository,* he could not consider the likelihood that the novelist's attention was called to that book before its publication date and while the conception of *The Pioneers* must still have been in a fairly plastic state.

ing Christmas with the Bracebridge family in *The Sketch Book* and throughout *Bracebridge Hall,* Irving's material bears a marked resemblance to Cooper's. Both authors focus their attention on the residence, domestic routine, and family affairs of a great landed proprietor. Both are concerned with developing the relationship of the proprietor and his household to the community which depends on them by showing their patronage of the village church and school, their benign encouragement of the village games and festivals, and their authoritative role in the enforcement of law and the administration of justice. Moreover, certain elements of the initial and concluding actions of *The Pioneers* follow those of Irving's Bracebridge sketches, taken in the order of their publication. Thus the opening chapters of Cooper's novel, like the three Bracebridge pieces in *The Sketch Book,* center on the celebration of Christmas: the reunion of the family, the feasting, and the church service. The last important episode in *Bracebridge Hall,* apart from the wedding in the final scene, deals with the arrest of the gypsy chieftain Starlight Tom for stealing sheep, his trial before Squire Bracebridge, and his escape on the night following his conviction. Similarly, late in *The Pioneers,* Natty Bumppo is charged with taking a deer out of season, is tried before Judge Temple, and makes his escape from jail that night. But the two authors are even closer to each other than these similar patterns of action alone would indicate. The relationship of Irving's gypsies to the village of Bracebridge, for example, is very nearly the same as that of Cooper's Leatherstocking and Mohegan to Templeton. The gypsies, Irving tells us, "are the denizens of nature, and maintain a primitive independence in spite of law and gospel, of county gaols and country magistrates." In their "obstinate adherence to the wild unsettled habits of savage life," they "are totally distinct from the busy, thrifty people about them. They seem to be like Indians, either above or below the ordinary cares and anxieties of mankind." Their leader, Starlight Tom, again suggests the life of primitive America by his "lofty, air [sic] something like I have seen in an Indian chieftain."[2] In the trial scenes, Squire Bracebridge shares with Judge Temple a reluctance to punish the lawbreaker. The squire conducts the examination of Tom "with great mildness and indulgence,...partly from the kindness of his nature, and partly, I suspect, because his heart yearned towards the culprit, who...had found great favour in his

[2]*Bracebridge Hall, or The Humourists. A Medley* (New York, 1822), II, 48, 126.

eyes."[3] Naturally benevolent and indebted to Natty for the rescue of his daughter, Judge Temple speaks to the accused "mildly," and he must struggle "to overcome his feelings" as he imposes sentence.[4] The specific parallels between Irving's two books and Cooper's by no means end here. One can find in a minor character like Elnathan Todd, the Yankee physician of Templeton, a face and figure that surely derive from Irving's schoolmaster of Sleepy Hollow; appropriately enough, Dr. Todd's father is named Ichabod. And even a character as important as Richard Jones, the bustling little bachelor cousin of Judge Temple, village favorite, and self-styled expert in everything, seems indebted to Irving's sketching. Among the few things that the review of *Bracebridge Hall* had found to praise was the characterization of Master Simon Bracebridge, the Squire's bachelor relation and general factotum, who had been introduced in *The Sketch Book* as "a tight brisk little man" with "a chirping, buoyant disposition."[5] The point that should be made, however, is not that Cooper borrowed certain elements of characterization and situation from Irving but that the pages of *The Sketch Book* and *Bracebridge Hall* bring into haphazard juxtaposition a substantial portion of the diverse materials from which *The Pioneers* was to be constructed: romantic outcasts, voracious Yankees, paternalistic proprietors and bustling bachelors, manor-house manners and tavern politics, village games and country churches. His task was to assemble those materials in a coherent and meaningful structure, to impose upon them systems of relationship and patterns of development that Irving's casual sketching did not permit.

Cooper, of course, had the novelist's advantage of being able to tie his materials to firm and sustained plot lines. If Irving had made an ineffectual gesture in this direction with the romance of the fair Julia and her handsome young officer, Cooper could shape a true narrative from the developing conflict of Natty Bumppo and Judge Temple and from the related action of Oliver Effingham's assumption of his rightful inheritance. Yet neither these two major lines of action nor any other conventional plots were adequate to sustain the huge burden of description that was necessary to the depiction of an

---

[3]*Bracebridge Hall,* II, 193.
[4]*The Pioneers* (New York, 1859), pp. 408, 410. All subsequent page references to this volume, the Townsend edition of the novel, will be made parenthetically in my text.
[5]*The Sketch Book of Goeffrey Crayon, Gent.,* No. 5 (New York, 1820), pp. 45, 46.

entire community in the transition from wilderness to civilization. To unify that mass of description, to prevent it from splintering into a succession of set pieces and genre sketches as it does in Irving's books, in Paulding's poem, and even in the novels of Maria Edgeworth and her followers, Cooper was forced to discover some principle of organization beyond those of the conventional narrative.

A clue to the nature of that discovery is offered by the label which Cooper affixed to *The Pioneers* on its title page, "A Descriptive Tale," for the phrase suggests that he considered the book as an attempt to join the methods of prose fiction to those of descriptive poetry. Centering on the interplay of human activity and the seasonal cycle of nature, the descriptive poem flourished well into the early decades of the nineteenth century.[6] Notwithstanding the new approaches to nature and rural life developed by the Lake Poets, the popularity of the older mode as practiced by Thomson, Cowper, and Crabbe persisted, so vigorously, in fact, that Thomson's *The Seasons* went through forty-four editions between 1800 and 1820.[7] To Cooper, always an admirer of Thomson,[8] the harmonious interweaving of extensive natural description, narrative episodes, and genre sketches of country labors and recreations in *The Seasons* must have seemed intensely relevant to the task he had set for himself in *The Pioneers*. Just as the two chapter epigraphs which he drew from *The Seasons* mark the presence of Thomson's poem in his consciousness, so the general movement of the novel and certain salient features of its design indicate the pervasive influence which Thomson and the descriptive poets generally exerted on that consciousness. Thus many of the stock elements of the eighteenth-century descriptive poem can be found in *The Pioneers*: the landscape painting, the attention paid to weather portents, the didactic descriptions of agricultural techniques such as the manufacture of maple sugar, the vignettes of seasonal activities like sleighing in winter and bass fishing in spring, the genre sketches of village games

[6]For a history of the genre and a full discussion of the central importance of *The Seasons* to it, see Dwight L. Durling, *Georgic Tradition in English Poetry*, Columbia Univ. Stud. in Engl. and Comp. Lit., No. 121 (New York, 1935); for a more compact account, see Robert A. Aubin, *Topographical Poetry in XVIII-Century England*, MLA Revolving Fund Ser., No. 6 (New York, 1936), pp. 46-55.

[7]See Durling, p. 49.

[8]According to Cooper's daughter, Thomson was among his five favorite authors: see Susan Fenimore Cooper, *Pages and Pictures, from the Writings of James Fenimore Cooper* (New York, 1861), p. 17.

like the Christmas turkey shoot—all are American counterparts of
the standard materials of British descriptive verse. Judge Temple's
advocacy of conservation and Natty's denouncements of the settlers'
"wasty ways" appear to be in some degree an outgrowth of the pattern of protest against the slaughter of birds and animals that Thomson introduced to English rural poetry, for Cooper's images of the
predatory citizens of Templeton correspond closely to Thomson's
view that "ensanguined Man /Is now become the lion of the plain, /
And worse."[9] The much discussed ambivalence of Cooper's attitudes in *The Pioneers* toward the polar values of wildness and
civilization seems less remarkable as a revelation of unique characteristics of his mind and art when one encounters precisely the
same tensions and contradictions in *The Seasons*.[10] But whatever
may have been the exact extent of the influence on Cooper of Thomson and the poetic tradition he established, there can be little doubt
that they contributed heavily to the grand design of *The Pioneers,*
its seasonal structure.

Thomson's poem is divided into four major parts of approximate-
ly equal length, each named for a season and descriptive of it. *Spring*
is developed by means of a systematic series of descriptions of the
effect of the season on inanimate matter, then on vegetation, and
finally on man. *Summer* consists of the account of a single typical
summer day, beginning with the dawn and closing with nightfall.
Autumn and *Winter* are more loosely organized than the two preceding sections, but both involve a progressive movement in time
through their respective seasons. Since the pattern of seasonal
change itself is not Cooper's exclusive subject, as it is Thomson's,
The Pioneers lacks the symmetry of Thomson's organization, and
yet the time scheme of the novel is carefully designed to achieve
Thomson's major effect, a sense of the incessant flux in nature and

[9]*Spring,* II. 340-342; the text of all quotations from Thomson is that of *The Poetical Works of James Thomson,* ed. F. J. Child, 2 vols. (Boston, n.d.). For a discussion
of the priority and influence of Thomson's humane concern for wildlife, see Ray-
ner Unwin, *The Rural Muse: Studies in the Peasant Poetry of England* (London,
1954), p. 43.

[10]The best treatment of this aspect of Cooper's thought in *The Pioneers* is Henry
Nash Smith, *Virgin Land: The American West as Symbol and Myth* (New York,
1957), pp. 66-70. For discussions of Thomson's contradictory attitudes toward primitive values and the progress of civilization, see Raymond D. Havens, "Primitivism
and the Idea of Progress in Thomson," *SP,* xxix (1932), 41-52, and Alan D. Mc-
Killop, *The Background of Thomson's Seasons* (Minneapolis, 1942), pp. 89-128.

human activity and of the sharp contrasts in the scenes that the seasonal cycle brings successively into view. Thus Chapters i-xix are devoted to winter, concentrating on the three days from 24 December to 26 December. Chapters xx-xxv supply three vignettes of spring: first the time of alternate thaw and frost in late March (Chapters xx-xxi), then the breaking up of the ice on the lake and the migration of birds in late April (Chapter xxii), and finally the balmy days and mild evenings of May (Chapters xxiii-xxv). Chapters xxvi-xl cover the events of three days in the intense heat and drought of late July,[11] while fall is represented only in the concluding chapter of the novel, set on a bracing morning in mid-October.

At each turn of the seasonal wheel, Cooper summarizes the changes in nature and in the human community during the intervening period, carefully establishes the appearance and mood of the natural world at the time of the present action, and then leads adroitly into the doings and dialogue of his characters, a transition that usually establishes an immediate relation either of contrast or similitude between the natural scene and the human emotions he is about to depict. The opening of Chapter xxii, the account of the slaughter of the passenger pigeons by the inhabitants of Templeton, illustrates Cooper's method. He first bridges the gap between the preceding scene, set in late March, and this one:

> From this time to the close of April the weather continued to be a succession of great and rapid changes. One day, the soft airs of spring seemed to be stealing along the valley, and in unison with an invigorating sun, attempting covertly to rouse the dormant powers of the vegetable world; while on the next, the surly blasts from the north would sweep across the lake, and erase every impression left by their gentle adversaries. The snow, however, finally disappeared, and the green wheat-fields were seen in every direction, spotted with the dark and charred stumps that had, the preceding season, supported some of the proudest trees of the forest. Ploughs were in motion,, wherever those useful implements could be used.... The lake had lost the

[11] Cooper's handling of time in this section of the novel involves a curious double movement. Like Thomson's *Summer,* Chs. xxvi-xxxi trace the happenings of a single day from early morning to evening. This day is first said to be "in the beginning of July" (p. 312). Later we learn that it is sometime after the Fourth of July (p. 361), and at last the day is designated as 20 July (p. 368). The effect is to produce at once an extreme concentration of action and the impression that the heat and dryness are increasing as one might expect them to do only with the passage of several weeks.

beauty of a field of ice, but still a dark and gloomy covering concealed its waters, for the absence of currents left them yet hidden under a porous crust. ... Large flocks of wild geese were seen passing over the country, which hovered, for a time, around the hidden sheet of water, apparently searching for a resting-place; and then, on finding themselves excluded by the chill covering, would soar away to the north, filling the air with discordant screams, as if venting their complaints at the tardy operations of nature.   (p. 265)

To see the general resemblance of Cooper's technique to Thomson's, one need only compare this passage with the opening lines of *Spring:*

> And see where surly WINTER passes off,
> Far to the North, and calls his ruffian Blasts:
> His Blasts obey, and quit the howling hill,
> The shatter'd forest, and the ravaged vale;
> While softer Gales succeed, at whose kind touch,
> Dissolving snows in livid torrents lost,
> The Mountains lift their green heads to the skies.
>
> As yet the trembling Year is unconfirm'd,
> And WINTER oft at eve resumes the breeze,
> Chills the pale Morn, and bids his driving sleets
> Deform the Day delightless: so that scarce
> The Bittern knows his time, with bill ingulf'd,
> To shake the sounding marsh; or from the shore
> The Plovers when to scatter o'er the heath,
> And sing their wild notes to the listening waste.
>
> Joyous, the impatient Husbandman perceives
> Relenting Nature, and his lusty steers
> Drives from their stalls, to where the well used plough
> Lies in the furrow, loosen'd from the frost.
>
> Nor only through the lenient air this change,
> Delicious, breathes; the penetrative sun,
> His force deep-darting to the dark retreat
> Of Vegetation, sets the steaming Power
> At large, to wander o'er the vernant Earth.

(ll. 11-25, 34-37, 78-82)

The personified powers of the contending seasons, the release of woods and fields from their covering of snow, the revivifying effect of the sun on the vegetation, the resumption of plowing, the weather-baffled birds, all testify to the kinship of the two treatments of seasonal change. And just as *Spring* as a whole moves from the effect of the season on nature to its effect on man, not only by painting scenes of typical seasonal activities but by introducing narrative episodes illustrative of man's dependence on and response to his natural environment, so Cooper gradually links his description of the oncoming spring to the human world. But his method is more complex and subtle than Thomson's. Surveying the still-frozen surface of Lake Otsego, Cooper seizes on a single point of detail, that the lake was now in the "undisturbed possession of two eagles, who alighted on the centre of its field, and sat eying their undisputed territory":

> During the presence of these monarchs of the air, the flocks of migrating birds avoided crossing the plain of ice, by turning into the hills, apparently seeking the protection of the forests, while the white and bald heads of the tenants of the lake were turned upwards, with a look of contempt. But the time had come, when even these kings of birds were to be dispossessed. An opening had been gradually increasing at the lower extremity of the lake, and…the fresh southerly winds, that now breathed freely upon the valley, made an impression on the waters. Mimic waves began to curl over the margin of the frozen field, which exhibited an outline of crystallizations that slowly receded towards the north. At each step the power of the winds and waves increased, until, after a struggle of a few hours, the turbulent little billows succeeded in setting the whole field in motion, when it was driven beyond the reach of the eye, with a rapidity that was as magical as the change produced in the scene by this expulsion of the lingering remnant of winter. Just as the last sheet of agitated ice was disappearing in the distance, the eagles rose, and soared with a wide sweep above the clouds, while the waves tossed their little caps of snow into the air, as if rioting in their release from a thraldom of five months' duration.   (p. 266)

In a total view of the novel, this passage becomes an important symbolic reference to two of Cooper's major themes, the meanings of legitimate right and the contest between freedom and authority. The two eagles, those "monarchs of the air" who eye the birds of passage with disdain, those "kings of birds" who assert their claim to be the rightful owners and rulers of their domain and who nevertheless are dispossessed by the winds of change, are intimately linked to the ultimate significance of the dispute over the ownership of the land which Judge Temple holds. Similarly, the rebellious waves are one in a whole series of images of the opposition of liberty, license, and anarchy on the one hand and discipline, restraint, and oppression on the other. The scene, however, also serves to establish an immediate relation between nature and man. In denying the lake to the other birds, the eagles function as symbols of the reign of winter, at last overthrown with the disintegration of the ice sheet. Their dispossession signals a liberation and awakening and points backward to the preceding paragraph, in which the "invigorating sun" attempts "to rouse the dormant powers of the vegetable world," and forward to the release of the waves from their winter thraldom. With the keynotes of motion, release, and reanimation thus clearly sounded, Cooper moves swiftly from the natural sphere to the human one:

> The following morning Elizabeth was awakened by the exhilarating sounds of the martins, who were quarrelling and chattering around the little boxes suspended above her windows, and the cries of Richard, who was calling in tones animating as the signs of the season itself—
>
> "Awake! awake! my fair lady! the gulls are hovering over the lake already, and the heavens are alive with pigeons."   (p. 266)

Unable to resist this "animated appeal," Elizabeth Temple joins the group who are "impatiently waiting" to begin the pigeon shoot and finds that "if the heavens were alive with pigeons, the whole village seemed equally in motion" (p. 267). With man and nature stirred into buzzing activity by the advent of spring, Cooper can now begin the narration of the episode.

The opening paragraphs of Chapter xxii, then, serve not only as an indication of the resemblance in concept and technique of Thomson's *The Seasons* and important segments of *The Pioneers* but as an example of the method by which Cooper introduces nearly all the major episodes of the novel, a method which at once fixes the natural setting of the present action amid the flux of seasonal change and establishes an immediate connection between the tempo and mood of that natural scene and the human action which it is to surround. But since Cooper's final concern is with the drama of human relationships in the process of settlement and not, as in Thomson, with the seasonal panorama of nature, the question remains whether descriptive passages like the one just discussed are not at last primarily decorative in function, beautiful and often powerful set pieces that incidentally help to bridge the gaps between the episodes of what might otherwise be an annoyingly disjointed narrative. Do they contribute to the unity of the novel in any way more radical than their service as transitions? Is there an organic relation between Cooper's natural history of the year and the complex of human actions that his novel charts?

III

The initial and most forceful impression conveyed by the passages of natural description in *The Pioneers* is that nothing is static or permanent in nature but that everything is caught up in a cycle of incessant transformation. The only certainty in the natural world is the fact of change itself. When Cooper extends the field of vision in his landscapes to include the works of man as well as the objects of nature, he makes it apparent that the human community of Templeton is involved also in the flow of change, change to which it both responds and contributes. In the previously quoted description of the April landscape, for example, the forest has not been devastated by the fury of winter, as it had in the parallel passage from Thomson; rather, in the background of Cooper's landscape are the ravages of man, "the dark and charred stumps that had, the preceding season, supported some of the proudest trees of the forest." Indeed, "so rapid were the changes" worked by the settlers that Elizabeth Temple, newly returned to her father's domain after an absence of four years, imagines "they were enlarging under her eye, while she was gazing, in mute wonder, at the alterations that a few short years had made in the aspect of the country" (pp. 40-41). Within the village itself, Elizabeth finds that the process of change goes on still more swiftly. On the signboards, "not only new occupations, but names that were strangers to her ears, met her gaze at every step. ... The very houses seemed changed. This had been altered by an addition; that had been painted: another had been erected on the site of an old acquaintance, which had been banished from the earth almost as soon as it made its appearance on it" (p. 122). In no way a rock of permanence amid this stream of change, Judge Temple's mansion, which has set the architectural fashion for the surrounding area, is modeled on "the composite order," a style "intended to be the most useful of all, for it admitted into its construction such alterations as convenience or circumstances might require" (p. 43). Like the buildings they inhabit, the people of Templeton continually undergo drastic changes, alterations, transformations. At one end of the social scale is the shiftless Jotham Riddel, who, according to Judge Temple, "'changes his county every three years, his farm every six months, and his occupation every season!...that epitome of all the unsteady and profitless propensities of the settlers'" (p. 349). At the other end, within the Judge's own household, is Richard Jones with his flexible purposes and his innovating imagination, would-be marksman, musician, physician, architect, religious authority, animal breeder, mathematician, prospector: the sheriff and presiding spirit of the county. Marmaduke Temple himself is not exempt from change; the former Quaker merchant is now a great landed proprietor, an Episcopalian, a judge and member of the state legislature. Contemplating the transformation of Oliver Effingham from rude forester to genteel private secretary, Elizabeth observes that "'everything in this magical country seems to border on the marvellous,...and among all the changes, this is certainly not the least wonderful. The actors are as unique as the scenery'" (pp. 233-234).

The setting of *The Pioneers,* then, is "that changeful country" (p. 236) where both nature and man exist in ceaseless and rapid fluxion. But the mere condition of change is not the only tie between the natural and human worlds of the novel. There is first, and most obviously, a direct correlation of human activity with the seasonal cycle. Thus, at the approach of spring, "the inhabitants of the country gradually changed their pursuits from the social and bustling movements of the time of snow, to the laborious and domestic engagements of the coming season. ... Everything seemed indicative of a mighty change, not only in the earth, but in those who derived their sources of comfort and happiness from its bosom" (pp. 238-239). It is this aspect of the novel, the governance of typical human activities by the revolution of the seasonal wheel, that makes it seem most Thomsonian and reminds readers of the whole pastoral tradition that lies behind both *The Pioneers* and *The Seasons.* On first reading *The Pioneers,* William Cullen Bryant discovered in Cooper "the poet of rural life in this country—our Hesiod, our Theocritus, except that he writes without the restraint of numbers, and is a greater poet than they."[12] Donald Ringe finds in the descriptive portions of the book "a kind of pastoral idyll," while Charles Brady, emphasizing the retrospective mood of the book, remarks that "here is Vergil more than Hesiod or Herrick."[13] But the pastoral quality of *The Pioneers* is most evident in those scenes which take a sweeping and generalized view, as when the plow is seen moving in a distant hillside clearing, or to those readers whose response to the novel is equally sweeping and generalized. To stress, as does Bryant, the cheerful harmony of the people of Templeton among themselves and with nature, or to seize, as does D. H. Lawrence, on the unalloyed beauty of the scenes in the tavern or at the pigeon shoot is to submit to vivid but superficial first impressions, to mistake the tone of the book, and to fail to attend to Cooper's intricate conception of the relation of man and nature, the basis of the thematic and structural unity of the novel. *The Pioneers* appears idyllic only at long range and in dim light.[14]

If the novel must be associated with the pastoral, it is best viewed as an ironic treatment of the genre. As James Grossman observes, "the mood of the book is that of the sophisticated pastoral that mocks, as tenderly as it loves, the wholesome life it portrays, and is as skeptical as it is sentimental about its pictures of sweet rural cooperation and communal labors affectionately shared. In Cooper the doubt is not whether this simple world ever existed but whether men ever liked it."[15] Looked at closely, the episodes of the novel reveal anything but harmony and loving cooperation in the affairs of men.

[12]"Discourse on the Life and Genius of Cooper," in *Memorial of James Fenimore Cooper* (New York, 1852), p. 47.

[13]Ringe,: [*James Fenimore Cooper* (New Haven, 1962)] p. 33; Charles A. Brady, "James Fenimore Cooper, 1789-1851: Myth-maker and Christian Romancer," in *American Classics Reconsidered: A Christian Appraisal,* ed. Harold C. Gardiner (New York, 1958), p. 84.

[14]In *Studies in Classic American Literature* (New York, 1953), p. 64, Lawrence makes the strange judgment that *The Pioneers* "is a beautiful, resplendent picture of life. Fenimore puts in only the glamour." It is perhaps significant that the highly impressionistic comments of Bryant and Lawrence are both marked by factual errors. Bryant has Mohegan taking part in the turkey shoot, while Lawrence gives the setting of the novel as the shores of Lake Champlain.

[15]*James Fenimore Cooper* (New York, 1949), p. 30.

[16]For a balanced and perceptive treatment of these aspects of *The Pioneers,* see Ringe, pp. 33-37.

From the opening scene of the dispute over the deer that has been shot on the road to Templeton to the final confrontation of Natty and the forces of Judge Temple's law in the penultimate chapter, the novel is infused with a spirit of angry contention, with resentment and boasting, with competition and the jealous assertion of rival claims. Every serious commentator on *The Pioneers* has dealt at length with the conflict between the primitive freedom of Natty Bumppo and Judge Temple's attempts to foster the institutions of civilization, and some have gone on to discuss the still larger conflict between the self-discipline which both Natty and the Judge champion and the wanton destructiveness of the community at large.[16] But conflict is by no means limited to these two characters or to these particular issues. In Remarkable Pettibone's resentment against Elizabeth Temple's authority in the Judge's household, in the general hostility to the attempts of Richard Jones and the Judge to establish Episcopalianism as the official mode of worship in Templeton, in the quarrels between Ben Pump and Billy Kirby over the respective merits of salt water and fresh, everywhere in the novel one encounters bickering and baiting, grudges and grumbling. The Temples' housekeeper and their steward settle down with their grog for a Christmas Eve chat but soon fall to squabbling and separate, hurling insults at each other. The turkey shoot brings the "jealous rivalry" of Natty Bumppo and Billy Kirby into "open collision" (p. 209) and is marred by repeated angry disputes over the rules of the sport. The fishing expedition violates the stillness of the lake at night with the invectives that express "the turbulent passions of the party"; Judge Temple fears that "'there will soon be ill-blood'" between the wranglers (p. 280). Perhaps the best example of the characteristic mood and movement of Cooper's episodes is offered by the tavern scene. Having attended the church service on Christmas Eve, the male citizens of Templeton gather in the Bold Dragoon. One would expect a demonstration of Christmas fellowship and good cheer, but the scene opens ominously as Lippet, the village lawyer, and Hiram Doolittle, the carpenter and justice of the peace, entertain the pleasing possibility of a lawsuit against Judge Temple. When the Judge and Natty join the group, the two start to argue about the game laws which the state legislature has recently enacted at Temple's instigation. As Natty lapses into sullen bitterness and Mohegan begins to mutter his war chant, Richard Jones pipes up with a new song that he has composed:

> Then let us be jolly, and prove that we are
> A set of good fellows, who seem very rare,
> And can laugh and sing all the day.

The song continues while Natty, speaking in Delaware to Mohegan, identifies the Judge as their true enemy. The drunken Indian, his eyes "glaring with an expression of wild resentment," fumbles at his belt for his tomahawk and then collapses in total inebriation. "'Well, old John is soon sowed up,'" Jones remarks, and he resumes his cheery ditty (pp. 178-181).

The tavern scene not only exemplifies the pattern of development of the majority of the episodes of *The Pioneers;* it represents in miniature the progression of the novel as a whole, the movement from suppressed enmity to the verge of violence. And by viewing that progression against the changing seasonal background, the reader begins to discern the full intricacy and subtlety of the system of relationships that binds together Cooper's depictions of the spheres of man and nature. In the opening Christmas scenes the relation between the human world and the natural one at first appears to be simple indeed, in the words of one critic "a winter contrast, as old as Horace, between the snow-capped mountain without the roaring fire within."[17] As the episode in the tavern shows, however, the conventional connotations of the hearth—security, sociality, comfort, intimacy—are inverted by Cooper's manner of developing the winter scenes; even Richard Jones's quickness with his Christmas greetings is not an indication of abounding good will but of his compulsive "zeal for preeminence" (p. 196). Yet for the most part the resentment, rivalry, and hostility of the winter scenes remain safely suppressed beneath the forms of social cooperation and civic harmony. The citizens of Templeton, including those who subscribe to the "conference" of dissenters, dutifully attend the Episcopalian service on Christmas Eve; at its conclusion "sundry looks of private dissatisfaction were exchanged between Hiram and one or two of the leading members of the *conference,* but the feeling went no further at that time" (p. 141). The frozen earth and ice-locked lake image the surface calm of the population of Templeton. For the time, the discipline imposed by social forms, whether they be the decorum of the church service or the rules of the shooting

---

[17]Brady, p. 84.

match, is sufficient to prevent the latent enmity that pervades the community from expressing itself in action.

As we have seen, the advent of spring stirs both the natural and human worlds into motion. The sap rises in the sugar maples, the waves of the lake are free to toss, swift flights of pigeons crowd the air, the water is alive with bass. The villagers, too, erupt in activity, rushing to their stations for the pigeon shoot or laboring at the lines of the bass seine. In such episodes as the slaughter of the pigeons and the massacre of the bass, the citizens, organized by Richard Jones in what is by this point clearly a parody of communal cooperation, give vent to the destructive impulses that the winter discipline has stifled. The frenzy is upon everyone. Although Judge Temple had contemplated his part in the pigeon shoot "with that kind of feeling that many a man has experienced before him, who discovers, after the excitement of the moment has passed, that he has purchased pleasure at the price of misery to others" (p. 274), he nevertheless is seized once again by the desire to destroy in the fishing scene, "yielding to the excitement of the moment, and laying his hands to the net, with no trifling addition to the force" (p. 284). Even Elizabeth and Louisa Grant, the minister's daughter, are "greatly excited and highly gratified by seeing two thousand captives...drawn from the bosom of the lake, and laid prisoners at their feet" (p. 284). The springtime quickening, then, sharply raises the level of activity and passion in the human world of the novel, but the change is not simply a harmonious response by man to the swifter tempo of nature. The flow of the sap, the migration of the pigeons to their northern breeding grounds, the shoals of spawning bass are all manifestations of the creative vitality of nature, a vitality which man here intercepts and truncates with the needless ravages of his ax, gun, and seine. A heavy irony thus qualifies the paralleled renewal of motion in the natural and human worlds. The processes of nature yield life and plentitude; man's activity is productive only of wounds and death. But, for the season, nature serves as a convenient outlet for the destructive impulses that might otherwise act within the community, shattering its pretense of unity.

The pace of activity and the intensity of passion rise to a climax in the scenes set in July. Significantly, the initial incident draws Natty and Mohegan into an abandonment of the self-control and restraint that had distinguished them from the rest of the characters during the pigeon shoot and bass fishing. As Natty watches his dogs drive a deer into the lake, he no longer is the calm advocate of disciplined moderation. He knows that the venison is lean in July, knows that he will get into trouble with the law if he hunts out of season, and yet the sight of the swimming buck is too much for him: "'The creater's a fool to tempt a man this way'" (p. 326). Even Mohegan, his dark eye "dancing in his head with a wild animation" (p. 328), loses the stoic resignation that only drink before had violated. They kill the deer, and Natty exclaims, "'This warms a body's blood, old John'" (p. 328). In the dry heat of July, the novel seems to suggest, everything succumbs to violence, not only the natural man but nature itself. Soon after Natty and Mohegan kill the buck, Elizabeth and Louisa narrowly escape the attack of a panther, whose "glaring eyes" and "horrid malignity" (p. 337) will long haunt Elizabeth's dreams. As the heat of the summer day increases, animosity spreads throughout the community. When Hiram Doolittle and Billy Kirby attempt to enter Natty's hut to find evidence of his violation of the game laws, the hunter assaults Doolittle and threatens Billy with his rifle. Now Judge Temple determines to arrest and try Natty, and Oliver is no longer able to maintain his pose of mild deference before the Judge: "Hitherto he had been deeply agitated by his emotions; but now the volcano burst its boundaries" (p. 380).

Fire and heat, implied in the imagery of this quotation and of earlier references to the passions and attitudes of the actors in the July scenes, now become an explicit motif of the action. Natty is arrested amid the smoldering ruins of his hut where he is "treading down the hot ashes and dying embers with callous feet" (p. 392), as if enacting his effort to smother his rage and submit peaceably to the officers of the court. But animosity and violence flicker throughout the scenes of Natty's trial and punishment in the stocks and break out once more as Natty, aided by Oliver, makes his escape from jail. The hue-and-cry in the village, "some earnest in the pursuit, and others joining it as in sport" (p. 443), takes us back to the scene of the pigeon shoot, but now the chase is a manhunt. In the action of the following day, the development of the motif of heat is resumed. As she climbs Mount Vision for a meeting with the fugitive, "the very atmosphere that Elizabeth inhaled was hot and dry" (p. 439). At the summit she encounters Mohegan, who sits there awaiting the approach of death, his eyes filled with "wildness and fire" (p. 440). Soon the figurative fire once more becomes literal; the torches of the posse that had pursued Natty have kindled the

dry woods on the mountain. The vivid scene of the ensuing con-
flagration on the summit coincides with the emotional climax of
the novel; in the desperation of the moment Oliver declares his
love for Elizabeth, and Mohegan, scorched and dying, rejects the
hope of Christian redemption held out to him by Mr. Grant and
returns to the proud stoicism of his pagan past. Although the forest
fire is extinguished by a sudden thunderstorm, the human world of
the novel remains in a "feverish state" (p. 470). Led by Richard
Jones, who is "burning with a desire" (p. 475) to examine Natty's
cave under the delusion that it contains a clue to the location of a
non-existent silver mine, the village militia assaults Natty's strong-
hold. At the moment when the action is about to turn from comic
violence to serious bloodshed, Judge Temple and Oliver call for
peace. The existence of Major Effingham, Oliver's grandfather and
the original owner of the territory around Templeton, is brought to
light, and Oliver's title to a portion of the Judge's holdings is acknowledged. With the marriage of Oliver and Elizabeth, the estate
is consolidated and established on a sure and lasting basis, for the
marriage unites the claims of its legal owner and of its developer.

Even a summary of this sort should make the central symbolic
significance of the forest fire evident. As we have seen, the fire in
nature serves as an emblem of the fierce passions that have engulfed
the human world. The gathering rancor of Natty Bumppo against
the civilization that is despoiling the wilderness, the reassertion
of savage dignity by the dying Mohegan, the emotional tension in
Oliver as he is pulled between his resentment of what he thinks has
been Judge Temple's usurpation of his birthright and his love for
the usurper's daughter, the aimless curiosity and acquisitiveness
of Richard Jones, the deeper avarice of his confederates Jotham
Riddel and Hiram Doolittle, and the restless impulse toward
destruction of the whole community of Templeton are mirrored by
their equally turbulent and dangerous natural counterpart. Moreover, the fire functions in a less obvious way as a punishment and a
purgative, for Jotham Riddel, the fullest embodiment of the itching
greed and anarchic instability that constitute Cooper's most pointed
indictment of the community at large, dies by its agency. Unwilling to abandon his hunt for the illusory silver, Riddel is overtaken
and nearly consumed by the flames. The fate of Riddel, "whose life
paid the forfeiture of his folly," conveys "a mortifying lesson" to
Richard Jones (p. 494), and the Temple household is henceforth free

of his schemes for exploiting the resources of the territory. Resonant in its implications and dramatic in its presentation, the scene of the forest fire thus represents Cooper's closest approach to the fulfillment of what would seem to be the major objective of the design of *The Pioneers*, the perfect fusion of natural setting and human action.

IV

Effective though the fire scene is, however, its suggestion of symbolic catharsis is not alone a sufficient resolution of the conflicts of the novel. Its primary relevance is to the circle that includes Richard Jones, Jotham Riddel, Hiram Doolittle, and those other citizens of Templeton who are similarly devoted to the causes of exploitation and innovation. The center of conflict in the novel, the tighter circle that encloses Natty, Mohegan, Oliver, and Judge Temple, seems less directly related to the fire and its meanings. It is true that the fire contributes to and coincides with the death of Mohegan, but surely we are not intended to regard his death as a retributive cleansing like Riddel's; on the contrary, all the emphases of Mohegan's death scene are on release and victory. We may well wonder, then, why his rejection of the white civilization to which he has resigned himself throughout the narrative and his triumphant resumption of savage purity should occur at this moment: what is the connection between the deaths of Riddel and Mohegan, and what is the significance of Mohegan's return to his Indian ways, as if some huge cycle had been or was about to be completed? Beyond these questions lies another. Are we to take the concluding chapter of the novel, in which Oliver gains his inheritance and marries Elizabeth and in which Natty conveniently removes himself as a source of conflict by moving westward, as what it at first appears to be, a highly arbitrary manipulation of character and action for the purpose of securing a happy (and spurious) ending? If the conflicting passions that the novel has stressed since its opening pages are meant to be forgotten amid the hopeful sentiments of young love and the pleasing pathos of Natty's departure, then the conclusion is no conclusion at all; it is only a scattering of the dust of sentimentality, under cover of which Cooper can make his exit.

The setting of the last chapter, it should be noted, is a fall day, "one of our mildest October mornings, when the sun seems a ball of silvery fire, and the elasticity of the air is felt while it is inhaled, imparting vigor and life to the whole system" (p. 494). The natural setting is thus an ideal one, reminiscent of that perpetual spring which Thomson imagines to have preceded the corruption of man and the cycle of seasonal change which came as his punishment. Fire is present in the sun, but it is remote, restrained, beneficent. The air itself is life-giving, refreshing, renewing. The mood is that of a benediction, again, as in the death of Mohegan, as if some sweeping cycle had concluded and a fresh beginning could now be made. Within the realm of nature, of course, just such a cycle is about to be completed as the sequence of the seasons swings toward its starting point in winter. That a similarly cyclical revolution has been accomplished in the realm of human affairs may be overlooked so long as we fix our attention to the last scene exclusively on Natty's departure. Viewed in that way, the ending of the novel seems to be only a realization of Natty's repeated fear that "might makes right," that the forces of the social order, personified and led by Judge Temple, have triumphed and that he, the representative of the natural order, has been displaced, driven deep into the western wilderness where, at least for the moment, he is beyond the reach of the destructive and all-powerful hand of civilization. This might well be Natty's interpretation of the outcome of the action. But Natty's angle of vision is a strangely limited one. In an important sense, he is more primitive, more profoundly embedded in savage isolation than are the Indians with whom he has lived. Not only is he the adversary of white society; he has no place in Indian society: no wife, no family, no shared religion, no political status. He is the advocate of animals and trees and the enemy of man and human values. During the pigeon shoot he shakes his head sadly at the sight of "'Mr. Oliver, as bad as the rest of them, firing into the flocks, as if he was shooting down nothing but Mingo warriors'" (p. 270). Natty regards the Iroquois as fit objects for slaughter, but "'the Lord won't see the waste of his creatures [animal, not human] for nothing'" (p. 270). Denouncing the agents of the society that persecutes him, he says that he has been driven "'to wish that the beasts of the forest...was his kindred and race'" (p. 393). That wish has long since been fulfilled.

Although the prolonged spectacle of the rancor and destructiveness of the little segment of society over which Judge Temple presides may tempt us to share Natty's point of view, the final position of the novel is not a simple primitivistic condemnation of civilization. We must not allow the pathos of Natty's displacement to distract us from the fact that Judge Temple has also been displaced, for his dominion is now in the hands of Oliver Effingham. So long as we dismiss Oliver as merely a stock romantic hero, a wooden young man who figures in the novel only as a sop to the interests of young female readers, the significance of his assumption of possession and authority will escape us. But careful attention to Oliver's place in the total scheme of the book suggests that he is designed to play a key role in Cooper's drama of societal evolution.

Seen in its widest dimension, *The Pioneers* encompasses the whole sweep of the first two hundred years of social change in America, the progression from the hunting culture of the forest Indians, through the initial processes of white settlement, to the establishment of a stable, ordered civilization.[18] Although the action of the novel involves only the middle phase, the narrative is framed, as it were, by the other two. Thus the central action concerns Natty Bumppo and Judge Temple, those embodiments of primitivism and progress who play out their intricate relationship within the period of transition. But neither Natty nor the Judge offers any basis on which the final structure of civilization can be erected. Natty, of course, rejects the very idea of a human community. And Judge Temple, the promoter of churches and schools, of roads and coal mines, of civil law and domestic decorum, ironically lacks the sanction of tradition and legitimacy, lacks the roots in the continuity of history that Cooper considers essential to a viable civilization. Judge Temple is a man of change, capable of stimulating and overseeing the process of transition but unable to consolidate and perpetuate its results, for, in Cooper's view, the innovator is necessarily the enemy of legitimacy and order. Within the scheme of the novel Temple must be depicted as a supporter of the rebellion against the crown, as a betrayer of his Quaker principles by his war-profiteering and his *de facto* ownership of a Negro slave, as a judge without legal training and with qualifications that "might make a Templar smile" (p. 37). As the proprietor of Templeton, the Judge may censure the excesses of the regicides in revolutionary France, and he may seek to establish the

---

[18]There is a hint of a still wider perspective in Cooper's Malthusian remark that the inhabitants of New York will find that "the evil day must arrive, when their possessions shall become unequal to their wants" (p. 15).

Anglicanism of the British past, but his position is undercut by the principle of change that his whole life has served. He is called "'duke'" by his friends and his house is known as the "castle"; his cousin Richard Jones thinks that Temple "'would make an excellent king'" and would give him a throne if it were in his power. (p. 199). But this same Jones, this ultra-Episcopalian and whimsical royalist, opens the court in which his cousin sits by flourishing a sword "that he was fond of saying his ancestors had carried in one of Cromwell's victories" (p. 396). Temple's reign is in reality a short-lived usurpation that must soon give way to the restoration of a fully legitimate authority.

Clearly Oliver Effingham is designed to be that legitimate authority, and equally clearly his inadequacy in the role is a major weakness of the novel. In part the trouble stems from Cooper's notorious tendency, especially marked in the early novels, to freeze his genteel young men in attitudes of stilted dignity and insufferable pride. But Oliver is further devitalized by his place in the general scheme of *The Pioneers*. He and Mohegan are framing characters; that is, they are figures intended to represent the two phases that enclose the period of transition on which the narrative focuses. As such, they are necessarily passive. Mohegan, to whom Natty pays "the utmost deference on all occasions" (p. 144), had been a great Delaware chieftain, but now his authority and his title to the land have ended. His function is that of a guardian, for he must see that the territory which his people have given in council to Major Effingham passes into the hands of Oliver, its rightful inheritor. Oliver, too, must watch and wait until the transition over which Judge Temple presides is accomplished. His part is to be played in the future; for now, he must stand in the wings, eclipsed by the energy of the transitional characters who hold the stage of the present action.

Cooper takes great pains, however, to qualify Oliver for his future role. He is heir to a long tradition of honor, of loyalty to established authority, of continuity in religion and social class. The Effingham line has been a race of soldiers and is distinguished by its chivalric idealism and its absolute integrity, qualities that contrast sharply with the shrewdness, flexibility, and expediency of the mercantile world in which Marmaduke Temple has been schooled. As the son of Edward Effingham, who had been exiled for his allegiance to the crown in the Revolution, Oliver has deep roots in the white past of America; and as the grandson of Major Effingham, who had been proclaimed a chief by the Delawares and adopted by Mohegan as a son, he is firmly linked to the Indian past. In the design of the novel the second relationship is the more important one, for it constitutes the major bridge between the wilderness that used to be and the city that is to come. Again and again Cooper insists on the fundamental parallelism of Mohegan and Oliver as embodiments of the legitimate authority to which Judge Temple cannot attain. If Mohegan's manner is "noble" and "Roman" in its dignity (p. 91), Oliver walks "with the air of an emperor" (p. 316); Elizabeth playfully wonders if he "'is in secret a king'" (p. 307). The village is united in the delusion that Oliver has Indian blood and is possibly the son, grandson, or grandnephew of Mohegan. By the end of the novel, Oliver is not only the legal heir to the estate which Judge Temple has held in trust for Edward Effingham, but symbolically he is the inheritor of the Indians' moral claim to the land. It is abundantly right that Mohegan, who has outlived the world to which he belongs, should find release in death at the moment when Oliver's title to the property is about to be established. Mohegan has accomplished the purpose of his guardianship; the stability and validity of the Indian possession of the land have been passed on intact to the representative of white civilization.

In this transfer of rightful authority, the human world of the novel completes the cycle of change which the seasonal progression in its natural world has echoed and reinforced. In both detail and grand design *The Pioneers* thus works steadily and effectively toward the full union of its diverse materials, constructing from them a powerful and meaningful image of American life and American landscape. Cooper's achievement in the novel is an important one. From the variety of influences and stimuli which contributed to the conception of the novel and in the interplay of natural and social change which gives the book its structure, he succeeded in devising a form that proceeds from the materials both functionally and with compelling beauty.

From the Ruins of History:
The Last of the Mohicans

by Terence Martin

I

Midway through *The Last of the Mohicans* (1826), Leather-stocking, his Mohican friends, and Duncan Heyward succeed in their efforts to get Cora and Alice Munro to their father at Fort William Henry. Up to this point, Leatherstocking, assisted by Uncas and Chingachgook, has directed the action through a preliminary (albeit lengthy) series of flights, pursuits, and skirmishes. But when the scene shifts inside the Fort, the outpost of civilization, Leatherstocking and the Mohicans disappear from the narrative. Through Heyward's eyes we once see Leatherstocking, a prisoner, being led in embarrassment toward the Fort, but we do not encounter him again until the Fort is in ruins. With Uncas and Chingachgook, the case is even more absolute: during the scenes at the Fort they drop completely out of the novel. Cooper does not subordinate these three characters; he dismisses them. They make no exit from the stage they have dominated so completely; they simply vanish.

As one might expect, the absence of Leatherstocking, Uncas, and Chingachgook signals a radical change in the kind of fiction Cooper is presenting. Once the action moves inside the Fort, the world of the novel is turned inside out. Cooper is, as we know, moving toward a scene of history (the massacre at Fort William Henry), coming to

"From the Ruins of History: *The Last of the Mohicans*, by Terence Martin." From *Novel: A Forum on Fiction* (Spring 1969), pp. 221-29. Reprinted by permission of *Novel*.

focus the lens of history on his narrative in a way that will require his imagination to work within the contours of a specific historical event. But he is still in a sense collecting his plot. Thus, despite the proximity of historical circumstance, he introduces in the Fort an interlude of domestic fiction. No longer are we concerned with moccasin tracks, broken twigs, and the danger of ambush; no longer do Leatherstocking and the Mohicans lead a forlorn group of characters to safety. Different concerns now become evident, allowing Duncan Heyward to demonstrate his efficiency as an officer of the King, providing Alice Munro a chance to appear gay and independent. When Heyward brings a message from Montcalm, Major Munro refuses to hear it; "Let the Frenchman and all his host go to the devil, sir. ... He is not yet master of William Henry. ... Thank heaven, we are not yet in such a strait that it can be said Munro is too much pressed to discharge the little domestic duties of his own family." Heyward the soldier is thus encouraged to become Heyward the suitor. The world of domestic fiction flourishes momentarily, with scenes such as Alice sitting on her father's lap and, during a promenade, chiding Heyward for not being a more attentive knight.

The conventions of domestic fiction allow Heyward to apply formally for the hand of Alice. But the scene between Heyward and Major Munro has a special and concomitant function, for it is here that we learn of Cora's negro blood. Brief as it is, the story of Cora's birth temporarily pushes all other concerns into the background; not only are Leatherstocking and the Mohicans still absent, but Montcalm might be in the far reaches of Canada, so thoroughly is he put at a distance. A native Virginian, Heyward recoils at Munro's revelation and is overjoyed to find that his beloved Alice is safely white. Cora, however, is now in a special class; she has come from a different and exotic world into one in which she has no destiny. In effect, despite Major Munro's defiant pride in her as a human being, she has been disqualified from the select (if somewhat wooden and conventional) group of those who belong to the world of domestic fiction. At the end of *The Last of the Mohicans,* only those who are fully eligible for that world will leave for the settlements. As the novel progresses, it becomes clear that Cora will not be among that number.

Interrupted by the episodes of domestic fiction, the large narrative movement from romance into a moment of history reaches its culmination as Cooper describes the massacre outside the Fort. In presenting the massacre he adopts the role of historian—to the extent that he later feels the need of retiring from Clio's "sacred precincts" to "the proper limits of our own vocation." Moreover, he comes up against one of the basic problems of the historical novelist—how to handle fictional characters when episodes of history take place—and resolves it by gradually dismissing his characters in the order of their fictional importance. It is obvious that Cooper does not want Leatherstocking and the Mohicans present at the time of the massacre. Not only do they lack historical existence, but the imaginative conception that brought them into being gives them such a forceful fictional life that, wherever they are, they will have an impact on the circumstances around them. Though they could hardly turn the tide of battle, Leatherstocking, Uncas, and Chingachgook might threaten to subvert or at least force Cooper to qualify his presentation of the massacre. Even Heyward and Major Munro, less powerfully conceived, lose their identity as characters during the scene outside the Fort. The more passive characters (Cora, Alice, David Gamut) remain briefly and afford a point of view from which to desscribe the action, until they, too, are withdrawn, leaving Cooper free to castigate Montcalm for his "cruel apathy" before resuming his story.

What characterizes the massacre for Cooper is that it happened, that it is a recorded event, that people know—or can know—about it. He respects it, in other words, as historical fact, something different in kind from the fiction he is inventing around it. He has contributed much to the conventions and strategies of what we call historical fiction; his characters of romance move easily and often meaningfully against a generalized historical backdrop; but he shies away from involving them in specific historical events. They are, in a sense, *of* history without being *in* it.

If he cannot penetrate the massacre with his fiction, Cooper does make it relevant, as we shall see, to the central concerns of his novel. And if the historical moment results in his major characters being temporarily set aside, it also allows him to re-introduce them later into a world of their own where their destinies take form beyond the reach of fact and specific event.

II

Cooper's treatment of the massacre of women and children at Fort William Henry points up explicitly a problem of moral responsibility, of means and ends, that was of fundamental significance to a civilization meeting savagism along its frontiers. From the beginning of the *Mohicans* he stresses the importance of the wilderness in shaping the course and conduct of battle. Recurrent metaphors of burial and of being swallowed by the forest emphasize the somberness, voraciousness, and primal strength of the wilderness. Cooper also characterizes the locale of the *Mohicans* by saying that "perhaps no district...can furnish a livelier picture of the cruelty and fierceness of the savage warfare of these periods." And he sees to it that the action of his novel bears out such a contention. The accumulating violence of the *Mohicans* reaches its apex in the massacre at Fort William Henry. With the French and Indian troops standing by, the conquered British soldiers issue from the Fort, followed by the women and children. Montcalm has granted the English an honorable surrender, and the soldiers of France know how to respect its terms. But not so their Indian allies, who are unable to appreciate the value of a tactical victory. Aflame with a desire for battle, an Indian precipitates an incident which leads to the general massacre. Flourishing tomahawks and knives, the Indians descend upon their victims, converting the scene to one of bloody triumph and abject terror. An Indian catches an infant by the feet, whirls it high in the air, explodes its head against a rock, then kills the distraught mother. Amid the chaos and cruelty, Cooper's Hurons kneel and drink the blood of their victims as it flows in rivulets along the earth. With modes of civilized warfare completely broken down, the scene becomes a carnival of atrocity, dominated by cruelty and savage violence.

Such violence, of course, inheres in the dramatic demands of the situation with which Cooper is dealing. But it also serves to pose the problem of moral responsibility to which I have alluded. In taking savage allies that one cannot, at crucial moments, control, one risks, almost invites, ruthless measures of warfare. Since the Indians have their own code of battle, to fight alongside them against a common enemy is to become a party to the result. To hope for the best, to hope that they will, in civilized terms, behave themselves, is at best self-delusion, at worst hypocrisy. Cooper levies a heavy responsibility on Montcalm for the massacre. Aware of the danger, Montcalm has mentioned his Huron allies to Duncan Heyward during a peace talk by saying, "I find it difficult, even now, to limit them to the usages of war." The remark, which is meant as a warning to force the British to an early surrender, serves also as an admission of limited authority. In this sense it is a confidence from one civilized man to another that danger is to be apprehended from the forces of savagery—the ultimate enemy. On the night before the battle Montcalm muses over the "deep responsibility they assume who disregard the means to attain their end, and of all the danger of setting in motion an engine which it exceeds human power to control." But he shakes off such reflections as evidences of weakness in the moment of triumph and takes no steps to avert the impending disaster.

The implications of the problem of moral responsibility are not at all limited to the massacre at Fort William Henry, though Cooper, to my knowledge, speaks nowhere else so directly to the point. Throughout the Leatherstocking novels the problem is related to the notion of cultural relativism by means of which Leatherstocking asserts his whiteness even as he accounts for Indian methods of warfare. What is right for an Indian, Leatherstocking believes, may be wrong for a white man. But Leatherstocking's notion of "gifts," so useful in explaining his relation to Indian friends and enemies, can seem inadequate when the problem of responsibility for the acts of Indian allies is brought explicitly to the fore.

When Leatherstocking and his party are making their way toward the Fort, for example, they are challenged in the darkness by a young French sentry. Answering in French (as only the gentleman hero could), Heyward succeeds in fooling the sentry. The young Frenchman gallantly bids the ladies good-night, assures them of Montcalm's hospitality, and hums a gay tune to himself as the party moves away. A moment later, Leatherstocking and Heyward hear a terrible groan, and Heyward notices that Chingachgook is missing from their group. While they hesitate in uncertainty, Chingachgook glides out of a thicket and rejoins them:"with one hand he attached the reeking scalp of the unfortunate young Frenchman to his girdle, and with the other he replaced the knife and tomahawk that had drunk his blood. He then took his wonted station, with the air of a man who believed he had done a deed of merit."

The sudden and shocking nature of the deed has its effect on Leatherstocking. He leans on his rifle, "musing in profound silence. Then shaking his head in a mournful manner, he muttered,—''t would have been a cruel and an unhuman act for a white-skin; but 't is the gift and natur' of an Indian, and I suppose it should not be denied. I could wish, though, it had befallen an accursed Mingo, rather than that gay young boy from the old countries.'" Cooper's handling of the incident suggests the dangers inherent in taking Indian allies and prefigures the larger massacre in which Montcalm is involved. Moreover, the killing of the French sentry strikes a note of moral ambiguity close to the center of the novel: Chingachgook is the old and trusted friend of Leatherstocking and the father of Uncas. In any struggle between the good guys and the bad guys one feels able to count on Chingachgook, a warrior of experience, bravery, wisdom, and craft. And, indeed, one can. Yet suddenly the sentry seems kind, generous, and civilized, while Chingachgook's violent deed proves embarrassing and saddening. Leatherstocking sees this clearly and can do nothing about it (except to wish that the victim had been an enemy Indian). There is no ground for a reprimand; there is no hope of change. To fight alongside Chingachgook, to accept his aid, is, inevitably, to risk involvement in this kind of incident. Just as Montcalm is implicated in the actions of his Indian allies, so is Leatherstocking implicated in the action of Chingachgook. The imaginary character and the figure from history bear a subtle relationship which Cooper does not otherwise stress—he could not have had Montcalm plead off on the idea of "gifts" any more than he could afford to castigate Leatherstocking for allying himself with Chingachgook. But he has displaced a troubling criticism of Leatherstocking by emphasizing the massacre at Fort William Henry and thereby blaming Montcalm for a kind of irresponsibility for which Leatherstocking is always liable.

The Huron allies of the French exemplify the wild and savage violence that Montcalm's (and Cooper's) civilization has supposedly grown beyond, that it has harnessed, repressed, or made latent by means of self-protective rules of warfare. When such violence, however latent, is unleashed, and Montcalm stands by, a spectator to the massacre, Cooper blames him as if he were participating in the atrocity. And Montcalm is of course participating: he has allied himself with savage forces, against which, when they erupt, the forms of civilization are helpless and meaningless. Cooper's large concern over the massacre comes ultimately, I believe, from his sense that civilization as he knows and respects it is crumpling, retrogressing, outside Ford William Henry, that primitive savagery, in some nightmarish way, is destroying in a moment the ponderous but commendable work of centuries. The Fort itself, that outpost of civilization in which Major Munro could hold Alice on his knee, in which Heyward could propose marriage, has in the process been destroyed as well. What remain are "the ruins of William Henry."

III

Leatherstocking, Uncas, and Chingachgook are re-admitted to the narrative three days after the savage massacre at the Fort. They survey a scene barren and desolate: the weather has undergone such a "frightful change" that corpses "which had blackened beneath the fierce heats of August, were stiffening in their deformity, before the blasts of a premature November." Cooper's imagination has worked, with moral distress, up to and through a moment of history. Now, without explaining their presence any more than he explained their absence, he summons the characters of romance back onto the stage. He brings them face to face with the results of an experience they have not been through, allows the horror of the scene to register on them, and delivers the narrative into their hands.

Traditionally, the ruins of history are the matrix of legend and romance. Traditionally, too, they appeal to the imagination through a mist of years, replete with wonder and nostalgia. American writers in the first half of the nineteenth century recognized the importance of ruins, of history crumbling into legend, even as they lamented (and celebrated) the absence of such things in their country. "Romance and poetry, ivy, lichens, and wall-flowers, need ruin to make them grow," wrote Hawthorne in his preface to *The Marble Faun* as he explained the difficulty of setting a romance in America. The United States abounds with beautiful scenery, Irving admitted in *The Sketch-Book;* but Europe beckons with "the charms of storied and poetical association. ... Her very ruins told the history of times gone by." Cooper, we see, is giving a different twist to the familiar association between ruins and romance. In the *Mohicans* he provides us with ruins that are shocking rather than pleasurable to contemplate, forbidding rather than inviting to the imagination; moreover, they are temporary rather than permanent, the result of sudden violence rather than the result of age. Yet they afford him the moment, the occasion, he needs to begin his narrative anew and to point it toward the more innocent and more congenial ground of romance.

Together with Heyward and Major Munro, Leatherstocking and the Mohicans spend a night among the ruins of the Fort while deciding on a plan of pursuit which will control the action from this point onward. In the first half of the *Mohicans,* Cora and Alice Munro try to reach their father; in the second half the father (in Cooper's words) is "in quest of his children." Thus the pattern of the chase, one of Cooper's legacies to American fiction and popular culture, is inverted and reinvigorated. Major Munro, however, has almost as little to do in the wilderness as Leatherstocking and the Mohicans had to do in the Fort. In a trance-like state, he is virtually dragged along on the "quest" because his presence is demanded by the plot. The chief work falls to Leatherstocking, Heyward, and, of course, Uncas, who assumes an increasingly important role as the novel moves from the ruins of history toward a final world of legend and romance.

"My boy," says Chingachgook to Leatherstocking when speaking of the ancient glory of his tribe, "is the last of the Mohicans." According to the title, it is thus Uncas' story we are reading. But it is also, in a technical and limited sense, Duncan Heyward's story, for Heyward is the gentleman or romantic hero that no Cooper novel can be without, who allows the novel to fulfill the requirement of being a love story. And, as we know, in a larger sense the novel is also a part of Leatherstocking's story.

The Last of the Mohicans is thus a novel with three kinds of protagonist, one savage, one civilized, one standing between. Such a configuration of characters is not unusual in Cooper's work: in *The Prairie* (1827), for example, Hard Heart seems another version of Uncas and Duncan Middleton is the grandson of Duncan Heyward. But despite the fact that they stand on either side of Leatherstocking at the time of his death, neither Hard Heart nor Middleton figures as importantly in *The Prairie* as do their counterparts in the *Mohicans.* In the latter novel Cooper has conceived his three protagonists almost as a unit; with few exceptions they are together throughout the story, each acting out his own kind of heroism, each complementing the others even as he is complemented by them. During a fierce skirmish with the Hurons (in which Heyward arms himself with a tomahawk), the three dispatch an enemy in a trinity of violence: "the tomahawk of Heyward and the rifle of Hawkeye descended on the skull of the Huron, at the same moment that the knife of Uncas reached his heart." This may well be the deadest Indian in American literature.

Uncas, the last of the Mohicans and the savage hero, is significantly exempt from much of the violence and ferocity which pervade the novel. After the above mentioned skirmish with the Hurons, Chingachgook moves silently about, taking the scalps of the enemy dead. "But Uncas," says Cooper, "denying his habits, we had almost said his nature, flew with instinctive delicacy, accompanied by Heyward, to the assistance of the females." The sight of Cora and Alice in each other's arms moves Heyward to manly tears; as for Uncas, he "stood fresh and blood-stained from the combat, a calm, and, apparently, an unmoved looker-on, it is true, but with eyes that had already lost their fierceness, and were beaming with a sympathy that elevated him far above the intelligence, and advanced him probably centuries before the practices of his nation."

But Uncas lacks nothing in the way of bravery, manliness, and an Indian thirst for battle. In the forest he repeatedly displays greater perception than either his father or Leatherstocking; in battle he is athletic and fearless. And Uncas does take a scalp. In the ruins of Fort William Henry, when a Mingo shoots at Chingachgook from the dark, Uncas conquers the would-be assassin and returns to the campfire with a fresh scalp at his belt. But we note that Cora and Alice are not present at this scene and perceive further that Cooper never has Uncas perform such an act of violence when the ladies are present. Uncas, the image of Indian nobility, is made an exception to qualify him for his special place in the novel and in the world of Cooper's fiction. For Uncas, as we know, is attracted to Cora, whom he admires silently, courteously, but unmistakably. In waiting on the girls (an exceptional thing in itself), Uncas shows a preference for Cora; in the first rescue of Heyward's party he leaps instinctively to her assistance; during the final pursuit of Magua and Cora, he bounds far ahead of Heyward and Leatherstocking, impelled by a more personal if otherwise unexpressed feeling.

It is in relation to Uncas (and to Magua, his anti-type, as we shall see) that Cora's negro-ness has a definite function in *The Last of the Mohicans.* By making her not only the dark woman but the partly negro woman, Cooper has put Cora within the range of Uncas' admiration. To have Uncas (no matter how noble) attracted to the blonde, innocent, and white Alice would be inconceivable for Cooper. By rights of social and novelistic convention Alice belongs to Heyward, the gentleman hero from Virginia, who, we recall, protests his freedom from prejudice when he learns Cora's story from Munro, but who writhes inwardly with a "deeply rooted," almost "ingrafted" feeling as he listens to the revelation. But Cora is an extra (and a different kind of) heroine, provided, I believe, because of Uncas' heroic stature in the novel, made partly—but unrecognizably—negro to placate the social requirements of Cooper's imagination.

From the beginning, Cora's response to Indians differs from that of Alice. When Alice trembles with suspicion of Magua, and even Heyward hesitates to follow him, Cora asks, "coldly": "Should we distrust this man because...his skin is dark?" With respect to Uncas, Alice renders an esthetic and impersonal appreciation; he is, to her, a magnificent bit of sculpture endowed with life. Cora, on the other hand, wonders if anyone who looks at this "creature of nature" can "remember the shade of his skin." Cooper's numerous suggestions regarding the mutual admiration of Cora and Uncas are subdued, qualified by Uncas' reserved demeanor as well as by Cora's modesty; but the suggestions are nonetheless clear; and it is equally clear, I believe, that Cora's negro ancestry makes them possible.

IV

Perhaps the most perplexing problem facing Cooper in *The Last of the Mohicans* was the creation of an antagonist. The triple protagonists, Uncas, Leatherstocking, and Heyward, ably assisted by Chingachgook, present a formidable array of intelligence and craft, strength and determination. Combating them is Magua, who certainly has his work cut out for him. In attempting to solve his problem, Cooper appears to have surrendered to the exigencies of plot, to have permitted the demands of his story to reshape his conception of Magua as the novel progressed. At first, Magua appears base, almost cowardly, a hopeless renegade: his tribe has cast him out, apparently because of his conduct while he was repeatedly drunk; he has joined the British forces fighting against his own tribe, but has been humiliated by a whipping administered on orders from Major Munro. In short, we are presented initially with an outcast who lives by treachery and betrayal, who seems only a foil for the Indian virtues of Uncas. After the battle at Glenn's Falls, however, Magua is somehow in command of a band of Hurons. Before the massacre at Fort William Henry he appears mysteriously in the dark to a brooding Montcalm, a virtual embodiment of Montcalm's uneasy conscience, and speaks to the French commander in authoritative tones. Later, in his tribal village, he is revealed as a powerful orator, crafty and overly conscious of his skill, to be sure, but capable of influencing the decisions of his tribe; he is said to be intelligent, "far above the vulgar superstitions" of his people. We learn finally that he is a chief, that he has completely regained the confidence of his tribe, that he has become, "in truth, their ruler." At this point he is even compared to "the Prince of Darkness, brooding on his own fancied wrongs and plotting evil," an image far from that of the early Magua skulking treacherously through the forest.

Magua, we see, undergoes a remarkable increase in stature as the novel unfolds. His capacity for evil multiplies until he suggests an image of Satan. And the process, anomalous and improbable as it is, serves Cooper's purpose; for Magua must finally confront Uncas on something like equal terms if the climax of the novel is to prove effective. The enemy of Leatherstocking, Chingachgook, and Heyward, Magua ultimately stands opposed to Uncas, whose nobility of character demands a significant antagonist.

More than anything else, of course, Magua's desire for Cora puts him in direct competition with Uncas. Attracted by her dark beauty, aware too that she is contemptuous of him, he is motivated to possess her primarily by his desire for revenge against Major Munro. In *The Last of the Mohicans* (as in other Leatherstocking novels), the ladies are prizes, precious objects, moved about first by one group then another in a series of flights and pursuits. The pattern emerging from the varied action of the chase is clear: all movement toward the girls' father is good, all movement away is bad. The grand aim of Leatherstocking-Uncas-Heyward is to restore Cora and Alice to their father; the design of Magua is to take them away from their father, and, out of spite and attraction, to keep Cora for himself.

Magua thus forces the action in one direction, the protagonists in another. And because Magua makes Alice a hostage as the best way of insuring Cora's acquiescence in flight, Heyward, as well as Uncas, is emotionally involved in the pursuit. But Alice, technical heroine though she is, is here a decoy. The most deadly opposition, between Magua and Uncas, concerns Cora.

Born into fiction ahead of her time, manifestly unable to belong to any coherent world Cooper could fashion imaginatively, Cora comes to represent fatality in the terms of the novel. Uncas, who is doomed in a larger sense by the advance of civilization, takes extreme risks on her account and finally dies in a frantic attempt to rescue her. For Uncas and Cora, as opposed to Heyward and Alice, Cooper sees no future. When the Indian maidens chant of their reunion in another world Leatherstocking shakes his head negatively, "like one who knew the error of their simple creed." Happily for the self-command of Heyward and Munro, says Cooper, "they knew not the meaning of the wild sounds they heard." Cora's mixture of blood, which allows for the admiration of Uncas, proves in the end a fatal inheritance. For Uncas is himself the last of a high race, a warrior of "unmixed" blood, whose purity of descent accounts for his dignity and nobility. He exemplifies a principle of order in the midst of the wild disorder of the world in which he lives, where tribes fight related tribes in a hopeless confusion of loyalties caused by the influx of civilization.

Magua, on the other hand, is an example of how the vices of civilization may corrupt savage nobility; with features of potential greatness about him, Magua has fallen, victim, end-product, and finally breeder of disorder. Since social order for Cooper seems to depend upon solidarity, unity, and purity of race, Cora, the dark lady of the narrative, introduces her own legacy of disorder which involves Magua and precipitates the death of the high-born Uncas.

The sense of absolute finality in Uncas' death and burial is the most powerful effect in the novel—and perhaps in the entire Leatherstocking series. A feeling of shock pervades the final scenes; so well does Cooper manage the mood that without the ponderous and formal movement of the death ritual, it is as if the characters might freeze in attitudes of woe. The scene at the grave of Uncas stands at the opposite pole from those involving Fort William Henry. The characters who derive from domestic fiction have departed for the settlements—they, in their turn, have been dismissed from the novel. History has given way to legend, manners to ritual. At times clumsily, at times adventitiously, Cooper has taken us in *The Last of the Mohicans* from conventional romance to a moment of history which, by means of violence and atrocity, burns itself to ruins. Then, with all preparations made, he has led us from the ruins of history to mourn the death of Uncas in the most exalted world of romance of which he was capable. And in the course of all this he has managed to uncover issues and concerns which are of startling relevance to the American (and human) experience, both in his time and ours.

Beyond Definition: A Reading of *The Prairie*

by Wayne Fields

I

Seeing in a wilderness requires a vantage point: either sufficient elevation so that the turmoil of vegetation and the idiosyncrasies of geography are subdued, or a clearing that pushes back the wild and makes it in some small way comprehensible. Nineteenth-century painters sought elevation; nineteenth-century writers sought clearings. In his wilderness novels, James Fenimore Cooper chooses some break in the thicket—a lake like Glimmerglass, a settlement like Templeton, an Oak Opening or a Ravensnest. Defined by a framing forest, such places allow us to see characters and action by getting the trees out of our way. They are openings where the forces of the novel come to light, converge, and are at last reconciled, but always with the shadow of forest threatening and reassuring as it outlines the stage for each particular drama. These clearings are essential to the most enticing of New World experiences, allowing both character and reader to be in a dark continent and yet to stand in their own small patch of light. The arrangement is reciprocal: Without the forest there would be no opening, no stage, and without the opening the forest would be unperceivable. Viewer and landscape are bound together in a mutual act of definition. The viewer struggles to order his physical surroundings, to find coherence, and simultaneously is himself located or defined in relationship to those surroundings.[1]

"Beyond Definition: A Reading of *The Prairie*" by Wayne Fields. This article appears for the first time in this volume.

[1]This, of course, involves more than physical perception. The reciprocity of the arrangement inevitably makes "seeing" in a wilderness an effort of psychological and moral perception as well.

But not all is forest. There is another American wilderness where no mountains elevate nor clearings give perspective. "Virtually the whole of this immense region," says Cooper, "is a plain extending nearly 1500 miles east and west, and 600 north and south." The American prairie is, he suggest, the immense floor of some ancient sea, and, if the forests east of the Mississippi have in other Cooper novels suggested a youthful continent, alive with vegetation and promise, this place is old and a desert. It, not the Western ocean, is terminus: the "final gathering-place of the red men," the place where an aged Leatherstocking comes to die, and finally the great wasteland toward which America is tending. The landscape is inverted. Characters are drawn not toward openings—all is open—but toward clumps of trees, rocky outcroppings, even stands of high grass. There is no defining frame; the action drifts across an immense waste where readers, like most of the characters, are dislocated. We are beyond cultivation in a dying, autumnal world, sea-like in both its vastness and vacancy.

In one way the perceptual demands of the prairie are much like those of the woods. In the plentitude of a forest, space allows the perspective seeing requires, while on a prairie physical objects provide focal points around which the rest of the landscape can be arranged. Yet the two experiences remain fundamentally different. It is easier to make something of plenty than of scarcity, easier for both individuals and communities to be defined in the enclosure of a clearing than in vast open terrain. To come into the prairie is to try in the extreme one's sense of both place and self precisely because, without boundaries, it lacks the coherencies of more conventional landscapes. It provides a neutral ground where Cooper's characters are tested less for their ability to survive physically than for their ability to order their worlds and themselves.

II

Ishmael Bush has come to the prairie to escape the restrictions of settlements, its indefinite nature having drawn him out of the Kentucky forests. "I have come...into these districts," he declares, "because I found the law setting too tight upon me. ..." Later he elaborates, "I have come five hundred miles to find a place where no man can ding the words of the law in my ears. ..." Though he is alluding to a particular conflict with authority, he is also speaking, more abstractly, of all the restraints imposed by the communities he has left behind. "Why," he asks,

> do not the surveyors of the States set their compasses and run their lines over our heads as well as beneath our feet? Why do they not cover their shining sheep-skins with big words, giving to the land-holder, or perhaps he should be called airholder, so many rods of heaven, with the use of such a star for a boundary-mark, and such a cloud to turn a mill?

Assuming that Leatherstocking is a kindred spirit, Ishmael adds, "neither of us, I reckon has ever had much to do with title-deeds, or county clerks, or blazed trees; therefore we will not waste words on fooleries."

Ishmael's instinctive linking of civil law and the surveyor's lines suggests how analogous in this novel are the boundaries of geography and those of human conduct. Both provide the guidelines that keep us on familiar ground, the first by defining a landscape and the second by setting limits governing behavior. To escape surveyed boundaries is to step beyond the restraints of civil authority and to take upon oneself the task of ordering the moral as well as the physical world. Thus Ishmael strides across the prairie, following no particular path and moving toward no particular destination, satisfied to have outdistanced surveyor and judge and arrogantly confident of his family's sufficiency in this uncharted place. He seems oblivious to landscape except as it serves his needs and appetites, regarding it in all its enormity merely as the elbow room he and his brood require. Scornful of the settlements in which more conventional people live, he has chosen an alternative that retains a seductive power in America: He has withdrawn into the clan, a social unit that appears to allow both radical individualism and community.

Nothing so indicates Ishmael's independence and pride as his clothing. Instead of the mixture of homespun and leather typical among borderers, Cooper provides a much more flamboyant costume:

> In place of the usual deer-skin belt, he wore around his body a tarnished silken sash of the most gaudy colors; the buckhorn haft of his knife was profusely decorated with plates of silver; the marten's fur of his cap was of a fineness and shadowing that a queen might covet;

the buttons of his rude and soiled blanket-coat were of the glittering coinage of Mexico; the stock of his rifle was of beautiful mahogany, riveted and banded with the same precious metal; and the trinkets of no less than three worthless watches dangled from different parts of his person.

Ishmael's dress would be the envy of pirate or gypsy, nobleman or savage, asserting his independence from all social hierarchies by mixing deerskin and buckhorn with marten fur and mahogany. It proclaims him nationless as well as classless, an outrider for whom coins are no more than buttons and watches no more than trinkets. In addition, Cooper tells us, he carries "a keen and bright wood axe" through land nearly devoid of trees. Whether weapon or ornament, he bears it effortlessly and arrogantly wherever he walks.

Ishmael dares live beyond the physical and psychological protection of the settlements in a landscape which would demoralize and destroy a lesser man. Set apart from the average by his size, his confidence, and his dress, he seems to belong on the prairie since he, too, defies definition and since the conventions of the settlements would be too confining for so unconventional a man.

But while Ishmael is emphatic in his contempt for civil authority, he has an obsessive preoccupation with law. His conversations turn again and again to talk of courts and justice. Confident of his moral as well as his physical strength, he has, in fact, come to the prairie not to live without law but to be the law. After his oldest son strikes Abiram, his brother-in-law, Ishmael declares, "When the law of the land is weak, it is right the law of nature should be strong." He then says to the man who has just insulted him as well as his son, "As for you, Abiram, the child has done you wrong, and it is my place to see you righted. Remember; I tell you justice shall be done; it is enough." In the patriarchy that now governs the Bush clan, Ishmael is the law, but in his exchange with Abiram he claims that this power will not be used arbitrarily; that it will be guided by an innate knowledge of right and wrong. For Ishmael the simplicity of his system of governance is the basis for its superiority over statutes and courts, whose very complexity he sees as corrupting.[2]

Although they enter the book as American borderers of the early nineteenth century, the Bush family resemble, in both their notions

[2]See John P. McWilliams's discussion of *The Prairie* in *Political Justice in a Republic* (Berkeley, Calif.: University of California Press), pp. 259-76, for an excellent study Ishmael and the law of retribution. Mary E. Rucker, in "Natural, Tribal

of law and their physical stature, a more ancient tribe. The sons—
bearing such names as Abner, Enoch, and Asa—are, like their father,
"vast" and powerful, and under Ishmael's control seem an irresis-
tible force striding across the prairie without fear or self-doubt.
"It was only at moments, however," the narrator says of the father,
"as some slight impediment opposed itself to his loitering progress,
that his person, which, in its ordinary gait seemed so lounging and
nerveless, displayed any of those energies which lay latent in his
system, like the slumbering and unwieldy, but terrible, strength of
the elephant." The same mixture of grace and power marks the description of Asa as he chops down a tall cottonwood, one of the
novel's few trees:

> He stood a moment regarding the effect of the blow, with that sort of
> contempt with which a giant might be supposed to contemplate the
> puny resistance of a dwarf, and then flourishing the implement [his
> ax] above his head, with the grace and dexterity with which a master
> of the art of offence would wield his nobler though less useful weapon,
> he quickly severed the trunk of the tree, bringing its tall top crash-
> ing to the earth in submission to his prowess.

He is the giant dwarfing the tree; his is the grace and power of a
mythic race subduing the earth.

For the most part, Ishmael leads his family through their desert
trials with awesome success. Whole Indian tribes do not frighten
them, and, even horseless, they seem capable adversaries for the
Sioux war party. Tough in mind and body, they never give in to
confusion or doubt and, on occasions, rise nearly to the level of a
natural nobility. But for all the American innovations they bring to
their roles, and despite Ishmael's arrogant assumption that he has
found a new path in a new world, they are cast in an old drama and
finally must act out a familiar dilemma. Their movement away from
settlements does not enable them to transcend society and law but
instead locates them in a different society governed by a different
law.[3] Their movement is, in fact, one of regression to a stage of

---

and of Civil Law in Cooper's *The Prairie," Western American Literature* (Nov.
1972), pp. 215-22, explores many of the themes with which this essay is concerned,
though from a different perspective.

[3] See Henry Nash Smith's "Introduction" to *The Prairie* (New York: Holt, Rine-
hart and Winston, 1950) for a most valuable discussion of the novel and, in particular, a helpful explanation of Condorcet's theory of social evolution and its influence on Cooper.

social development inherently limited by what Ishmael thinks is its greatest strength: the reliance upon tribe or family.

Ishmael's is essentially a drama in two acts: The first takes place in Chapters 11 and 12 and the second in Chapters 31 and 32. When Chapter 11 opens, descriptions of the prairie have, temporarily, shifted from images of desert and waste to images of plenitude. The land has become a "wild pasture" supporting "vast herds" while, ironically, "endless flocks of aquatic birds" fly overhead. Like all other life on the prairie, the flocks and herds are migratory, but for the moment they are present in abundance. In the darkening evening Ishmael and his sons, laden with game, return from the hunt and gather round the fire for the evening meal. Cooper then provides the first in a series of powerful scenes that endow the family with a primitive grandeur:

> The reader will remember that the citadel of Ishmael stood insulated, lofty, ragged, and nearly inaccessible. A bright, flashing fire that was burning on the centre of its summit, and around which the busy group was clustered, lent it the appearance of some tall Pharos placed in the centre of the deserts, to light such adventurers as wandered through their broad wastes. The flashing flame gleamed from one sunburnt contenance to another, exhibiting every variety of expression, from the juvenile simplicity of the children, mingled, as it was, with a shade of the wildness peculiar to their semi-barbarous lives, to the dull and immovable apathy that dwelt on the features of the squatter when unexcited. Occasionally a gust of wind would farr the embers; and, as a brighter light shot upwards, the little solitary tent was seen as it were suspended in the gloom of the upper air. All beyond was enveloped, as usual at that hour, in an impenetrable body of darkness.

One of the family, however, is missing from this circle and remains in the darkness. Asa has not returned from the hunt, and his absence is inextricably linked with that small tent ominously "hovering" at the edge of Cooper's picture. Although they have placed it outside their circle, the flames reveal an alien presence they have brought into the familial unit, tying them to a world they claim to have left behind, and the scene prefigures the moral weakness that inevitably must negate Ishmael's arrogant claims of family self-sufficiency. In rejecting civil authority, he has drawn back into the tight circle we see in the firelight, but he has also brought into it—no matter how concealed—the instrument of its destruction. In this scene the family is in a clearing, a clearing of light, but the following day they will venture out to find the son whom the firelight does not touch. For the moment, they are aloof, "inaccessible" on their citadel, but that too will be left behind. The next morning, Esther, until now little more than a frontier shrew, pushes Ishmael aside and Fury-like drives her sons in search of the missing child. When they falter she cries out: "Follow *me*!... I am leader to-day, and I *will* be followed." Signs of tragedy abound as winds gust and dark clouds rush across a sky "beneath which interminable flocks of aquatic birds were again on the wing, holding their toilsome and heavy way towards the distant waters of the south." At last, as vultures wheel and dogs howl, the family finds Asa's corpse.

A desert comes to life with herds and flocks, not that a pastoral might be enacted, but so its antithesis will be all the more striking and ironic. It is not as easy to order either the physical or the moral realms as Ishmael has assumed. Light and darkness, life and death do not stay neatly in place but swirl up, confounding the boundaries assigned to them. For Ishmael to have expected otherwise testifies to his ignorance of both history and human nature. That in his bewilderment he has been pushed aside by his wife indicates the enormity of his presumption in coming to the prairie. Cooper's descriptions, filled with portenous signs, reverberate with the cadences of older stories about the insufficiency of tribal law. What to Ishmael is a break with the established and the conventional becomes, in these passages, the reenactment of a tragic plot at least as old as the *Oresteia*.[4] Though his confidence in the system of order he has chosen is not yet broken, the eventual consequences of Asa's death will completely undercut the viability of that choice.

As long as Ishmael believes Leatherstocking to be the killer, he is able, despite his personal grief, to deal with the trauma of death, even murder, within the context of his tribal system. Together with his surviving sons he awaits a time of retribution. But when at last he discovers that the murderer is a kinsman rather than a stranger, the principles upon which he has ordered his wilderness life are negated. Families are bound to revenge blood with blood, but they

---

[4]Joel Porte suggests a connection between *The Prairie* and *The Eumenides* in *The Romance in America* (Middleton, Conn.: Wesleyan University Press 1969), p. 47, and Mary Rucker observes "the tragedy of his [Ishmael's] plight...lies in his being compelled to execute a member of his family in order to attain a just recompense" ("Natural, Tribal and Civil Law," p. 219).

are equally bound not to shed familial blood. The code works only so long as family members sustain one another and when that internal loyalty breaks down, the code fails; the "we" and "they" upon which it depends become indistinguishable. Orestes was urged by a god to avenge his dead father, then was pursued by the Furies for taking the life of his mother. When Natty identifies the murderer, declaring it "a shame and a disgrace...that he is of the blood and family of the dead," Abiram threatens his brother-in-law with the very taboo he has violated: "I'll call on God to curse ye if you touch me!"

The kinship between judge and judged dominates the final act of the familial drama. Abiram repeatedly addresses Esther as sister and Ishmael as brother, and they in turn allude to the family tie in references to him. Nor do Ishmael and Esther ever forget the terrible burden placed upon them by that tie. "And yet Ishmael," says Esther, "my blood and the blood of my children is in his veins!" But Ishmael, fully aware of that bond's significance, is resolved:

> I had brought my mind to the punishment of that houseless trapper, with no great strivings, for the man had done me few favors, and God forgive me if I suspected him wrongfully of much evil! This is, however, bringing shame in at one door of my cabin in order to drive it out at the other. But shall a son of mine be murdered, and he who did it go at large?—the boy would never rest!

They came giantlike onto the prairie, and giantlike they return. Now moving eastward, Ishmael marches instinctively past all obstacles, crossing in a day what seemed throughout the novel hundreds of miles. "Water-courses were waded, plains were passed and rolling ascents risen and descended, without producing the smallest change." When at last the rolling prairie is "interrupted by irregular hillocks, occasional masses of rock, and broad belts of forest," Abiram is killed. But the act is not the revenge Ishmael would have exacted of Natty or any other outsider. He does not shoot the murderer in an act of personal vengeance but, appealing to "the laws of God *and man*" [my italics], forces Abiram to hang himself in an act of impersonal justice.

This day, as the day on which Asa's body was discovered, opened with an oddly pastoral description of a prairie turned "soft, calm, and soothing," but night falls on the most autumnal scene in the novel: "For the first time, in a life of so much wild adventure, Ishmael felt a keen sense of solitude." The tribal unit has been irreparably broken, and the prairies, which were to become the plantations of his children, he sees, for the first time, "as illimitable and dreary wastes." Abiram hangs from the dead cottonwood, its leaves together with the leaves of Esther's Bible blowing around his feet. With his burial we are told, "All was then finished." There can be no turning back to the old law of tribe and retribution. Ishmael realizes this, and his dreams of vast western plantations, his titan's will, and his claims to radical independence are defeated. His law, like the law which governed Orestes, must now be either set aside or turned against him, and so his family goes back to the leveling law of the settlements, their wagons and lives blending in with all the others, never to be heard from again.

Throughout the novel Cooper has prepared the reader for Ishmael's ultimate defeat by constant emphasis on the intellectual dullness that flaws the Bush family. The persistence of these references suggests the author's concern that the reader not mistake ignorance and presumption for heroism (claims of self-sufficiency are almost inevitably the mark of fools in Cooper's stories). It would be a mistake, however, to think that the Bush family need the external restraint of civil law merely because they are ignorant. What their story finally suggests is not their uniqueness but their representative nature. The whites who pursue Ishmael, inasmuch as they are wiser than he, recognize their need to be guided by the laws of the settlements. They also are inadequate in this waste, often appearing in the peculiar optics of the prairie as stunted and with their very humanity threatened by the indefiniteness of the landscape. They, too, require external guidance to pull them from confusion and lethargy, and their appetites can be as rapacious as Ishmael's. The likable Hover declares, "I deny myself nothing," and wants to kill his buffalo a day so that he might eat only the best portion; but he, together with his feminine counterpart, Ellen, eventually recognizes his limitations and allies himself with the more restrained Middleton. And Inez, who comes from a society—Spanish and Catholic—that Cooper portrays as equal in indolence and superior in decadence to anything achieved by the Bush family, is, like her native Louisiana, redeemed only by the virtue and energy of proper Anglo-Saxon Protestant government.

The white leader, ultimately, is Middleton, the even stuffier reincarnation of all the other Middletons and Effinghams who enter

Cooper's novels. A man defined by the boundaries of rank and law, he has in this novel been forced into a landscape where those boundaries do not reach. His promise is apparent but so is the severity of his limitations. He cannot cope with the powerful forces that sweep across the prairie, and is saved, together with the rest of his party, only because in crisis after crisis he defers to Leatherstocking. His younger eyes cannot see what the old trapper can discern, and, though less a captive of his emotions, like Hover he also falters, a victim of rashness or despair. Because he interprets what he sees and experiences through the conventions of his culture, he misperceives much of what, removed from that culture, he encounters in this place (as when he thinks the approaching grass fire a glorious sunrise). In the last chapter his return to the prairie as commander of a military company foreshadows the ultimate conflict between his world and Hard-Heart's. When he comes to the Indian camp to see Natty one last time, he misunderstands his reception by the Pawnees and, unguided by Leatherstocking and secure in his rank, prepares his soldiers for battle.

So at last all those who were heading westward when the novel began must turn back to the settlements and to the guidance and imposed restraint of civil authority. There Middleton can exercise the civic virtue that republican governments require. There Hover can grow from the boyish enthusiast we see on the prairie to the respected legislator we are told he eventually becomes. The arrogant claim that the new breed of humanity spawned in America can live independent of such restraints—either as individuals or as tribes—is refuted, but with the consolation that laws can be enlightened and communities dynamic in this newer world.

III

Between the chapters in which the body of Asa is discovered and that in which the identity of his killer is revealed (nearly a third of the novel), Ishmael and his family cease to dominate the action, and conflict between Pawnee and Sioux displaces conflict between whites. In many of these interim chapters the whites are merely observers; Middleton and Hover lie bound on one fringe of the action while the Bush family, once more "inert," lounge on the other. The

Indians who dominate these pages are familiar enough to Cooper's readers. There is a clear distinction between good Indians and bad Indians. The Mingoes of the East, still contaminated by contact with the Catholic French of Canada, have become the Sioux of the West, and the Pawnees of this novel are so like the Delaware of Leatherstocking's earlier life that Natty thinks Hard-Heart surely a relative of Uncas. Even as Middleton is interchangeable with his grandfather *(Last of the Mohicans)* or with Oliver Effingham *(The Pioneers)*, so the Indians of *The Prairie* are those of the earlier tales with new names. Yet the drama they enact, familiar as it is in most respects, is subtly changed when it is played against this setting and as an interlude for the Bush family's drama.

In the encounter between Pawnee and Sioux we see people who belong on the prairie, who, like the other forces that sweep across its surface, are native expressions of this landscape. They seek neither to order nor to subdue but rather struggle to bring their own lives into harmony with the world around them. They live by a tribal law not unlike that to which Ishmael aspires, and, as the whites look on, the basis of that law is tested by a people for whom it is a more natural principle of social order.

The Indian episodes provide elaborate parallels to the characters and events presented in the white chapters surrounding them. At the center of the Sioux-Pawnee action is another act of vengeance and another trial, but this trial involves a different kind of testing than those over which Ishmael presides. It is a taunting, a complex effort to humiliate an old enemy, where abstract notions of justice of the sort Ishmael indulges are totally alien. Here captor and captive are bound together in a symbiotic relationship that tries the character of all participants and in which the vanquished can be noble and the conqueror ignoble. Hard-Heart's trial is a ritual of barbaric simplicity that cannot be translated into terms appropriate to the world of settlements. Inasmuch as it adheres to the Indians' tribal code, this revenge ritual exposes, by contrast, the odd mixture of incompatible values that Ishmael's law represents and thereby suggests the ultimate absurdity of his efforts to pursue justice and revenge simultaneously.

While the Indian chapters judge Ishmael's regression by contrasting a "natural" tribal society with his own peculiar creation, they also reinforce the inevitability of his downfall through the contrasting characterizations of Mahtoree and Hard-Heart. Mahtoree, the undisputed leader of the Sioux, is an awesome warrior, but his nobility has been lost:

> We have everywhere endeavored to show that while Mahtoree was in all essentials a warrior of the prairies, he was much in advance of his people in those acquirements which announce the dawnings of civilization. He had held frequent communion with the traders and troops of the Canadas, and the intercourse had unsettled many of those wild opinions which were his birthright, without perhaps substituting any others of a nature sufficiently definite to be profitable. His reasoning was rather subtle than true, and his philosophy far more audacious than profound. Like thousands of more enlightened beings who fancy they are able to go through the trials of human existence without any other support than their own resolutions, his morals were accommodating and his motives selfish.

Though he still is the acknowledged leader of his tribe, he does not bend his own will to serve the interests of his people; rather, he manipulates his followers in the service of his own desires. Like the whites whose excesses Natty continually decries, he is without self-restraint. His speech before the council lacks the natural dignity (even borders on the obscene) of the oratory delivered by the noblest of Cooper's Indians. Like Ishmael, he is a man who stands between two stages of civilization, a man "unsettled" because he has abandoned one system of order without substituting another "sufficiently definite to be profitable." He is "one of those bold spirits who overstep the limits which use and education fix to the opinions of man in every state of society," and his failings as a man as well as a leader result from the presumptuous claim that he, "like thousands of more enlightened beings," makes of being "able to go through the trials of human existence without any other support than their own resolution. ..." That presumption brings his death and the destruction of his tribe.

His Pawnee antagonist, Hard-Heart, has had little contact with whites and, by holding to the principles of his people, achieves the nobility of a true tribal leader. First described as "apollo like," he is, the narrator declares, a fit model for the art of an Allston or a Greenough. "The outlines of his lineaments were strikingly noble, and nearly approaching to Roman. ..." Although carrying, like a warrior from antiquity, a shield emblazoned with "some daring exploit," he disdains artifice. Whereas Mahtoree speaks "in the haughty tones of absolute power" combined with an affected humility, Hard-Heart speaks simply and openly; he is always the leader who serves rather than is served. Like the Sioux chief, he too is attracted to Inez, yet he does not yield to that attraction and, instead, subordinates his own desires to the dignity of his office.

The opposite of Middleton in many ways, Hard-Heart shares with him an unshakable commitment to the established laws of his culture and is never tempted, as are Mahtoree and Ishmael, into the role of moral entrepreneur. His strength, like that of his white counterpart, lies in his unswerving loyalty to the principles of order that have evolved among his people. In the trials of his captivity, it is not Hard-Heart but Mahtoree who falters, falters because he steps out of the role defined by custom and begins to improvise for his own corrupt purposes. Neither he nor Ishmael can redefine his world out of his own character: Both can only use such talk as camouflage for morals that are "accommodating" and motives that are "selfish."

Hard-Heart does not see the prairie as the site of future plantations or as a place needing the validation of maps and names but as a constantly changing world in which individuals survive through the common sustenance of a tribe. Defined by his ties to a transient community rather than by a fixed geographical location, he and his people find in the bonds of kinship and custom the coherence that makes life on the prairie possible and are never deluded by the thought that they are somehow capable of living unchecked and unsustained beyond the boundaries of that community. In the Sioux camp Hover and Middleton—who spend much of the novel either crouching or prone—lie tied together on the ground, the one calling out ineffectual curses and the other fainting in despair; Hard-Heart stands bound to a stake just a few yards away. Far from the ordering principles of their own culture and cast in roles for which they are totally unprepared, the best of the settlement whites are impotent. But Hard-Heart, resigned yet watchful for some unexpected opportunity, fits into the cruel ritual being performed by captive and captors; he is a necessary part of a primitive aesthetic as he serves the expectations his people hold for a Pawnee chief. While Middleton, because he is civilized, swoons in frustration, his savage counterpart is the heroic center of this scene, but only because he is so thoroughly primitive. Ishmael underestimated the awful burdens of tribal society, and Middleton is sufficiently civilized and reasonable not to be tempted by its primitive grandeur; but for Hard-Heart, who has not yet left Indian gifts behind, the life is still a noble one.

IV

The point of Ishmael's story—and of Hover's and Middleton's—is that people cannot live without boundaries and laws. And, as the story of Hard-Heart and Mahtoree makes clear, even individuals in more primitive stages of social development require the external definition of social customs and values if they are to lead worthwhile lives. Leatherstocking says early in the novel, "The Law—'tis bad to have it, but I sometimes think it is worse to be entirely without it. ... Yes—yes, the law is needed when such as have not the gifts of strength and wisdom are to be taken care of." Before discussing why Leatherstocking, alone among the characters of the novel, has such gifts and is capable of ordering his life and world without the sustenance of either tribe or settlement, it is necessary to consider why he is present in this novel, or more particularly on this landscape, at all. Though such a question may seem digressive, finding Natty on the prairie is so enormous an improbability that the issue cannot be ignored. Furthermore, the question can inform in yet another way our understanding of the themes of law and coherency.

A child of the woods and the mountains, Leatherstocking has come to a flat, barren land to die, all the time believing "trees... are to the 'arth, as fruits are to a garden; without them nothing can be pleasant, or thoroughly useful." The sound of the ax has driven him out of his native hills: "I came west in search of quiet." Yet he walks into this novel moving in the opposite direction. He has been west—incredibly, since Lewis and Clark are, by the time the novel opens, just beyond the Great Divide—all the way west, so that he can now declare, "I have seen the waters of the two seas." Thus the Leatherstocking who comes to the prairie so outstripped the choppers that he reached the Pacific at least a decade before Jefferson's party of exploration managed the same feat. He has crossed the Rockies, whose western slope was, in 1805, still beyond the territorial claims of the United States, and yet we are to believe that he has left the pristine forests of that west to return to a landscape he abhors.

Though it defies history and characterization, Natty's return to the prairie is essential to Cooper's broadest thematic concerns. Leatherstocking's shadow, cast eastward by the setting sun, enters the novel a page before he does. And, in retrospect, his shadow seems always to have been ahead, leading him. In the morning he moved west to Glimmerglass and then, even though his own morning had fled, to the Pacific. But by 1805 the sun has crested and Natty, in one final trek, reenters the world of the prairie with his face toward the East. Thus the line of his movement intersects with that of the immigrants, and when Ishmael and his family, pulling the growing weight of their own shadow westward against the sun, first meet Leatherstocking, they see not a man but a "colossal" figure, a "supernatural agency" thrust forward by the dying light. If, as the narrator later suggests, coming events (and more especially the course of civilization) cast their shadows before them, Natty's journey prophetically anticipates America's future.

Leatherstocking has followed the path that American settlement was eventually to follow: After years of preparation in the East Americans surged west, stopping only when the West itself stopped, and then at last returned to the prairies. But Natty is enacting more than a migratory pattern. In the unyielding light of this land, more is revealed than the final point of national settlement. This is terminus also as judgment. The prairie is the spiritual fate toward which America is tending. As he approaches his own death, content with the life he brings to this ultimate reckoning, Natty warns of the judgment that awaits an unrestrained America. The exploiters, "when they have cut their path from the eastern to the western waters," will "find that a hand, which can lay the 'arth bare at a blow, has been here and swept the country, in very mockery of their wickedness. They will turn on their tracks like a fox that doubles, and then the rank smell of their own footsteps will show them the madness of their waste." Then will they all face the judgment awaiting Ishmael: "The very stumps of Kentucky and Tennessee cry out agin ye."

Here is where an explanation of Leatherstocking's presence in this place returns us to the theme of order, for Natty's Jeremiad is not simply a conservationist's complaint. Just as the indefiniteness of the prairie judges the inadequacy of individuals, so it judges a society that promotes wantonness rather than restraint and panders to avarice rather than cultivates reason. This desert, Natty argues, is a moral as well as a natural phenomenon. Obed Bat tells Leather-stocking that the monuments in the Egyptian desert prove the "former greatness" of those lands "now that they lie stripped of their fertility." The absence of similar ruins on the prairie, he continues, proves the prairie a place without a past. But Natty remembers a Moravian teaching about the Biblical world, "that the Blessed Land was once as fertile as the bottoms of the Mississippi, and groaning with its stores of grain and fruits; but that the judgment has since fallen upon it, and that it is now more remarkable for its barrenness than any qualities to boast of." Desert, he concludes, is judgment, the consequence of "wickedness," "pride," and "waste." Therefore, it must follow that a great civilization once inhabited these regions, but so devastating was the judgment upon it, that no evidence of its existence endures. Though he speaks of what has been but is no more, his words provide a prophetic warning of what might lie ahead.[5]

In Chapter 23, after the prairie fire has passed, Leatherstocking looks out across the burned-over landscape, and, when the others ask him what he sees, answers:

> What the world of America is coming to, and where the machinations and inventions of its people are to have an end, the Lord, he only knows. I have seen, in my day, the chief who, in his time, had beheld the first Christian that placed his wicked foot in the regions of York! How much has the beauty of the wilderness been deformed in two short lives!

What the world of America is coming to is the prairie. Even as the novel's events are taking place, Lewis and Clark are systematically enclosing the wilderness, naming and mapping as they make their surveying way west. Ishmael is already here, and though he strives to place himself above those who live in the settlements, he comes with ax slung over his shoulder to cut down any tree that mirac-ulously stands in these wastes. He cries out against the property claims of those he left behind and yet, with incredible appetite, declares this vast district his own. He aspires to be self-sufficient but is too voracious to do more than plunder.

Only Leatherstocking has the self-possession to live in the prairie. In the midst of lethargy he alone is awake — and not just because he

[5]Merrill Lewis explores this subject in "Lost and Found in the Wilderness; The Desert Metaphor in Cooper's *The Prairie*," in *Western American Literature* (Fall, 1970), pp. 195-204.

perceives what Hover and Middleton cannot discern. For Natty, man is to be awake in a profounder sense; he has been created in the image of God inasmuch as he has been given reason, and he is most fully human when he sets aside his bestial passions to live a disciplined life in which he possesses nothing but himself. When the prairie fire and buffalo stampede panic Hover and Middleton, it is Natty who, at the right moment, causes those vast irrational forces to flow around him. When the others would rush to certain death, he uses buffalo to divide the herd and fire to deprive the larger fire of fuel. When captured, Hover and Middleton are made helpless by despair; Natty, though resigned to an almost certain death, remains watchful.

In the Dacotah camp, where the strengths and weaknesses of all the central characters are revealed, Natty stands apart even as he moves, aiding and comforting, among the others. When we see him in the council circle beside Obed Bat—that parody of reason here decorated so that he is also a parody of man—he is described "musing on the course he should now adopt, with the singular mixture of decision and resignation that proceeded from his habits and his humility, and which united to form a character, in which excessive energy, and the most meek submission to the will of Providence, were oddly enough combined." Only Natty has, as Joel Porte suggests, "through great strength and purity of intention...seemingly redeemed himself from Adam's curse, thereby wholly and singly meriting the great unspoiled land that is his bride."[6] He is the center of this novel both because, as Hard-Heart declares, he has "seen all that is to be seen in this country" and because, as Middleton says, he is "endowed with the choicest and perhaps rarest gift of nature: that of distinguishing good from evil."

Leatherstocking alone realizes the alternative to being defined by external boundaries: to be definitive in one's own being, like Wallace Stevens's jar in Tennessee or Thoreau at Walden, the point from which all else is measured. He is that man, more profoundly liberated than Ishmael could imagine, around whom the landscape radiates and is itself defined. The ultimate American hero, he enters a wilderness chaos and not only keeps his own identity intact but also gives order to the surrounding landscape without use of courtroom or surveyor's transit. It is this role that Obed Bat's presence underscores by contrast. The arrogant bungler who wants so des-

[6]Porte, *The Romance in America,* p. 52.

perately to be Adamic—the namer—Bat cannot deal with direct experience but must continually locate things in rigid, scholastic systems. He settles for apparent coherence by glibly categorizing all that he encounters and, consequently, is forever missing the essential in a dedication to the superfluous.

When, at the moment of death Leatherstocking calls "Here!," he simultaneously answers a final roll call and establishes a definitive point in the desolation of the prairie. Cooper's friend Horatio Greenough once observed in a discussion of the Washington monument that the function of an obelisk is, "in its form and character, to call attention to a spot memorable in history. It says but one word, but it speaks it loud. If I understand its voice, it says, 'Here!' It says no more." Leatherstocking's "Here!" is such a marker, and the stone that Middleton eventually erects over the trapper's grave—a marker bearing the name unspoken in the novel—is a definitive point around which the prairie radiates.

Leatherstocking is not a representative man, nor does he exemplify the American of the future. Although he is presented as the ultimate wilderness hero whose presence is the moral and aesthetic center of this novel, there is a sense in which he is also strangely absent. This is a novel about—among other things—vacancies. We are made to see this landscape, as often as not, in terms of what it lacks, as though emptiness has become palpable. Natty, too, as crucial as his presence in the novel is, is also an indicator of something absent. Eventually the vacancy will be that which in death he leaves between Hard-Heart and Middleton and the cultures they represent. But there is more. He enters the novel as a shadow, and when he is first described, it is in terms—"emaciated," "shrunken," "withered"—of what is missing rather than of what remains. After a career as "Deerslayer," "Pathfinder," "Hawkeye," "The Long Rifle," he is at last only an old trapper, a title that, together with the withered body, mockingly reminds the reader of what has been lost.

The one character who is capable of self-definition in this undefined world—who embodies in his rationality and his compassion the fullest expression of the humane—suggests not what we might be so much as what we cannot be. Unlike us he is free of the passions that disrupt even Middleton's life; he demands little in the way of family or possessions, and he cannot be distracted, even in his dotage, from virtue. Leatherstocking is an ideal and as such exposes what is missing in us just as his adequacy throws into sharper relief the inadequacy of all other characters in the novel. Having given us a hero who seems so like the new men Emerson and Thoreau celebrate, Cooper does not claim, as do the transcendentalists, that we are to become such heroes ourselves. He is never so optimistic about human nature as to suggest that we can live with such freedom or such responsibility. Our kinship with the novel's other whites is much stronger than our resemblance to Leatherstocking, and, like them, we require the ordering influence of an enlightened community. If, by comparison with grander claims for America and Americans, this seems unduly pessimistic, there is affirmation as well. True, the Bush family, leveled and chastened, returns to the settlements; and Ellen and Hover can hope for no greater purpose than to follow the leadership of Middleton and Inez; and Middleton, in all his well-intentioned stuffiness, returns to the world of regiments; yet something is reclaimed. I do not mean the recovery of Inez (and, allegorically, Louisiana) from both Spanish Catholicism and her kidnappers, nor do I mean the displacement of Ishmael's wantonness by the enlightened leadership of Middleton—though both are accomplishments not to be underestimated. Rather, I mean that even though Leatherstocking is not presented as an example of what we can be and though he does not vindicate the deepest myth of American individualism, still as an ideal, a figure so self-contained and true that out of his very humanity he orders the chaos around him, he provides us with a perspective from which to view both a new world and those of us who have come to inhabit it.

Love and Sexuality in *The Pathfinder*

by Annette Kolodny

The Natty Bumppo of *The Pathfinder* (1840),[1] like his earlier incarnations, insists upon his attachment to the dim but embracing enclosures of the forest, and claims that anyone who "'would lead me out of the shade of the woods, to put me in the sun of the clearin's!'" (p. 185), can be no friend to his happiness. But, as a now middle-aged Natty begins to fall in love with Mabel Dunham, we hear him make other, equally fervent protestations of quite a different sort: "'But I am human a'ter all; yes, I find I'm very human in some of my feelin's'" (p. 281). In assertions like these and in Cooper's attempt to convince us that Natty *could* fall in love, we have the author's last ditch attempt to make a psychologically whole man out of the character to whom he had attributed so many of the externals of manhood. Obviously, of course, Cooper never intended us to take seriously the possibility of Pathfinder's marriage, and so he introduced Jasper Western at the very beginning of the story as a more appropriate suitor; what he wanted to do, really, was to give his character a dimension that he felt had been missing from his makeup.

The central focus of the novel then becomes the contest, between the two competing feminines, for Natty's affections. For a time the comforts of the forest virtually disappear as the narrative follows Natty into the environs of the fort. Here there is a psychological, as

"Love and Sexuality in *The Pathfinder*" (editor's title). From Annette Kolodny, *The Lay of the Land: Metaphor as Experience and History in American Life and Letters* (Chapel Hill, N.C., University of North Carolina Press, 1975) (pp. 105-9). Copyright 1975, The University of North Carolina Press. Reprinted by permission of the publisher.

[1][All citations from *The Pathfinder* refer to *The Works of James Fenimore Cooper,* vol. 3 (New York: G. P. Putnam's Sons, 1893).-Ed.]

well as a physical, displacement of the character, most dramatically illustrated by Natty's "wantonly" shooting two birds from the air, an act of which we would not ordinarily have thought him capable, and completely contradicting earlier statements he has made about himself in the novel (p. 177). However, as the act is performed during what we might consider a courting scene, Natty's prowess with the rifle, his one objective phallic emblem, becomes not only an appropriate way of impressing Mabel, but also demonstrates, rather graphically, the quality of relationship he hopes to experience with her.

In response, nature has her own attractions to pit against the "'pleasant looks, and...winning ways'" (p. 199) of human females. On board the scud, viewing from its deck the passing "outlines of trees...and...large bays that lay embosomed in woods," Natty realizes that "notwithstanding he found it so grateful to be near Mabel...his soul [did] pine to be wandering beneath the high arches of the maples, oaks, and lindens, where his habits had induced him to fancy lasting and true joys were only to be found" (p. 305).

The initial resolution of the tension occurs, not dramatically, but psychoanalytically, as Natty relates a recent dream to Mabel:

> "...the very last night we stayed in the garrison, I imagined I had a cabin in a grove of sugar maples, and at the root of every tree was a Mabel Dunham, while the birds that were among the branches sang ballads, instead of notes that natur' gave, and even the deer stopped to listen. I tried to shoot a fa'an, but Killdeer missed fire, and the creatur' laughed in my face, as pleasantly as a young girl laughs in her merriment, and then it bounded away, looking back as if expecting me to follow." [p. 291-92]

The dream is not, as David Noble suggests, an evocation of Natty's desire "to exchange physical nature for human companionship,"[2] but rather, a revelation of the two competing feminines between whom Natty finds himself torn. The cabin, which in dreams represents not so much a physical shelter as a symbol of psychological identity, is here particularly placed "in a grove of sugar maples," enclosing it thereby within the embrace of nature; Natty's internal reality, then, is complete only as the two things harmonize — the

[2][David Noble, "Cooper, Leatherstocking and the Death of the American Adam," *American Quarterly* 16 (1964): 424.-Ed.]

cabin *within* the grove—and both the human and the natural elements seem equally important. The sugar maple, as we know from *The Pioneers,* is that delightful tree that gives forth the sweetness of its sap, singularly nurturing and appealing. "At the root" of each of these unique trees "was a Mabel Dunham," who, as the maternal feminine, or Earth Mother symbol, gives nurture to the roots of all growing things. In this case, it is particularly sweet and positive nurturance; and the femininity is not that of a discrete person in any real sense, but rather the impersonal but nevertheless positive femininity of the Mother. Mabel, of course, the only woman to whom Natty has ever responded with personal feeling, is thereby an appropriate emblem through which his unconscious may image the archetypal feminine in nature.

Then Natty does something quite odd, for him: he aims at a fawn, without giving it the benefit of the chase, and, more unusual yet, Killdeer misfires. Subsequently, the fawn takes on flirtatious, coquettish qualities, laughs in the dreamer's face, and then bounds away, "'looking back as if expecting me to follow.'" Why, we wonder does a fawn laugh at her hunter and beckon her potential destroyer to follow? Because that destroyer has been rendered impotent; she may flirt all she wants and still be safe from his aggressions. Quite different from the maternal-feminine aspect of Mabel, seated at the root of every tree, the fawn is feminine nature's sexual face. Once we understand the psychological significance of the fawn within Natty's unconscious and internal reality, we also understand why, for the first time in any novel, his trusty gun does not go off. His overwhelming attraction for the real-world sexual Mabel has somewhat severed him from his previous and total embracement within the natural world. But the fawn's flirtation encourages him to think that the natural world, too, will permit a sexual intimacy. That the gun misfires proves that dream to be, once more, an illusion. The Mother *will* not be violated—even if, to keep her hold on Natty, she *appears* to promise such total gratification. That Natty himself could not face the incest possibility is made clear by the fact that it is his own unconscious that, in the dream, deflects that potential threat. Now, having been awakened by Mabel to the possibility of his own sexuality, Pathfinder complains that, "'instead of sleeping as sound as natur' at midnight, as I used to could, I dream nightly of Mabel Dunham'" (p. 476).

His previous containment within the unconscious sleep of the maternal has been seriously threatened, and, in order to elaborate upon and emphasize the psychological implications of the dream, Cooper has Natty repeat it to Jasper Western: "'The young does sport before me; and when I raise Killdeer in order to take a little venison, the animals look back, and it seems as if they all had Mabel's sweet countenance, laughing in my face, and looking as if they said, "Shoot me if you dare!"'" (p. 476). Natty's potentially destructive powers are being defused; the apparently innocent act of taking "'a little venison'" is now being experienced as aggression against something essentially feminine, beloved, desirable, and vulnerable. As a result, Natty finds he cannot accept the implicit challenge to assert himself: he would not dare to shoot.

This is the only dream recorded in all five of the Leatherstocking novels, and, as such, it is Cooper's first and only attempt to image for us Natty's internal reality. Its fundamental meaning is subsequently reinforced as Cooper, apparently recognizing for the first time the psychological significance of his creation, describes Natty's mind as "almost infantine in its simplicity and nature" (p. 294). The regressive aspect of the man whose psychic reality could be imaged within an embrace of nature, the cabin in the maple grove, for instance, has been admitted at last! It is a containment that has never been challenged, and suggests that Natty has been, all along, presexual, his movements those of the son and not the lover. That this late experience with the sexuality of woman has been "'so painful and so deep'" as "'to harrow the very soul,'" underscores Natty's unfamiliarity with this aspect of his own masculinity. "Indeed, in this respect," as Cooper tells us, "the Pathfinder was a mere child," and he drives the point home again in comparing him to an "infant" (p. 294). Still, Cooper insists, the external details of Natty's life and mien maintain the appearance of masculine identity—"so stern, stoical, masculine, and severe, in all that touched his ordinary pursuits" (p. 294). Which is exactly what had us all so confused; even the admiring Simms had noted the contradiction, disturbed by what he saw as Cooper's repeated failure "to hit the true line that divides the simplicity of nature, from the puerility of ignorance or child-hood."[3] But now we realize that Natty's apparently masculine out-ward identity had no real internal or psychological correlative. Cooper had been merely taking it for granted. As the language of the previous narratives had hinted—with their insistence on the enclosure motif in Natty's world—and now, as the incidents of this fourth novel make clear, Natty had all along been a psychological child, still contained within a world that was predominantly mater-nal. That was the secret of the almost nonviolating harmony, the second-paradisal intimacy, which he alone, of all the Leatherstock-ing whites, had been able to maintain within the natural world.

The novel's conclusion suggests that if the primal harmony Natty had previously known is now seriously threatened, it is not com-pletely destroyed. Natty cannot assimilate Mabel, as the forest has assimilated him, into a parental embrace, and through her, he remains forever tied to the possibility of his own sexuality; he continues to pay homage to that possibility in the "valuable presents of furs" he sends her "at intervals of years" (p. 500). And, in spite of his pain and his inability "'to march quite as light-hearted as I once used to could, or to sleep as sound for some time to come,'" Natty acknowledges the positive power of conscious light breaking into the unconscious and embracing slumber. "'How could I be sorry that a ray of the sun came across the gloom,'" he asks, or "'that light has broken in upon darkness, though it remained so short a time!'" (p. 491). But whether that "light" will be fully realized, even without Mabel's presence, or whether it is doomed to remain only "so short a time," is the psychological impetus for the final novel in the series. With the close of *The Pathfinder* we know only that Natty intends to "return to the wilderness and my Maker'" (p. 492), and our final view of him is as a man receding from our sight, "lost in the depths of the forest" (p. 500).

---

[3][William Gilmore Simms, "Writings of James Fenimore Cooper," in *Views and Reviews in American Literature, History and Fiction,* ed. C. Hugh Holman (Cam-bridge, Mass: Harvard University Press, 1962), p. 273.-Ed.]

Moral and Physical Action in *The Deerslayer*

by Marius Bewley

The five Leatherstocking novels are, as a group, Cooper's greatest work. They were composed at long intervals across his active career, *The Pioneers* appearing in 1823, while the last of the series, *The Deerslayer,* was not published until 1841. The continuity in these novels is provided by the character of Leatherstocking himself—the hunter, Natty Bumppo; but the novels do not record a consistent chronological record of Natty's life. He is an old man in the first; he dies in the third novel, *The Prairie;* while in *The Deerslayer,* in which the conception of Natty's character is fully matured, he is a young man on his first warpath. *The Deerslayer* is probably the best thing Cooper ever wrote, and it is one of the important masterpieces of American literature. We see here his conception of an action as the form of a novel—that conception we have already discussed in relation to the minor novels—perfectly realized here in his art.

The action of *The Deerslayer* takes place at the beginning of the French and Indian War, but the adventures it records are only indirectly associated with that struggle. The novel opens, as so often with Cooper, with a vision of the American forest:

> Whatever may be the changes produced by man, the eternal round of the seasons is unbroken. Summer and winter, seedtime and harvest, return in their stated order with a sublime precision, affording to man one of the noblest of all the occasions he enjoys of proving the high powers of his far-reaching mind, in compassing the laws that control their exact uniformity, and in calculating their never-ending revolu-

"Moral and Physical Action in *The Deerslayer*" (editor's title). Reprinted from Marius Bewley: *The Eccentric Design* (New York: Columbia University Press, 1963), pp. 87-100, by permission of Columbia University Press and Chatto and Windus Ltd.

tions. Centuries of summer suns had warmed the tops of the same noble oaks and pines, sending their heats even to the tenacious roots, when voices were heard calling to each other, in the depths of a forest, of which the leafy surface lay bathed in the brilliant light of a cloudless day in June, while the trunks of the trees rose in gloomy grandeur in the shades beneath. The calls were in different tones, evidently proceeding from two men who had lost their way, and were searching in different directions for their path.

"...two men who had lost their way, and were searching in different directions for their path." We shall not be portentous if we bring a maximum of meaning to this line. When the two men emerge from the forest into the little clearing we are face to face with the handsome hunter, Hurry Harry, and his companion, Deerslayer, who is Natty Bumppo as a young man in his early twenties. In the long novel that here opens we begin to trace, beyond the pattern of violent physical action, two opposing moral visions of life which are embodied in these two woodsmen. This is the true form and drama of *The Deerslayer,* which is played out against a background of Indian attack and ambuscade—played out on a stage almost classically circumscribed, and over a period of only several days. These severe limits of place and duration impart a unity to the novel that, despite the incidents, which are more than usually densely gathered for Cooper, gives a prominence to the moral theme and its deeper meaning. Deerslayer's values are not only defined through the action, their influence becomes the diffused atmosphere that the others breathe. They do not exist as a separable commentary on the action; they are in the heart of the action itself.

As *The Deerslayer* is no longer inevitably read, even by children, my comments may be more intelligible if I offer a brief résumé of the plot. Reduced to these proportions, it is nothing more than a somewhat exaggerated adventure tale. Deerslayer has lived with, and been educated by, the Delawares, a tribe of Indians for whom Cooper always showed a particular fondness. Among the Delawares his special friend has been the handsome and noble young chief, Chingachgook, betrothed to the Delaware maiden, Wah-ta!-Wah. Before the story opens, Wah-ta!-Wah, coveted for her beauty by many young braves, has been kidnapped by Briarthorne, a traitor to his tribe, and carried into the western wilderness where a hunting expedition of Hurons, or Mingoes, are encamped on the shores of Lake Otsego, which goes under the name of the Glimmerglass. The

Hurons, friendly to the French, have travelled this far from the Canadas, and, in their present encampment, are trespassing on English territory, although the remoteness of the spot enables them to do so with impunity. Chingachgook, learning that Wah-ta!Wah has been carried here, makes an engagement with his friend, Deerslayer, to undertake the rescue of his betrothed—and the two are to meet, at a certain time, by a certain rock, on the shores of the Glimmerglass. It is while travelling to keep this meeting that Deerslayer meets Hurry Harry in the wilderness. They two have known each other before, and as Hurry is also headed for the Glimmerglass, the two join forces. The purpose of Hurry's expedition is to visit a family that lives in this isolated spot, Tom Hutter and his daughters, the beautiful Judith and her feeble-minded sister, Hetty. Despite Judith's reputed indiscretions with the officers of an English garrison a day's march away in the wilderness, Hurry is infatuated with Judith's beauty and wishes to marry her. The Hutter family (with the exception of poor Hetty, who becomes a bore) is very well done. Cooper was always at his best when creating rather sinister old men; and Tom Hutter, who has withdrawn into the wilderness because of a price on his head for piracy, compares favourably with Aaron Thousandacres in *The Chainbearer,* and with Ishmael Bush in *The Prairie.* For the sake of security against Indian attacks Tom Hutter has built a log house, referred to as the Castle, on piles near the middle of the lake; and for additional security and convenience, he has constructed a large flat-bottomed boat, called the *ark,* in which he and his daughters live during the summer. The ark and the castle, with occasional sojourns on the lake shore, become the scene of the crowded action that follows.

The Hurons have just learned of the outbreak of hostilities between the French and the English, and as adherents of the former, they are reluctant to break up their summer encampment without bearing away, as trophies of their trip into enemy country, the scalps of the whites on the Glimmerglass. They are met half-way in their desire by Hutter and Hurry, who desire Indian scalps to collect the bounty the British colonial government has placed on that commodity. The action is complicated by the arrival of Chingachgook, who, from more honourable motives, joins in the scalping expeditions of the white men. It is not necessary to detail the incidents that follow in quick succession. Reduced to a synopsis most plots sound exaggerated or silly, and this is particularly true of Cooper.

Much of the persuasiveness of his actions comes from a perfect sense of dramatic timing, and this quality is especially strong in *The Deerslayer*. As the novel progresses towards the later chapters, it comes to resemble a complicated choreography whose intricate measures resolve themselves into several lucid basic movements. There is, first of all, the opposition of two basic points of view represented in action by Deerslayer and Hurry Harry; there is also the opposition of two racial viewpoints for which identical acts may mean honour or dishonour; and, finally, there is the essential theme of Deerslayer's dedication to his own vision of truth. Cooper had never been able to resolve the division in American experience that divided, for example, his European political novels from the Littlepage trilogy, and which made the Effinghams such grotesque failures; but here the conflict is completely transmuted into other terms that are amenable to artistic resolution, and Natty, even though he cannot read, is more of a gentleman in the wilderness than the Effinghams were in their drawing-rooms. But I shall be more explicit about this in the next chapter when I discuss Natty Bumppo as a critical symbol of American experience.

A great part of the effectiveness of *The Deerslayer* arises from Cooper's control of the natural moods of sky, light, and darkness on the Glimmerglass to intensify the emotional movement of the action. The Glimmerglass, which is the confined and the confining scene of all that happens, in its variety of natural moods between midnight, noon, and midnight, constantly suggests that equilibrium in nature which is the serene and indifferent resolution of all violence and blood. But if, after violence, Cooper describes it again and again in some tranquil dusk of early morning or burst of cheerful sunlight to suggest the returning dominance of nature after an interval of human strife, he uses it also to enforce the dramatic necessities of the action at any given time. The following description of night on the Glimmerglass is long, but I quote it because it illustrates the quality of Cooper's writing, which is better in this novel than usual. Because of the threatened hostilities of the Hurons against the Castle during the night, Hutter and Deerslayer decide to embark their whole party in the ark, which is more expedient, both for defence and escape. It is already night when they embark in the large slow-moving boat, whose biblical name is itself something of a portent:

The vicinity of the hills, with their drapery of pines, had the effect to render nights that were obscure, darker than common on the lake. As usual, however, a belt of comparative light was stretched through the centre of the sheet, while it was within the shadow of the mountains, that the gloom rested most heavily on the water. The island, or castle, stood in this belt of comparative light, but still the night was so dark, as to cover the departure of the ark. At the distance of an observer on the shore, her movements could not be seen at all, more particularly as a background of dark hillside filled up the perspective of every view that was taken diagonally or directly across the water. The prevalent wind on the lakes of that region is west, but owing to the avenues formed by the mountains, it is frequently impossible to tell the true direction of the currents as they often vary within short distances, and brief differences of time. This is truer in light fluctuating puffs of air, than in steady breezes; though the squalls of even the latter are familiarly known to be uncertain and baffling in all mountainous regions and narrow waters. On the present occasion, Hutter himself (as he shoved the ark from her berth at the side of the platform) was at a loss to pronounce which way the wind blew. In common, this difficulty was solved by the clouds, which, floating over the hill tops, as a matter of course, obeyed the currents; but now the whole vault of heaven seemed a gloomy wall. Not an opening of any sort was visible. ...

The action of *The Deerslayer* is convincing because the world in which it occurs is created with vividly realized circumstantial detail. It is less mere description than it is the evocation of the tangible reality of *things*. The passage just quoted loses a good deal by being torn from context. Its pressure on the nerves depends on the way it focuses, in the appalling, empty atmosphere of surrounding black, the suspense that has been built up through pages. It bears an interesting similarity with a passage from Cooper's great admirer, Joseph Conrad ("F. Cooper is a rare artist. He has been one of my masters. He is my constant companion," letter to Arthur Symonds, 1908). The passage I am referring to is that famous description of the night Nostromo and Martin Decoud spend in a lighter on the Gulf with the silver shipment to the Gould mine:

A great recrudescence of obscurity embraced the boat. The sea in the gulf was as black as the clouds above. Nostromo, after striking a couple of matches to get glimpses of the boat compass he had with him in the lighter, steered by the feel of the wind on his cheek.

It was a new experience for Decoud, this mysteriousness of the great waters spread out strangely smooth, as if their restlessness had been crushed by the weight of that dense night. The Placido was sleeping soundly under its black poncho.

The main thing now was to get away from the coast and gain the middle of the gulf before day broke. The Isabels were somewhere at hand. "On your left as you look forward, senor," said Nostromo suddenly. When his voice ceased, the enormous stillness, without light or sound, seemed to affect Decoud's senses like a powerful drug. He didn't even know at times whether he were asleep or awake. Like a man lost in slumber, he heard nothing, he saw nothing.

In both passages the blackness is so palpable that it is more concrete than the reality it conceals. And it provides a medium that confers a startling intensity on the actions that it feigns to smother. Both Cooper and Conrad share this extraordinary ability of rendering transient sensations and evocations of atmosphere with a psychological immediacy that can be terrifying. Although it is too long to quote here, an admirable instance of this quality in Cooper occurs in Chapter VI. Tom Hutter and Hurry Harry, impelled by the desire to secure the bounty on Indian scalps, have made an expedition to shore under cover of the darkness to visit the Huron encampment which, they believe, is on this occasion inhabited solely by squaws and children, the warriors having withdrawn for the night to another part of the lake shore. Deerslayer, unable to prevent this excursion, is drawn up in a canoe among the rushes. Cooper evokes the atmosphere of the darkness brooding on the Glimmerglass with great effectiveness—"a gloom of night which threw its shadowy and fantastic forms around the lake, the forest, and the hills. ... The size of the lake brought all within the reach of the human senses. ..." Suddenly, through this solitude comes the quavering call of a loon from the opposite shore of the lake: "Shrill, tremulous, loud, and sufficiently prolonged, it seems the very cry of warning." And then, as the cry of the loon subsides a second time, "the profound stillness of night and solitude was broken by a cry so startling as to drive all recollection of the more melancholy call of the loon from the speaker's mind. It was a shriek of agony that came either from one of the female sex, or from a boy so young as not yet to have attained a manly voice. ... Heart-rending terror—if not writhing agony— was in the sounds, and the anguish that had awakened them was as sudden as it was fearful."

Tom Hutter and Hurry Harry are not simple cases of moral

depravity. Their villainy, which, as we see it, is confined to a habit
of scalping Indians, is strictly legal, and encouraged by the government, and Cooper is fully aware of all their implications for American society. For if Hurry and Tom Hutter are not the Americans of
the new age, they seem to have their relations with them. Their
impressiveness in the book, however, springs from the concrete
richness with which they are realized. They are before us, not only
as superbly solid physical embodiments of the American wilderness-
man, but the nature of the violent, if narrow, action is exactly calculated to illuminate the restricted stage of their moral consciousness. In an early dialogue between Deerslayer and Hurry on the
subject of Indians, we have a finely drawn picture of Hurry's mental
processes — a picture so typical of a pattern that was to become
representative of one line of American rationalizing that in Hurry
we almost feel we have the artistic progenitor of Senator McCarran's
racial ideal:

"I look upon the red-men to be quite as human as we are ourselves,
Hurry. They have their gifts, and their religion, it's true; but that
makes no difference in the end, when each will be judged according to
his deeds, and not according to his skin."

"That's downright missionary, and will find little favour up in this
part of the country, where the Moravians don't congregate. Now, skin
makes the man. This is reason; else how are people to judge of each
other. The skin is put on, over all, in order that when a creatur', or a
mortal, is fairly seen, you may know at once what to make of him. You
know a bear from a hog, by his skin, and a grey squirrel from a black."

"True, Hurry," said the other looking back and smiling; "nevertheless, they are both squirrels."

"Who denies it? But you'll not say that a red man and a white man
are both Injins?"

"No; but I *do* say they are both men. Men of different races and
colours, and having different gifts and traditions, but, in the main,
with the same natur'. Both have souls; and both will be held account-
able for their deeds in this life."

Hurry was one of those theorists who believed in the inferiority of
all the human race who were not white. His notions on the subject
were not very clear, nor were his definitions at all well settled; but
his opinions were none the !ess dogmatical or fierce. His conscience
accused him of sundry lawless acts against the Indians, and he had
found it an exceedingly easy mode of quieting it, by putting the whole
family of red men, incontinently, without the category of human

rights. Nothing angered him sooner than to deny his proposition, more especially if the denial were accompanied by a show of plausible argument; and he did not listen to his companion's remarks with much composure of either manner or feeling.

Hurry as a moralist is a type we have with us still in American literature. This passage might be compared with the long argument on Indian-killing in Melville's *The Confidence Man*. But Cooper is more successful because Hurry is a thoroughly realistic figure, whereas Melville's Indian-killer, Colonel Moredock, although an actual historical person, exists in the medium of Melville's irony with an unsatisfactory (that is to say, a muddy) ambiguity. Melville would have rejected the clear-cut "placing" of values which the presence of Deerslayer achieves. And moving up from Melville, we can find Hurry's mental type persisting in the wealthy and socially secure Tom Buchanan of Scott Fitzgerald's *The Great Gatsby:*

> "Civilization's going to pieces," broke out Tom violently. "I've gotten to be a terrible pessimist about things. Have you read *The Rise of the Coloured Races* by this man Goddard? ... Well, it's a fine book, and everybody ought to read it. The idea is if we don't look out the white race will be—will be utterly submerged. It's all scientific stuff; it's been proved."

Or, going on from fiction to more "responsible" utterances, we have this from Teddy Roosevelt in his pre-Presidential years:

> I don't go so far as to think that the only good Indians are the dead Indians, but I believe that nine out of every ten are, and I shouldn't like to enquire too closely into the case of the tenth. The most vicious cowboy has more moral principle than the average Indian.

In Hurry Harry and his moral vision of life we have an early representative of a type that was to become a dominant element in American civilization as it moved along towards the Gilded Age— a type that could supplant moral motives by motives of commercial expediency, and pretend, even to itself, that the substitution had never been made. Cooper's perceptions in creating Hurry Harry are profound and accurate. Although he does not perceptibly wince at the idea of scalping Indian children for the bounty, he is a pattern of the forthright, impulsive, attractive young American. Much of Cooper's genius is shown in the way he effectively suggests the squalid reality behind the romantic figure of the woods. And it is well to bear in mind that this brand of American romanticism was partly cultivated in Cooper's day for the sake of putting some colour of attractive decorum on the crimes of the American wilderness, without which the expansion of the frontier would have notably lagged, or so it seemed. The delicacy of Cooper's distinctions is poised and precise. If he gives the dark side of Hurry, he never identifies him with the overt criminality of old Tom Hutter, the ex-pirate:

> But neither of these two rude beings, so ruthless in all that touches the rights and interests of the red man, though possessing veins of human feeling on other matters, was much actuated by any other desire than a heartless longing for profit. Hurry had felt angered at his sufferings, when first liberated, it is true, but that emotion had soon disappeared in a habitual love of gold, which he sought with the reckless avidity of a needy spendthrift, rather than with the ceaseless longings of a miser. In short, the motive that urged them both so soon to go against the Hurons, was an habitual contempt of their enemy, acting on the unceasing cupidity of prodigality. The additional chances of success, however, had their place in the formation of the second enterprise. It was known that a large portion of the warriors—perhaps all—were encamped for the night, abreast of the castle, and it was hoped that the scalps of helpless victims would be the consequence. To confess the truth, Hutter in particular—he who had just left two daughters behind him, expected to find few but women and children in the camp. This fact had been but slightly alluded to in his communications with Hurry, and with Chingachgook it had been kept entirely out of view.

Hurry Harry is the portent of how things were to go in America. Hurry is a woodsman, but his relation with the wilderness is opposed to Deerslayer's. His true roots are in the settlements, and the wilderness exists for him essentially as a business that he may make periodic visits to "civilization" with his pockets jingling. Hurry is an indication of how things *will* be, Deerslayer of how they *might* have been. Deerslayer exists on a different level of the imagination than Hurry. He is essentially a poetic evocation, and his conception inevitably incorporates an element of myth in so far as myth may be defined as the incarnation of racial aspiration and memory. His vision of life is best summed up in this speech from Chapter XV:

As for farms, they have their uses, and there's them that like to pass their lives on 'em; but, what comfort can a man look for in a clearin' that he can't find in double quantities in the forest? If air, and room, and light, are a little craved, the wind-rows and the streams will furnish 'em, or here are the lakes for such as have bigger longings in that way; but where are you to find your shades, and laughing springs, and leaping brooks, and venerable trees, a thousand years old, in a clearin'? You don't find *them,* but you find their disabled trunks, marking the 'arth like head-stones in a graveyard? It seems to me that the people who live in such places, must be always thinkin' of their own ends, and of natural decay; and that, too, not of the decay that is brought about by time and natur', but the decay that follows waste and violence. Then as to churches, they are good, I suppose, else wouldn't good men uphold 'em. But they are not altogether necessary. They call 'em the temples of the Lord; but Judith, the whole 'arth is a temple of the Lord to such as have right minds. Moreover, all is contradiction in the settlements, while all is concord in the woods. Forts and churches almost always go together, and yet they're downright contradictions; churches being for peace, and forts for war.

Tolerance is a somewhat imprecise word to use in a discussion such as the present one, but tolerance is nothing more than intelligence and sensitive understanding—perception deep enough to find the substantial likeness under the shadows of division. If there is a poetry of tolerance, Deerslayer is its expression. It is what radically distinguishes him from the more characteristically American Hurry Harry. The following exchange between them may seem to add but little to a quotation I have already given, but so important in this quality for understanding Deerslayer and his role that some repetition is justified:

"God made us all, white, black, and red; and, no doubt, had his own wise intentions in colouring us differently. Still, he made us, in the main, much the same in feelings; though I'll not deny he gave each race its gifts. A white man's gifts are christianized, while a red-skin's are more for the wilderness. Thus, it would be a great offence for the white man to scalp the dead; whereas it's a signal vartue in an Indian. Then ag'in a white man can't amboosh women and children in war, while a red-skin may. 'Tis a *cruel* work, I'll allow; but for them it's *lawful* work, while for us it would be grievous work."

"That depends on your inimy. As for scalping, or even skinning a savage, I look upon them pretty much the same as cutting off the ears of wolves, for the bounty, or stripping a bear of its hide. And then

you're out significantly, as to taking the poll of a redskin in hand, seeing that the very Colony has offered a bounty for the job; all the same
as it pays for wolves' ears, and crows' heads."

Cooper never forgets that Hurry's scalping practices are legally
sanctioned and encouraged by the government under which Deerslayer also lives. Perversely, it is Hurry, not Deerslayer, who follows the pattern set down by the Colony for the preservation of law,
order, and the more doubtful decencies. This obviously relates to
the dilemma that confronted Cooper in his other novels, and which
is at the base of much of his social criticism. In some ways Deerslayer is as much of an outsider in the American wilderness as the
Effinghams were in the American drawing-rooms that shattered
their sensibilities. But as a positive norm, Deerslayer is both a moral
and an artistic triumph.

But the mere statement of Deerslayer's tolerance, as it comes out
in such passages of dialogue as the one here quoted, does an injustice
to the living figure of Deerslayer as it exists in the novel. The whole
action is animated by Deerslayer's vision. It takes firm control of the
action, elevating it above plot mechanics into the realm of life and
moral form. Closely related to, and growing out of this tolerant
understanding of life is a reverence for life itself. One of the most
moving passages in *The Deerslayer* occurs in Chapter VII when
Deerslayer kills his first Indian in self-defence. Mr. Yvor Winters
in *Maule's Curse* has quoted lengthily from this passage, which he
refers to as 'probably the best single passage of prose in Cooper'. I
have not the space to deal with it here, but its importance lies, not
only as Mr. Winters maintains, in powerfully communicating "the
tremendous impersonal quiet of the American wilderness" (though
it certainly does that), but in registering, both with tenderness and
surgical realism, the tensions of a highly developed and refined
moral consciousness under the shock of a brutal necessity.

Dramatically, the central episode of *The Deerslayer* is that in
which Natty, a captive of the Hurons, is released on his honour for a
period of twenty-four hours, but at the end of that time is obligated
to return to captivity with the almost certain knowledge that he will
be put to torture and death. Natty keeps the terms of his promise to
the letter, although to do so appears madness to his companions, and
probably seems ludicrous heroics to most readers. Nevertheless, this
episode is the key to the significance of Deerslayer's life, which is

moulded in the imagination with the firm spiritual contours of the saint. It reveals Natty's vision of life to us as a passionate dedication to truth—and truth, not as the pragmatical nothingness it was to become in American life, but as a religious conception. To Hurry Harry's argument against his returning to the Hurons ("What's an Injin or a word passed, or a furlough taken from creaturs like them, that have neither souls nor names?"), Deerslayer replies:

> "If they've got neither souls nor names, you and I have both, Harry March, and one is accountable for the other. This furlough is not, as you seem to think, altogether a matter atween me and the Mingoes, seeing it is a solemn bargain atween me and God. He who thinks that he can say what he pleases, in his distress, and that 'twill all pass for nothing, because 'tis uttered in the forest, and into red men's ears, knows little of his situation, and hopes, and wants. The words are said to the ears of the Almighty. The air is his breath, and the light of the sun is little more than a glance of his eye."

What I have said here about *The Deerslayer* I hope will illustrate my remark at the opening of this chapter that "for Cooper at his best, an action is the intensified motion of life in which the spiritual and moral faculties of men are no less engaged than their physical selves. Cooper writes adventure stories; but an adventure is only the conventional boundary of this motion of life...." In *The Deerslayer* the moral and the physical action are intrinsically dependent on each other, and this was something new in the English novel since Jane Austen. It is highly probable that Cooper himself was not aware of his achievement along these lines, but it was possible because Cooper's motives in writing were deeply embedded in the new American experience he was trying to express. He may have wished to entertain his readers, but whether consciously or not there was a deeper creative urge at work which made him strive to clarify his own experience as an American.

The Unstable Element

by Kay Seymour House

So familiar to us now are the great sea novels in which the sea "inter-penetrates with life" that it is difficult to realize that Cooper's *The Pilot* (1823) was greeted as the first book in a new literary genre.[1] The sea offered Cooper both sublimity of scene and almost infinite variation of adventure. In his novels, as in Rachel Carson's *The Sea Around Us,* the sea is an entity that corresponds to fact: the earth is a waterworld in which continents are casual (and, in Cooper, dangerous) intrusions. Thus Cooper's seamen regard the world, and at least one (a cabin boy, Zephyr) has never touched land. He can only speculate about what going on shore would be like.

[1]See Marcel Clavel, *Fenimore Cooper and His Critics* (Aix-en-Provence, 1938), pp. 183-263. The *American Quarterly Review* and the *North American Review* in this country; *Blackwood's,* Marryatt's *Metropolitan Magazine,* and the *Foreign Quarterly Review* in England; and Eugène Sue in France are among those who give Cooper credit for inventing the sea novel.

Thomas Philbrick's *James Fenimore Cooper and the Development of American Sea Fiction* (Cambridge, 1961) contributes to Cooper studies by placing his sea novels correctly with relation to his immediate predecessors and contemporaries who wrote of the sea.

The Headsman offers proof of Cooper's own consciousness of the ship as a microcosm: "The crowded and overloaded bark might have been compared to the vessel of human life, which floats at all times subject to the thousand accidents of a delicate and complicated machinery; the lake so smooth and alluring in its present tranquility, but so capable of lashing its iron-bound coasts with fury, to a treacherous world, whose smile is almost always as dangerous as its frown; and, to complete the picture, the idle, laughing, thoughtless, and yet inflammable group that surrounded the buffoon, to the unaccountable medley of human sympathies, of sudden and

"They say one can hardly walk, it is so steady! They say the ground is rough and difficult to walk on; that earthquakes shake it, and make holes to swallow cities; that men slay each other on the highways for money, and that the houses I see on the hills must always remain in the same spot." *(The Water-Witch,* 163)

Land is to the sailor, like the settlements to Natty Bumppo, a place of danger, crime, and immobility. Land is an aberration; the sea, reality. This attitude is important, for such a sea is like a universe ordered by Providence; it has its own ways and its own reality, and forces man to come to terms with it. The ships he builds, the skill with which he sails them, even naval discipline and rank are parts of the price he pays to stay afloat and alive on it.

R. W. B. Lewis has said that "for Cooper the forest and the sea shared the quality of boundlessness; they were the *apeiron* — the area of possibility."[2] In a general sense, Lewis is right; by going to sea man escapes, if he wishes, those facts of his biography which would have determined his character on land. Yet Richard Poirier's designation of Twain's raft, Melville's *Pequod,* and Faulkner's woods (of "The Bear") as "places of removal" comes even closer to the meaning of Cooper's sea. As Poirier remarks,

> Each of these places of removal sets the stage for a reordering of the social hierarchies which exist outside it. The reordering is accomplished in terms of aspirations and achievements which cannot express themselves in a society based upon practical utility and traditional manners.[3]

Poirier's "reordering of social hierarchies" stresses the societal nature of life at sea. Cooper's shipboard functions much as the Marxist's ideal society; it is a synthetic community in which each man can fulfill his potential and where artificial and arbitrary distinctions can be minimized or escaped altogether. Here, if anywhere, the Negro Neb can succeed; Roswell Gardiner *(The Sea Lions)* can here be most easily awed out of his hubris; national enemies and temperamental opposites such as the British Captain Cuffe and the

---

fierce passions, of fun and frolic; so inexplicably mingled with the grossest egotism that enters into the heart of man. ..." (58)

This and subsequent citations from Cooper texts refer to the G. P. Putnam's Sons edition (New York, n.d.).

[2]*The American Adam* (Chicago, 1955), p. 99.

[3]*The Comic Sense of Henry James* (New York, 1960), p. 34.

French Raoul Yvard *(Wing-and-Wing)* can here feel mutual respect. Merit, or the lack of it, is more quickly visible at sea than on shore, and a man who places his own interest above that of the society of the ship creates a dramatizable danger. At the same time, merely prudish restraints can be cast off with the mooring lines. Captain Truck explains how this applies to freedom of speech, for instance.

> "Those fellows, after they have been choked off and jammed by the religion ashore for a month or two, would break out like a hurricane when they had made an offing, and were once fairly out of hearing of the parsons and deacons." *(Homeward Bound,* 243)

At sea, in short, Cooper's theories about the nature of man and society could be objectified; staved hulls, jagged reefs, ingenious escapes, and navigation—whether by stars, instinct, or wild theory—all become ways of talking about men.

Furthermore, the seaman's language furnishes the vocabulary. Becoming more than just salty sayings used and misused to characterize the sailor at least since Smollett's novels, seamen's terms are often metaphors. Some are as fancifully inflated as Trysail's comment in *The Water-Witch.*

> "I have often thought, sir, that the ocean was like human life,—a blind track for all that is ahead, and none of the clearest as respects that which has been passed over. Many a man runs headlong to his own destruction, and many a ship steers for a reef under a press of canvas. Tomorrow is a fog, into which none of us can see; and even the present time is little better than thick weather, into which we look without getting much information."   (245)

At its most commodious, the metaphor fills a whole novel, and four books are metaphysical voyages that discover mature values *(Afloat and Ashore),* the relation of man and society *(The Crater),* society's errors *(The Monikins),* and religious faith *(The Sea Lions).*

Cooper's water world is morally neutral. And while the sea does, as Conrad said, interpenetrate with life, Cooper's portrayal of the sea and seamen's lives is affected by his interest in man's psychological and political nature. Thus we find that the sea offers Americans roughly the same kind of opportunity that America itself promised the European immigrant.[4] Some characters, like some immigrants, ship their cultural baggage with them, and for these the

---

[4]Cooper thought this was as it should be; and *Jack Tier* contains a bitter protest at the government's neglecting long and meritorious service in order to "extend the

free (but ordered) life at sea can do little. Ithuel Bolt and Daggett are such characters; they remain essentially Yankee landsmen even while they venture forth briefly to harvest the sea. Still other characters bear aboard the psychological chains that keep them from profiting from the sea's freedom. To any man willing to start anew, however, the sea offers a second beginning. The history of one such, comparatively wealthy, character is told in the picaresque tale that runs through the two volumes of *Afloat and Ashore* and *Miles Wallingford* (see Chapter IX). As for the less well educated, Cooper suggested in his first sea novel that the sea was one place in which a man might be common without being mediocre.

Of the many common seamen in Cooper's novels who make no pretense to superiority but whose skills earn privileges and respect, *The Pilot's* Tom Coffin is the most familiar. He and Natty Bumppo appeared in the same year (1823), and Tom is as much a marine animal as Natty is a native of the forests. Born on a "chebacco-man" and trained at sea, Tom considers land useful only for raising vegetables and drying fish; otherwise it is a hostile element, the sight of which makes him uncomfortable (12) and on which he is impotent: "'I never could make any headway on dry land'" (193). So very salty is Tom that Grossman's objection of "mechanical extravagance" is justified. Tom's speech is too thickly brined with such aphorisms as "'a tumbling sea, with a lee-tide, on a lee-shore, makes a sad lee-way'" (283).

Much like the aging Natty Bumppo, Tom laughs silently (thus showing his caution and self-control), worries about "waste" (of an eighty-barrel whale being eaten by sharks), and has strong prejudices based on his experience. What Mingos are to Natty, soldiers are to Tom, who ranks "'a messmate, before a shipmate; a shipmate, before a stranger, a stranger, before a dog—but a dog before a soldier'" (259). Like Natty, he is proud of his family's talents: "'My father was a Coffin, and my mother was a Joy; and the two names can count more flukes than all the rest of the island [Nantucket] together'" (268). He is also like Natty in being privileged because of his special skills. His opinions, Cooper tells us, "in all matters of seamanship, were regarded as oracles by the crew, and were listened

---

circle of vulgar political patronage" by appointing "strangers" over men who had earned promotions (363).

to by his commander with no little demonstration of respect…" (199).

Tom's physique, skills, and inclination separate him from the rest of the crew, and his essential identification is with his nine-pound gun just as Natty is linked with his rifle. Like Natty, Tom divides phenomena into two categories; some things call for an exertion of skills (the winds and weather "'are given for a seafaring man to guard against, by making or shortening sail'" 282), while others are Providential and demand submission ("'It is never worth a man's while to strive to dodge a shot; for they are all commissioned to do their work'" 282).

Tom becomes, for the rest of the characters, a human link with the natural world. His training and instincts let him be the first to detect a northeaster; and he is in a limited sense the superior of his captain, to whom he explains that none get to know the signs of the weather "'but such as study little else, or feel but little else'" (245). By thus limiting his very life to that of the ship and its environment, Tom qualifies for his oracular and symbolic functions. When he is lost overboard and presumed dead during a battle, his loss strengthens the crew's efforts; they are still avenging him when he reappears in time to end the fray.

> …A wild-looking figure appeared in the cutter's channels at that moment, issuing from the sea, and gaining the deck at the same instant. It was Long Tom, with his iron visage rendered fierce by his previous discomfiture, and his grizzled locks drenched with the briny element from which he had risen, looking like Neptune with his trident. Without speaking, he poised his harpoon, and, with a powerful effort, pinned the unfortunate Englishman to the mast of his own vessel. (205)

Tom himself identifies his life and fortunes with those of the *Ariel,* and he reacts strongly to a vision of her sinking. "'I thought I saw her a wrack,'" he says, "'…and, I will own it, for it's as natural to love the craft you sail in as it is to love one's self, I will own that my manhood fetched a heavy sea-lurch at the sight'" (284). When Tom's premonition proves correct, his refusal to leave the ship and his unwillingess to outlive her make his death a suicide. The crew reports that he "'always thought it sinful to desert a wrack, and that he did not even strike out once for his life, though he has been known to swim an hour when a whale has stove his boat'" (297). Consequently, even though Tom verbally committed his life to Providence shortly before the *Ariel* sank, he required Providence to save him, if it meant to, in spite of his own willful refusal to swim. His body is never found; "with reason," Cooper adds, "for the sea was never known to give up the body of the man who might be emphatically called its own dead" (298).

Long Tom Coffin sets a standard for the American sailor. Casting off his connections with the shore, he ships abroad the *Ariel* everything worth living for and rises to be captain of a gun. He desires no further promotion, but fills comfortably a berth fit for a man who believes

> "...riches and honor are for the great and the larned, and there's nothing left for poor Tom Coffin to do, but to veer and haul on his own rolling-tackle, that he may ride out the rest of the gale of life without springing any of his old spars."   (210)

His unquestionable merits do not indicate that he has been unjustly denied command; Tom fits his station as naturally as a line-tub fits a whale-boat. Like Wallace, the second lieutenant in *Jack Tier,* or Stephen Stimson, a religious seaman in *The Sea Lions,* he is wise enough to recognize his limitations. As though he were consciously obeying the Delphic mottoes, "Know yourself" and "Nothing too much," Tom finds at sea the highest contentment of which he is capable.

When professionally competent and honest men remain contentedly as minor officers in a ship, we begin to look among Cooper's characters for the qualities which fit a man for command. He needs, it seems, an extraordinary vitality, high intelligence, superior skill, and the ability to become (to use Melville's image) a keel along which the isolatoes that form the crew can federate. With the exception of Peyton Dunwoodie as seen on the battlefields of *The Spy,* Cooper does not give us, on land, characters to match his sea captains. They can be found, however, in nineteenth-century American histories, and Prescott's Cortez is such a man.

The most memorable of Cooper's commanders have the romantic historical hero's ability to inspire and control men even while the leader's responsibilities, recognized and willingly accepted, isolate him from the crew. The captains of Cooper's merchant or government ships must reconcile their orders with their own consciences, with their responsibility for the crew, and with the occurrences of the voyage. The free-booters, supranational and beholden to none, need satisfy only their own and their crews' demands. These latter, more colorful, leaders owe much to such Byronic figures as the Corsair, Lara, the Giaour, or Childe Harold; they are also indebted to such actual pirates as Sir Harry Morgan, whose becoming governor of Jamaica made piracy almost as respectable as it was glamorous.

There is, however, one important difference between Cooper's pirates and Byron's. Byron's characters are a throb of reaction; if they are, as he would have us believe, the last link in a chain of experiences, the chain itself has disappeared. By contrast, even the most romantic of Cooper's captains set to sea with orders or ideas, and Cooper attempts to analyze their reconciliation of these with the experiences of the tale. As a result, a Byronic figure may be the hero of a novel which makes an anti-romantic statement.

The mysterious "Mr. Gray" who is the titular hero of *The Pilot* (1823) is only a volunteer American, but he is worth a moment's consideration because he is the most purely Byronic of Cooper's naval commanders. The character incorporates as many characteristics of the romantic hero as Cooper could reconcile with the historical figure of John Paul Jones. No one was satisfied with the amalgam.[5] The Pilot's complaints are those of Childe Harold; he feels his country has failed him (145) and asserts, usually speaking "proudly" or "scornfully" his right to a buccaneer's supranational freedom. "'I was born on this orb, and I claim to be a citizen of it. A man with a soul [is] not to be limited by the arbitrary boundaries of tyrants and hirelings...'" (148). His skill is superb, but his ego is even more outstanding; "'This it is,'" he says, "'to be marked, among men, above all others in your calling'" (379).

Although Jones's superior skills let him move about more will-

---

[5]See Marcel Clavel, *Critics*, pp. 183-263. Susan Fenimore Cooper later wrote that Cooper himself was dissatisfied with the character. "It was not sufficiently true to reality. The pilot of the frigate was represented as a man of higher views and aims, in a moral sense, than the facts of the life of Paul Jones would justify."—*Pages and Pictures* (New York, 1865), p. 77. The *North American's* reviewer (April, 1824) gave Cooper credit for having invented here a character to replace, in modern literature, "the gods of ancient writers and the witches, fairies, and other supernatural beings" who both created and resolved improbable situations.

fully than most men can, he is denied freedom. Fame is a psychological necessity for him, and he is, consequently, a driven man and a slave to his own obsession. The tale suggests a correspondence between Jones's psychological state and his political activity. He is portrayed as something of a professional revolutionary dashing from one troubled spot to another and perverting his superior abilities to serve a tawdry goal. His motivation is that of the mercenary except that Jones asks to be paid in glory. Griffith, the American officer who speaks Cooper's mind, suggests the antidote to such "romantic notions" as those Jones is possessed by. Jones should have

> "lived in a time and under circumstances when his consummate knowledge of his profession, his cool, deliberate, and even desperate courage could have been exercised in a regular and well-supported navy, and the habits of his youth [should have] better qualified him to have borne, meekly, the honors he acquired in his age...."
>
> (442)

As it is, however, Jones's obsession with glory makes him miserable as a man and prevents his becoming a hero.

There is no apparent connection between a man like Jones and the villainous Stephen Spike, a captain in *Jack Tier;* Spike is ugly, aging, insecure, greedy — mean in every ungolden sense of the word. Whereas Jones is a victim of his own "romantic notions," Spike is naturally evil and acts "under impulse of the lowest and most grovelling nature." Yet the two men have much in common; both are extraordinarily competent commanders, and what Cooper says of Spike is also true of Jones. He is "only great in a crisis and then merely as a seaman" (51). Both are morally unfit for command; but since Jones is only a pilot and is consequently restrained by officers of the navy, the damage he can do to others is slight. Spike, however, is a captain and that for one reason only: he owns the ship. His purchased power and unchecked evil nature destroy his subordinates and endanger his passengers. Spike's abuse of power, shown in some of the most brutal scenes Cooper ever wrote, clearly relates to Cooper's political concerns. Given an evil captain, the whole structure of government (here navel discipline) works for evil and even the good men in the crew find themselves involved in smuggling ammunition to America's enemies (the Mexicans) and murdering the passengers. Believing that no man was perfect and that some were thoroughly evil, Cooper tried to get Americans to understand that "the true practical secret of good government" consisted of "preventing vicious and selfish" leaders "from doing harm."[6] Cooper seems to have thought that men like Jones and Spike should be kept in subordinate positions; as junior officers, they could use their excellent training even while their flawed natures were controlled by their superiors in rank and morality. It would be interesting to know if Melville's *Billy Budd* deliberately challenges Cooper's optimism; Melville grants all Cooper's conditions, then shows that they are not enough to restrain evil.

One of Cooper's most popular sea captains (the titular hero of *Red Rover,* 1828) has certain of Jones's romantic characteristics but is the direct opposite of a commander like Stephen Spike. Red Rover is a typical swashbuckler (naturally good but apparently evil) whose basic character Cooper was to rework as Tom Tiller and the Skimmer of the Seas (pirates in *The Water-Witch,* 1831) and as the Frenchman Raoul Yvard *(Wing-and-Wing,* 1842). The Rover is also closely related to the amphibious outlaw who is the Italian hero of *The Bravo* (1831). "Red Rover" is the pseudonym of a Captain Heidegger, a native of the American colonies, who (like Jones) presents himself as a victim of English injustice and who has also become a citizen of the world. Unlike Jones, however, he is alienated for a real, not fancied, reason; he has wounded (presumably killed) a British officer who cursed the colonies. Consequently, his heart has a home even though his humor chooses the flag his ship flies.

Red Rover's crime suggests his weakness; he controls only with great difficulty his impassioned "fearful nature." Unsupported by religion or allegiance to the institutions of a settled homeland, he cannot know, much less trust, himself. He confesses his torment at one point:

> "...the innocent pillow their heads in quiet! Would to God the guilty might find some refuse, too, against the sting of thought! But we live in a world, and in a time, when men cannot be sure even of themselves."   (329)

Not Red Rover himself, but the cabin-boy Roderick, pays the full price of the older man's psychological chaos. Identifying his life with the Rover's and sensitive to each shifting mood, the boy refuses to leave the pirate and eventually goes mad. He is last seen

[6]*Letters and Journals,* II, 321.

alone with the Rover on the decks of the burning ship, gliding "like a lessened shadow of that restless figure" (461).[7]

Red Rover, like Paul Jones, has his observers also. In addition to the heroine and her mature female companion, Cooper uses a Griffith-like naval officer named Wilder as an analyst. The two men display the author's interest in human doubles; Cooper shares with Twain that curiosity about the effect of environment on personality that inspired Twain's human philopena in *Pudd'nhead Wilson* and *The Prince and the Pauper*. This is not the psychological duality of Wyandotté, but rather a comparative study of two men of almost identical temperaments. Wilder proves to be an officer of the regular navy and has strong religious precepts that restrain his pride and passions. Wilder is only temporarily on leave from the ship Cooper describes as having "the repose of high order and perfect discipline." Otherwise, they are much alike; crews respond to them, often like "mettled chargers," and they are both young, handsome, quick to volunteer for action or responsibility, quicker still to understand men and events. At one time each commands a ship and an impromptu sailing match is described from Wilder's point of view.

> To him [Wilder] there was neither obscurity nor doubt in the midst of his midnight path. His eye had long been familiar with every star that rose from out the dark and ragged outline of the sea, nor was there a blast that swept across the ocean, that his burning cheek could not tell from what quarter of the heavens it poured out its power. He knew, and understood, each inclination made by the bows of his ship; his mind kept pace with her wanderings; and he had little need to consult any of the accessories of his art, to tell him what course to steer, or in what manner to guide the movements of the nice machine he governed. Still he was unable to explain the extra-ordinary evolutions of the stranger [the *Dolphin*, sailed by Red Rover]. The smallest changes he ordered seemed rather anticipated than followed; and his hope of eluding a vigilance that proved so watchful was baffled by a facility of manoeuvring, and a superiority of sailing, that really began to assume, even to his intelligent eyes, the appearance of some unaccountable agency.   (225)

This treatment of the two men is typical of Cooper; one romantic hero is described at length but is, in turn, confounded by the hyper-

---

[7]Melville reviewed this novel for the *Literary World* in 1850 and seems to have found in it suggestions not only for Pip but for other scenes and the character of Black Guinea. (See Chapter III.)

romanticism of a second. The match continues until "the dim tracery of the stranger's form [the pirate ship] had been swallowed by a flood of misty light, which, by this time, rolled along the sea like drifting vapor, semi-pellucid, preternatural, and seemingly tangible" (227).

Although Red Rover and his ship may be here something of an ontological riddle to Wilder, the two men are hard to distinguish when aboard the same ship. Wilder is, however, the more controlled, and is consequently awarded the heroine, restored to his long-lost family, and made a hero in the American Revolution. Red Rover, too, is revealed, at the end of the book, as an American patriot; James Grossman protests that this attempt to redeem "the reader's morality" destroys "one of the serious and ironic themes of the novel, our own delight in the spectacle of polite wickedness."[8] This objection points out the most important difference between Wilder and Rover, for the themes of the novel intersect in the character of Red Rover. The exterior mystery and inner turmoil of the pirate allow Cooper to give him metaphysical extensions that cannot arise from the more circumspect behavior of Wilder. Beneath the surface story of adventure Cooper submerges his interest in American government and in appearance and reality.

The *Dolphin*, Rover's ship, like the colonies has no real identity. It is noted for its speed and for its sudden ability to change colors. (It is frequently repainted to suit the occasion.) One of Rover's marvelous ironies is his painting the *Dolphin* black and disguising her as a slaver, in order to berth her safely in a New England harbor and assure the townspeople's warm welcome to his crew. The crew itself, suitably for a ship that carries the flags of all nations, is chosen "from among all the different people of the Christian world" (372). Like the community in *Wyandotté*, the *Dolphin* contains American Indians as well as representatives of every other nation or con-

---

[8]James Grossman, *Cooper,* p. 59. Grossman considers the book's subject "the ability of decent attractive people to engage in an evil life" (59). Philbrick's thesis is that Cooper's sea novels are the outcome of his "maritime nationalism and romanticism" *(James Fenimore Cooper and the Development of American Sea Fiction,* p. 42). Grossman is the more correct; Cooper was interested in character rather than chauvinism. Yet Philbrick offers a needed qualification. The point of Red Rover's history is this: when decent attractive people are neglected in their youth and can find, in their maturity, no occupation which allows them to exercise their natural morality, they must exist outside society until they are given a chance to participate in a just action (the Revolution).

tinent that had furnished a part of the colonies' polyglot population. In one of the most interesting scenes of the novel, Rover analyzes for Wilder those racial characteristics that make his "a most dangerous and (considering their numbers) a resistless crew" (372). Their success, however, depends primarily on their being "directed by the mind [Rover's] which had known how to obtain and to continue its despotic ascendency over their efforts..." (372). Rover can rule them successfully because he identifies accurately and then indulges their temperamental peculiarities. Even better, he makes their racial weaknesses into assets by placing the men at posts that allow them to express their natural tendencies. He does not personally like certain of the men, but he gives each credit for his particular abilities and is tolerant of all. So long as his catholic attitude rules, even the natural antagonists among the crew can coexist harmoniously.

The crew, however, does not realize it is being superbly governed; the men only know that they cannot succeed without the Rover's superior intelligence and knowledge. Like Odysseus, Rover can communicate with the higher spheres, and so long as the crew remembers his ability it obeys. Threatened mutiny is based on materialism; just as Odysseus' crew unleashed the winds when they thought the bag held gold, Rover's fractious companions rebel when they have lost a prize and are quieted only by Rover's superior skills and his reminding them that without him all prizes will be lost. (303) At the end of the central action, Rover buys freedom for Wilder and the women by giving all the ship's booty to the crew. When everyone is satisfied, the Rover is left to pace the decks of his burning ship.

Having chosen this restless but superior individual as the central character, Cooper has little difficulty in creating an atmosphere of illusion. A moral pirate who governs successfully a shipload of men unable to govern themselves is already more than human; his own skill and seamen's superstitious beliefs make him ubiquitous as well. Cooper places the whole tale as close as possible to that hypothetical meridian where romance becomes myth. As seen by landsmen or other seamen, commander, crew, and ship seem unreal; and the myth of the Flying Dutchman is mentioned frequently. Various persons suggest that all aboard the *Dolphin* are leagued with the devil and receive supernatural aid. Throughout much of the book, consequently, the real meaning of this floating community is in doubt. Sometimes all those aboard the *Dolphin* seem to be the liberated; supranational and mobile without limit, they transcend petty distinctions and confining cultures. At other times (particularly when Wilder, the women, and a regular navy are the standards), they seem so much human waste tragically adrift on an indifferent sea. The reason for this ambivalence is that Rover is moral while his crew is not; evil (here presented as materialism and intolerance) is to be found on shore and in the crew of the *Dolphin*. The supernatural qualities belong properly to the ship and commander only; both are superior; but until the world offers them a proper place, they can only roam, like tormented spirits, endlessly at sea.[9]

When isolated for examination, such a captain as Red Rover seems extravagantly romantic; he would even seem so in the novel had Cooper limited his own perspective to the ship and used its decks as a stage. Joseph Conrad saw immediately how Cooper turned potential melodrama into meaningful statement:

> For James Fenimore Cooper nature was not the framework, it was an essential part of existence. He could hear its voice, he could understand its silence, and he could interpret both for us in his prose with all that felicity and sureness of effect that belong to a poetical conception alone. … His descriptions have the magistral ampleness of a gesture indicating the sweep of a vast horizon. They embrace the colours of sunset, the peace of starlight, the aspects of calm and storm, the great loneliness of waters, the stillness of watchful coasts, and the alert readiness which marks men who live face to face with the promise and the menace of the sea.[10]

[9]A certain amount of Red Rover's ambivalence (like Natty Bumppo's) may be due to Cooper's sympathy with the good man who has been driven from his natural home. *Red Rover* was published before Cooper felt the full brunt of his country's disaffection, but he wrote Horatio Greenough in July, 1832, that "I go home, if home I do go, Master Greenough, to take a near view for myself, and to ascertain whether for the rest of my life I am to have a country or not. The decision will be prompt, free from all humbug, and final. It is time that we understand one another. I am tired of wasting life, means, and comfort in behalf of those who return abuse for services, and who show so much greater reverence for fraud and selfishness than for any thing else. I can never change my principles except on conviction, but I should be a very dog to fawn on those who spurn me. I am heart-sick and will say no more on the ungrateful subject."—*Letters and Journals*, II, 268. See also Cooper's letter to William Dunlap, *ibid.*, II, 360.

[10]"Tales of the Sea," p. 55. Conrad acknowledges his indebtedness to Cooper in a letter to Arthur Symons (and apparently in answer to something Symons had

The menace as well as the promise of the sea means that these commanders live temporally in a series of crises and spatially in a world where waves sweep the decks, where wind and tide sometimes seem to conspire to smash them on reefs, and where a sound like a gunshot may be an attack or a broken mast. It is a world in which human life is expendable and the conservation of anything at all surprising. Almost every one of the sea novels has at least one Gothic spectacle: Dillon's body washes ashore in *The Pilot;* a seaman is eaten alive by sharks in *The Water-Witch;* in *The Red Rover,* the survivors of a sunken ship look upon a sight that foreshadows Melville's Fedallah.

> A human form was seen, erect, and half exposed, advancing in the midst of the broken crest which was still covering the dark declivity to the windward. For a moment it stood with the brine dripping from the drenched locks, like some being that had issued from the deep to turn its frightful features on the spectators; and then the lifeless body of a drowned man [drowned the day before] drove past the launch. (264)

The violence of Cooper's sea world supports the excesses of his heroes just as Malraux's terrorists are sustained by the world of *Man's Fate* while old Gisors, quietly smoking his pipe, seems anomalous. There is, on Cooper's sea, no resting place.

To go to sea in these novels is not to engage in any rite of purification; yet "sea change" is a valid phenomenon for Cooper. He wrote in *Jack Tier* that only the experienced seaman could "think, read, and pursue the customary train of reasoning on board a ship" (174) that he practiced ashore. The key word here is "customary," for the act of embarkation prompts man to reassess his experience at the same time that he becomes more sensitive and responsive to it. Cooper describes, in *Red Rover,* the psychological effect of going to sea:

> One hour of the free intercourse of a ship can do more towards softening the cold exterior in which the world encrusts the best of human feelings, than weeks of the unmeaning ceremonies of the land. He who has not felt this truth, would do well to distrust his own companionable qualities. It would seem that man, when he finds himself

---

written): "F. Cooper is a rare artist. He has been one of my masters. He is my constant companion."—*Joseph Conrad: Life and Letters* (New York, 1927), II, 73.

in the solitude of the ocean, most feels his dependency on others for happiness. He yields to sentiments with which he trifled in the wantonness of security, and is glad to seek relief in the sympathies of his kind. (195)

As the references to encrusted feelings and wanton security suggest, going to sea strips off hampering custom but exposes the nerves at the same time. As a consequence, the act prepares a man for an intensification of experience.

Considered in time, this intensification takes the form of an acceleration of processes. The formation of friendships or testing of character that might take years on land are possible, at sea, in the action of moments. Yet the results of such tests are valid. Deserving characters profit by this quality of sea life; the Negro Neb and a plain sailor like Tom Coffin earn at sea personal recognition that a lifetime of patient toil on land would not obtain for them. Conversely, the cowardice and greed of an Ithuel Bolt, or the desperate acquisitiveness of a Stephen Spike or Daggett are here quickly revealed. Where processes are concerned, the stability of the land exerts a braking action that, as compared with the sea, postpones rewards due and too long protects the meretricious.

Qualitatively, the intensification of experience functions much as Cooper's other devices of showing a character in crucial action, on his death bed or in old age. Such situations dissolve masking forms and reveal the essence of a man. The most complex analyses are made of European, not American, commanders caught in a conflict of principles, rigid institutions, and personal loyalties. Cooper's American captains have no complex social structures to battle since they are in the pre-Revolutionary or Revolutionary Navy or post-Revolutionary merchant marine. Consequently, they have enough latitude to succeed by seeing clearly, thinking honestly, and grounding their decisions on broad international law. Captain Truck's beloved Vattel is for him the same universally valid system based on natural law that the Constitution is for the gentry.[11] Personally, the plain commanders (like Captains Barnstable, Truck, Woolston, Poke, or Gardiner) share with the romantic ones a "parental responsibility from which the sea commander is never exempt" (*The*

[11] Emerich de Vattel, a Swiss philosopher and jurist, wrote a book translated in 1760, as the *Law of Nations,* that illustrated a growing concept of international law as resting on natural laws. Captain Truck, the American packet skipper of *Homeward Bound* and *Home as Found,* relates his every decision to Vattel.

Pilot, 286). Under their firm but benevolent paternalism, as under the gentry's, men can coexist in harmony and safety and can expand because protected from their own and their shipmates' natural weaknesses. When ruled by a good captain, the ship is, as we have said, an ideal community.

At the same time, however, Cooper denies this community any real sense of permanence. The seaman is denied the continuity that land represents for the gentry. For the unstable sea itself discourages plans for an earthly future and emphasizes the impermanence and sterility of shipboard life. Life's transiency, with all its promises and menace, is a recurring theme in Cooper and more than any other community the men of a ship realize fully that life is largely a striving and Heaven is the home of perfection. Thus it is a seaman who recognizes both a proper goal for society and the impossibility of its earthly attainment: "Content," he says, "is like the North Star— we seamen steer for it, while none can ever reach it" (*The Heidenmauer,* 65).

As individuals, Tom Coffin and a few others like him are exceptional; they are common men who become uncommon by submerging the self in the sea and whose life ends when the ship dies. Most of the seamen, however, return eventually to the land; the ship is only temporarily a place of removal. If we let actions speak, as actions do in Cooper, these men fit D. H. Lawrence's description of Americans as "a vast republic of escaped slaves. ... And a minority of earnest, self-tortured people." Long before Lawrence, Cooper had dramatized in fiction the question Lawrence then asks: "Which will win in America, the escaped slaves, or the new whole men?"[12]

---

[12]*Studies in Classic American Literature,* pp. 15, 18.

Light and Shadow in *The Bravo*

by Donald A. Ringe

The Bravo, a social and political novel of Venice, makes an even greater use of light and shadow than does *The Deerslayer.* The chiaroscuro is as broad as that which reinforces the structure of the later book, but the various elements function much more intimately in the action of the tale. Indeed, so closely related is the use of chiaroscuro to the thematic development that only a detailed analysis can indicate its true significance.

The general pattern of light and dark is easily discerned, for Cooper arranges his bright and shadowy scenes for maximum pictorial effect. The first seven chapters of *The Bravo,* for example, take place at night, and Cooper carefully paints his scenes in subdued tones, the shadowy courts and squares of Venice lit by torches and bathed in the soft glow of the moon. Chapter 8, however, begins with a passage that is obviously intended to dazzle: "A brighter day than that which succeeded the night last mentioned never dawned upon the massive domes, the gorgeous palaces, and the glittering canals of Venice" (p. 96).[1] Cooper goes on in this vein for the next three chapters. He describes the bright and colorful public ceremonies—the marriage with the Adriatic, and the various regattas—only to return in Chapter 11 to the dark and subdued tones with which he began the novel. Cooper repeats this contrast several times

"Light and Shadow in *The Bravo*" (editor's title). From Donald A. Ringe, *The Pictorial Mode: Space and Time in The Art of Bryant, Irving, and Cooper* (Lexington, Ky.: University of Kentucky Press, 1971), pp. 114-21. Copyright © 1971 by The University Press of Kentucky, Reprinted with permission of the publisher and author.

[1][Citations from Cooper's works refer to the Mohawk edition (New York: G. P. Putnam's Sons, 1896).-Ed.]

to establish the major pattern of light and dark that dominates the book.

The primary tone, however, is one of darkness. Twenty-five of the thirty-one chapters take place at night; the remaining six provide the highlights that intensify the prevailing gloom. Within the darkened chapters, moreover, Cooper introduces only dim or fitful light, best typified by the description of Venice in the first paragraphs of the book. As the story opens, just after sunset, the moon has already risen and bathes the tops of the public buildings—the Ducal Palace and the Cathedral of St. Mark—with a "solemn and appropriate light" (p. 3). Tall columns are silhouetted against the evening sky, while their bases lie in shadow. Beneath the arches of the buildings that face the piazza, lamps and torches cast a brilliant glare that contrasts sharply with the mellow glow of the moon. Hundreds of masked people hurry to and fro in the light of the torches—a strange and motley multitude bent on gaiety and pleasure. This description, recalled at intervals throughout the book and repeated at the conclusion, establishes the tone for the chapters that follow and suggests the symbolic values of each of the elements presented.

The darkness and silence of night, for example, are most frequently associated with the buildings of the state, the homes of the senators, and the workings of Venetian policy. Early in the book, during the first night of the action, Cooper describes the doge's palace in unequivocal terms. Dark and silent but for the rays of the moon and the footfalls of sentinels, it becomes "a fit emblem of that mysterious power which was known to preside over the fortunes of Venice and her citizens" (p. 35). The palace court, moreover, in contrast to the gaily lighted piazza, is consistently described as dark and forbidding. Indeed, even the homes of important senators partake of the general darkness. The palace of Signor Gradenigo, a member of the secret Council of Three, shows "more than common gloom" and, like the doge's palace, typifies the Venetian state. Within its walls, Cooper writes, "the noiseless steps and the air of silent distrust among the domestics, added to the gloomy grandeur of the apartments, rendered the abode no bad type of the Republic itself" (p. 53). Clearly, official Venice lives and acts in symbolic darkness.

This suggestion is strongly reinforced by Cooper's description of the secret tribunal which wields the real power in the state. Twice in the novel characters are summoned before the Council of Three.

Each time the dimness of the scene suggests the "gloomy and secret duties" (p. 367) that the council performs. One passage, however, the questioning of old Antonio, is particularly significant in the way that Cooper handles the lighting, for the scene perceptibly darkens as Antonio is brought to the council. First met on the quays by Jacopo, who is sent to summon him, Antonio is led through the "dimmer and broken light of the court," "along the gloomy gallery," and "through many dimly lighted and obscure passages," until he arrives at an apartment "of a dusky color, which the feeble light rendered still more gloomy" (pp. 140-41). Admitted to the council chamber, Antonio finds himself in a room draped in black and lighted by a single lamp. All the doors are concealed by the somber hangings which give "one general and chilling aspect of gloom to the whole scene" (pp. 149-50). The masked council members sit across the room, two dressed in robes of black, and one in a robe of crimson.

These men, who act anonymously in the name of the state, hold the power of life and death over all who are brought before them. Selected by lot from a larger body of senators, they are in effect the supreme power in Venice, whom the doge himself would not dare to disobey. Since they act in secret, they are responsible to no man for their deeds, and though they pretend in public to believe in justice, they are really concerned only with the protection of their own senatorial class. They decide all questions purely in terms of self-interest and do not scruple to kill to maintain their power. It is appropriate, therefore, that black be associated with these men, their institutions and their deeds, that their homes as well as the public buildings of Venice should suggest the ugly truth that lies concealed behind the imposing facades which these men and their state present to the world. It is appropriate, too, that their decrees be enacted under cover of darkness, that old Antonio, innocent of any serious wrong but considered dangerous to the state, should be secretly drowned in the Lagunes late at night by the council's agents. For the truth of Venice, Cooper clearly implies, is unremitted gloom.

Such a conclusion is only intensified by the brilliantly lighted chapters that contrast so sharply with the dim and shadowy ones. Cooper first uses the full light of day to depict the impressive public ceremonies of Venice. He describes the glittering canals, the brilliant spectacles, and the magnificent pageantry with obvious relish, but the careful reader immediately perceives the symbolic values of the sunlight. If the truth of Venice is shadow and silence, what shall we make of the brightness and clamor that dominate these chapters? A clue is immediately offered in the ceremony of the marriage with the Adriatic, a symbolic act of the doge to express the Venetian rule of the seas. At the time of the tale, however, Venetian power has already begun to decline, and the ambassadors from the northern maritime states are amused at Venetian pretension (p. 101). The doge himself, moreover, is only a figurehead, though he assumes the pomp and position of a powerful ruler. The reader soon comes to realize, therefore, that the Venice that greets his eye in the full light of day is an utterly false one, an empty show which hides the truth that the state cannot afford to reveal.

Venice by daylight must therefore be equated with falsehood and hypocrisy, an interpretation well borne out by all the sunlit passages. It is daylight when Don Camillo is courteously received among the senators in the Broglio, although the night before the council had stolen his bride, Donna Violetta, and had thwarted their plans for escape. It is broad daylight when the state gives old Antonio a lavish funeral to appease the rebellious fishermen who rise in protest over his murder. It is daylight too when the council calls for the arrest of Jacopo for a murder he did not commit. He is tried by day in the public courts, after secretly being condemned the night before by the Council of Three. Above all, it is a brilliant morning when, with a great display of justice, the state beheads him. Indeed, just after the execution, Cooper points up the brightness of the scene as Father Anselmo, who knows the truth of Antonio's death and Jacopo's innocence, looks up "at the windows of the palace, and at the sun which shone so gloriously in the heavens" (p. 413). Cooper is using bright light to reveal the flagrant falsehood of all that Venice professes to be and to intensify by contrast the black truth that is its reality.

The light of day, however, is not the only type that Cooper uses. Two other sources of light recur throughout his darkened chapters: the brilliant lamplight of the piazza and the mellow glow of the moon. The first may be quickly dismissed, for it obviously represents the false gaiety of the Venetian festa, the means that the bulk of the people use to escape, if only for a little while, the prying eyes and ruthless power of the soulless state. Cooper describes the piazza at night repeatedly in the book and crowds the details of the scene upon one another so rapidly that the reader is left with the impression of hundreds of people moving frenetically here and there across the square without serious purpose or direction. Thus, in the final paragraph of the book, "the gay laughed, the reckless trifled, the masker pursued his hidden purpose, the cantatrice and the grotesque acted their parts, and the million existed in that vacant enjoyment which distinguishes the pleasures of the thoughtless and the idle" (p. 413). So corrupt and corrupting is the vicious rule of the Venetian state that the mass of the people live only for themselves in the artificial pleasures of the piazza at night.

The moonlight, on the other hand, suggests the only positive values to be found in the book. Soft though it may be and generally unobtrusive in much of the description, it is repeatedly presented as contrasting with the other symbols developed in the novel. Thus, in the opening pages of the book, Cooper deliberately contrasts it with the torchlight of the piazza: "While all beneath the arches was gay and brilliant with the flare of torch and lamp," the great buildings of the city "were slumbering in the more mellow glow of the moon." "The base of the Campanile lay in shadow, but a hundred feet of its grey summit received the full rays of the moon along its eastern face" (pp. 2–3). The mellow glow can penetrate even the gloomy shadows of the palace court (p. 35). It imparts a "quivering brightness" to the waters of the canals and lends an air of "solemn but grand repose" to the buildings it touches. "Occasionally the front of a palace received the rays on its heavy cornices and labored columns, the gloomy stillness of the interior of the edifice furnishing, in every such instance, a striking contrast to the richness and architectural beauty without" (p. 43).

The light of the moon is intended, therefore, to contrast with both the darkness of official Venice and the false gaiety of the piazza. Indeed, it is most frequently associated with the uncorrupted characters in the novel. Thus, when Jacopo first meets Antonio on the square at night after the fisherman has vainly sought help from Signor Gradenigo for his grandson impressed in the galleys, the light of the moon bathes the poor fisherman with its gentle glow. Antonio's position brings "the whole of his muscular form and bronzed features beneath the rays of the moon," and his "dark, anxious, and stern eyes" gaze "upon the mild orb, as if their owner sought to penetrate into another world, in quest of that peace which he had never known in this" (p. 83). The full light of the moon repeatedly falls on the face of Jacopo; on Gelsomina, his fiancée; on

Father Anselmo when he pronounces the absolution after Antonio's last confession; indeed, even on the dead features of old Antonio when his body is brought by the protesting fishermen to the very palace of the doge. Thus, the moonlight seems intended to suggest the existence of a moral order that transcends the corrupt social order of Venice.

Such a conclusion is supported by Cooper's description of Venice on the night that Antonio is murdered. The moon is at its height as the chapter opens, and falls in a flood on domes and towers, "while the margin of the town [is] brilliantly defined by the glittering bay." Cooper chooses his words carefully here, for he wishes to suggest a kind of supernatural glory in the scene. "The natural and gorgeous setting was more than worthy of that picture of human magnificence; for at that moment, rich as was the Queen of the Adriatic in her works of art, the grandeur of her public monuments, the number and splendor of her palaces, and most else that the ingenuity and ambition of man could attempt, she was but secondary in the glories of the hour." To reinforce the impression that he wishes to create, Cooper deliberately enlarges the scene to include the infinite reaches of space which always in his novels suggest the power and glory of God. "Above was the firmament, gemmed with worlds, and sublime in immensity. Beneath lay the broad expanse of the Adriatic, endless to the eye, tranquil as the vault it reflected, and luminous with its borrowed light" (p. 192).

It is against this magnificent background that Antonio meets his end. The reader who comes upon the scene with a thorough awareness of what Cooper is doing with his light and shade is acutely conscious of the symbolic value of the moonlight that plays across the water. Antonio's boat lies "quivering in the rays of the moon" as Jacopo comes to seek him, and the old man tells his companion that he sees the image of his Savior in the natural world around him. He has "prayed much since the moon has risen" (pp. 193-94), and he needs only his confession to the Carmelite, who is later brought to the Lagunes by Antonio's assassins, to be completely at peace with his God. Antonio does not flee when the gondola of the state approaches, for he is not conscious of having committed any crime, but assumes that the agents of the senate are seeking Jacopo. The Bravo, however, withdraws along one of the "bright streaks that the moon drew on the water, and which, by dazzling the eye, effectually concealed the objects within its width" (p. 199). Jacopo is thus permitted to observe what occurs protected by the saving glow of the moon.

He sees the Carmelite pronounce the absolution, observes the gondola of the state approach a second time to remove the monk, and hears the fall of Antonio's body into the water. He tries to come to the rescue, his gondola flying "down the streak of light, like the swallow touching the water with its wing" (p. 205). But, although he arrives too late to save the old man's life, he, like the good Carmelite, has seen in the light of the moon what Venice would like to conceal in darkness or behind the brilliant display of its daylight pageantry. The moonlight is thus the truth-revealing element in the book. Both Jacopo and Father Anselmo fully perceive for the first time the utter cynicism of the aristocratic state, and both resolve to serve it no more. Father Anselmo returns to the palace of Donna Violetta so shocked by his experience that he marries Camillo and Violetta at once and resolves to help them escape. Jacopo, on the other hand, goes alone to the Lido, where he even contemplates suicide rather than return to the service of the senate.

In the ensuing action, Donna Violetta is kidnapped by a gondola of the state, and Don Camillo, who searches the harbor in an attempt to rescue her, eventually lands on the Lido, where he unexpectedly meets Jacopo. In a highly effective scene in symbolic moonlight, Don Camillo learns the truth of the Bravo's past and hears him swear that he will no longer do the senate's will. Since he has already served the state so long and so well, Jacopo knows much of its devious policy and the means it uses for accomplishing its ends. He enlists in Camillo's cause, therefore, and finally succeeds in retrieving the stolen bride and uniting the lovers on board a felucca, which, on the following moonlit night, carries them off to the States of the Church. Thus, each of the unwilling witnesses to Antonio's death contributes to the success of Don Camillo in subverting the plans of the senate, the only major incident in the book which shows a person able to evade the evil machinations of the state.

The patterns of light and dark that Cooper creates in *The Bravo* are clearly of the utmost importance in understanding the theme of the book and in perceiving its artistry. The dark and forbidding tone that dominates so much of the novel reinforces the impression that one receives from the action of the devious ways of the state and the secrecy of its true operation. The contrasting public acts, performed in the full light of the sun, represent, in essence, the mask behind which the state conceals its true nature. The fitful glare of the torchlit piazza at night becomes a symbol of the falsity of life under such a tyrannical system, and the full glow of the moon plainly suggests the presence of a transcendent moral order, adhered to by some of the characters, but largely ignored by the state and the bulk of its corrupt inhabitants. Taken together, all these elements reacting with one another create a rich and complex pattern that contributes much to the meaning of the novel and to the aesthetic pleasure that one derives from its perception.

Satanstoe: The Case for Permanence

by H. Daniel Peck

[We] recognize within the human soul the permanence of
a nucleus of childhood, an immobile but ever living childhood, outside history, hidden from the others, disguised
in history when it is recounted, but which has real being
only in its instants of illumination which is the same as
saying in the moment of its poetic existence.

GASTON BACHELARD
The Poetics of Reverie

The Deerslayer and *The Crater* have the same spatial design
(both depict "islands" surrounded by a vast wilderness), yet one
novel describes a world poised in an idyllic moment while the other
communicates a too urgent sense of danger. As a result, the "bounded-
ness" of *The Deerslayer* becomes the "boundary"—fiercely defended—of *The Crater.* As we have seen, the world of *The Deerslayer*
is protected not only by a spatial barrier but also by time; it is isolated in a moment of the nation's prehistory, a time before American
history is set in motion. *The Crater,* on the other hand, is Cooper's
ambitious and dogmatic attempt to allegorize the entire drama of
America's course of empire—its past, present, and future. The writer
allows time to flow into his paradise and to destroy it as a way of
exposing his enemies to attack.

Cooper's dominant tendency was to confront these enemies directly, and much of his fiction has a strongly argumentative quality.
But there are among his works several novels which demonstrate

the capacity to stand back from the battle. For example, the three romances written at the beginning of the 1840s *(The Pathfinder, The Deerslayer,* and the sea novel, *Wing-and-Wing)* all reveal the wish, as Thomas Philbrick has said, to "retreat from the oppressive reality of here and now."[1] Books like these suggest a temporary withdrawal from direct confrontation with the political and social issues that Cooper treated vigorously in the fiction of the 1830s and, with different emphasis, in the novels of the later 1840s. They appear to have been written in the interstices of his struggles, in periods when the polemicist in him was at rest.

To see Cooper's pastoral novels in this light is to regard them as almost fortuitous, happy accidents that resulted from the need to find respite in the world of the romance. The emergence of a book like *The Deerslayer* would seem to depend upon such an accident, one produced by the coincidence of two closely related conditions: a diminishing of the writer's desire to instruct his countrymen, and his choice of a time setting that prevents the intrusion of history. Yet Cooper wrote one remarkable book which forces us to extend the dimensions and define more fully the dynamics of his pastoralism. For *Satanstoe* is a most compelling pastoral novel that was written with polemical intent and whose moment is set in history.

Social and intellectual historians have been attracted to the Littlepage novels as a group because of the ideas they dramatize. But *Satanstoe* deserves to be treated on its own terms for, aesthetically, it stands apart from the didactic works that fill out the trilogy. Unlike *The Deerslayer,* it stands at the beginning of its series not only in respect to time setting but also in the order of composition. When Cooper published the first of the Leatherstocking tales *(The Pioneers)* in 1823, he was not planning a five-part series. And when he concluded *The Prairie* (1827) with Natty Bumppo's death, he felt he had put his character to rest for good. The resumption of the tales in the 1840s with *The Pathfinder* and *The Deerslayer* reveals several obvious discontinuities. In contrast, the Littlepage trilogy was designed as a composite statement about American society, and the

---

[1][Thomas Philbrick,] *James Fenimore Cooper and the Development of American Sea Fiction* [(Cambridge, Mass.: Harvard University Press, 1961) — Ed.], p. 12. Another sea novel from an earlier period which communicates a sense of pure romance is *The Water Witch* (1830). Written in Italy, a country which seems to have relaxed Cooper's rigid sensibilities, it obeys all the principles of the author's pastoralism. See my essay, "A Repossession of America."

three novels that comprise the series were written together, out of a preconceived narrative plan.

Cooper described the plan in a letter to his publisher. "The Family of Littlepage," he said, would "form three complete Tales, each perfectly distinct from the other as regards leading characters, love story &c," but connected by the fact that he would carry "the same family, the same localities, and same *things* generally through the three different books, but exhibiting the changes produced by time." As we saw earlier, Cooper regarded the Revolution as the event that had exposed (white) America to the full force of history. In this letter, he refers to the first book in the series as "Colony" and to the second as "Revolution," suggesting that *The Chainbearer* would describe the changes produced by time in the immediate postrevolutionary era. This second novel, Cooper went on, would depict a setting "in some respects resembling the Pioneers," a setting, in other words, characterized by the destructive forces of the settlement stage. The third novel, "Republic" *(The Redskins),* would treat "the present aspect of things, with an exhibition of the Anti-Rent commotion that now exists among us, and, which certainly threatens the destruction of our system" *(L&J,* 5:7).

Cooper intended, then, that *Satanstoe* would depict the nation's colonial youth, a time before the rapacious forces of the "outside" had gained strength. In *The Chainbearer* and *The Redskins,* he would show the damage being inflicted upon the world founded (and "found") in the first novel. Here we have a rare case in which the deliberateness of the writer's plan worked to aesthetic advantage, for in *Satanstoe* Cooper set out to create a pastoral, the ease and beauty of which would shame the turbulence and ugliness of later periods. Remarkably, he succeeded. In this novel, we do not hear the strident and intrusive voice of the social novels, in part because the writer knew he had reserved the opportunity to argue openly in the two later works. That is, by dramatizing the rise and fall of the landed gentry (on whose welfare Cooper believed America's destiny depended) in three separate novels, he avoided the necessity of forcing an entire historical development into one epic narrative, as he had done in *The Crater.* And perhaps it is also true that the first-person narration allowed him to inhabit the spirit of the ingenuous Corny Littlepage and to relax into the world of the romance.

Satanstoe, then, describes a simpler and more beautiful past, and the effect is similar to that of *The Deerslayer.* Yet different means are used to gain this effect, and the moments these two novels depict are not the same. While *The Deerslayer* focuses upon the adventures of a simple woodsman in a setting so isolated that it seems to exist "before" history, *Satanstoe* records the entry of America's gentry class into the affairs of national life. In the words of the young narrator-hero, the novel describes that moment when, "for the first time in the history of the colonies, the Littlepages had become the owners of what might be termed an estate" (157).[2]

Although the old family home of Satanstoe (near colonial New York City) is cherished by the Littlepage family, the unclaimed Mooseridge estate in the wilderness represents the *new* country Americans would possess for themselves after the Revolution. Therefore, Corny Littlepage's journey "in quest of the patent" (156), and Herman Mordaunt's parallel venture from his Hudson River home (Lilacsbush) to the wilderness settlement of Ravensnest, dramatize the initial stage of America's journey into the future.

That *Satanstoe* is organized by a symbolic journey suggests its relationship to *The Last of the Mohicans*. Both these novels describe a movement from a known world to the unknown northern wilderness, and, as Cooper notes in the letter cited above, they are set in the same period (the late 1750s) and region (the characters in *Satanstoe* pass by the ruin of Fort William Henry). But as we shall see, the similarity of structure and the intersection of time and place do not amount to a true correspondence. While the basic issue of both works—and of all of Cooper's fiction—is possession, *Satanstoe* is as different from *The Last of the Mohicans* as *The Deerslayer* is from *The Crater*. Just as Cooper could create an "island" that remained protected from the forces of destruction, he could also narrate a journey that was not characterized by "difficulty."

In every way, *Satanstoe* renders the sense of a beginning. The "journey to the north" (144) commences on March first, with spring about to break. Corny informs his readers that "winter was soon drawing to a close, and my twenty-first birthday was past" (156). This coincidence of the journey's beginning and Corny's coming of age signifies a parallel between the young hero's and the nation's development, a parallel of rich association which we shall examine

[2][All citations from Cooper's novels refer to the W. A. Townsend and Company edition (New York, 1859-61).—Ed.]

shortly. Before the expedition can begin, however, Cooper must first describe the family home of Satanstoe, for it is from this original site and its surrounding landscape that the journey draws its momentum. The first ten chapters of the novel treat in great detail and with "a loving sense of fact"[3] the charming ways and quaint manners of the prerevolutionary New York City region. But the most important background these early chapters provide is their rendering of Corny Littlepage's idyllic development through childhood to the moment of departure.

The circumstances of this fictional childhood suggest that, through Corny, the writer is offering an idealized version of his own growth, and it may be that this is the youth Cooper would have lived. There is much in the novel to indicate the author's origins, and many of the details, such as Corny's tutorship under an "English divine" (26),[4] are strictly autobiographical. It is true that the setting is removed from the Cooperstown region, yet this may be merely a displacement allowing a highly self-conscious writer to particularize the rest of the setting as his own.

In a voice which is self-promoting even as it pretends self-effacement, the narrator describes the highly favorable circumstances of his growing up. Born into prominence and wealth, properly educated (unlike Cooper, he graduates from college), the pride of his extended family, Corny represents himself as "special." As if to confirm this status, Cooper (the twelfth of thirteen children born into his family) makes his character a beloved only child. Although there "was a son who preceded me, and two daughters succeeded," Corny explains, "they all died in infancy, leaving me in effect the only offspring for my parents to cherish and educate" (15). Corny's "tender-hearted" mother is "full of anxiety in behalf of an only child" (58), and almost everyone in the novel, including the great Lord Howe (370), takes note of this fact about him—thus suggesting his crucial importance to his family's destiny.

We have seen how in *The Deerslayer* the father figure is rendered powerless by making him corrupt. In *Satanstoe*, there is only a hint of this—Corny's father "had the reputation of a gadabout" (57)— but the displacement is just as effective. It is hard to imagine a novel

---

[3]Richard Chase, *The American Novel and Its Tradition,* p. 51. Cf. A. N. Kaul, *The American Vision,* p. 90.

[4]In the fall of his eleventh year, Cooper was sent from Cooperstown to Albany to study with a clergyman whose allegiance to his native England was strong.

concerning the destiny of a family in which the father is more invisible. Much attention is given to Corny's loving relationship with his mother—as in *The Deerslayer*, a maternal presence pervades the world of the book—but the father is barely acknowledged. As we shall see, certain "pioneering" aspects of the paternal role are transferred to the heroine's father, Herman Mordaunt. But at another level, Corny himself takes this role. That is, he "fathers" the Littlepage destiny by exploring and helping to secure the Mooseridge and Ravensnest estates. It is to him as the founder that all subsequent generations will look back with reverence. Cooper himself was acutely aware that, though he had "embellished [Otsego Hall] a little," it was his father, William Cooper, who had "founded the place, and it is the first man who becomes identified with any thing of this sort" (L&J. 5:369). Perhaps, through Corny Littlepage, Cooper imaginatively becomes "the first man" and gathers to himself the full identification he may have (unconsciously) desired. This interpretation, however, is less important to our analysis than the narrative implications of Corny's role as founder, a role which places him at the absolute center of the novel's stage.

Despite his heavy responsibility as the carrier of his family's destiny, Corny's is a life remarkably free of disruption and protected from the tragedy that Cooper himself knew in childhood.[5] In *Satanstoe*, the writer appears to have taken the basic facts of his youth and imposed upon them an order and felicity which his own life (or any real life) could not sustain. Cooper seems to invest Corny's development with all of those things that, as an aging author, he had come to value. For example, he makes his character an Episcopalian from birth, thereby giving him the religion to which he himself became committed only much later.[6] Similarly, Corny's wooing of Anneke Mordaunt—recognizable as an analogue of Cooper's own romance with Susan DeLancey[7]—is a case of giving to the entire span of the character's life those "treasures" that came to the writer only in increments. Cooper extends this romance all the

[5]Cooper's beloved sister Hannah died tragically when he was ten years old. Her death was a loss from which he never fully recovered. See *L&J*, 6:99.

[6]Cooper, whose father was of Quaker background, became active in Episcopal diocesan affairs in his later life and was confirmed by the church shortly before his death.

[7]Cooper met and fell in love with Susan DeLancey after returning from naval service. In *Satanstoe*, he seems to invest Anneke Mordaunt's home, Lilacsbush, with his affection for the DeLancey mansion at Mamaroneck, N.Y.

way back into Corny's childhood and allows his child-hero to save Anneke from both a bully and a circus lion. Such episodes suggest wish fulfillment, and they demonstrate the way in which Cooper idealizes his character's development and spares him from "difficulty."

The ten chapters, then, that precede the "journey to the north" are more than preliminary. They describe both Corny's and his region's idyllic past and communicate the love the hero feels for his childhood home of Satanstoe. When the journey begins, we experience no sudden departure from that valued past; rather, the quality of amenity established in the first section of the novel is carried forward and informs all of the events the narrative will bring. Thus, while one of the purposes of the journey is to test Corny's emerging manhood, it is a test so lovingly and carefully managed by the author that its outcome is never in doubt. Although this novel ostensibly treats a character's growth, there is no development in the modern sense. Corny simply becomes what he was destined to become, and while he travels into regions unknown to him, he never really leaves the landscape of home.

It is entirely in keeping with the spirit of *Satanstoe* that the journey into the wilderness is delayed by a sustained and beautiful interlude in colonial Albany. Dutch geniality pervades this scene of feasting, young love, and adventure.[8] Most importantly, Albany provides the setting for the development of the romance between Corny and Anneke. The young suitor must prove himself a man, and, as we saw in *The Pathfinder,* women are always the final arbiters of adulthood in Cooper's fiction. When Anneke discovers Corny and his friend Guert Ten Eyck sledding playfully, her sarcastic refusal to join them makes her role clear: "'when Miss Wallace or I wish to ride down hill, and become little girls again, we will trust ourselves with boys, whose constant practice will be likely to render them more expert than men can be, who have had time to forget the habits of their childhood'" (193). The issue, then, is Corny's growth from childhood to maturity, and this growth will be measured by events. Corny, of course, does prove his manhood— most conclusively by saving Anneke from a terrifying upheaval of ice on the Hudson, an event which in several ways is the climactic, and most skillfully rendered, scene of the novel. Yet this heroic act

---

[8]The Dutch give this same quality of geniality to *The Water-Witch.* Cf. Washington Irving's and James K. Paulding's treatment of the Dutch.

is not qualitatively different from those rescues Corny performed earlier in childhood. Together, they form a continuum, and it is hard to locate a moment of genuine initiation (later scenes in which Corny fights bravely against French troops and a party of hostile Indians have a largely perfunctory quality). But Cooper clearly intends that we regard the ice scene as a major turning point in the hero's development (and in his relationship to Anneke), and as readers we accept this even as we realize how carefully this development has been controlled. As if to affirm the continuity of his character's growth, Cooper has Anneke tell Corny at the novel's conclusion that she has never loved anyone but him, even from childhood. His success was never in doubt, and all that was required of him was to carry through his preordained destiny. Corny remains as earnest and naive at the novel's conclusion as he was at the beginning. His maturation has been formal rather than developmental; it exhibits none of the turbulence and pain of adolescence, only the tranquillity of an "immobile" childhood.

On one level, Anneke's rejection of the suave and aggressive Major Bulstrode symbolizes Cooper's rejection of English influence in American life. But on another, Bull-strode's name as well as his behavior indicate that he represents an adult sexuality which the writer excludes from this world of romance. Just as much as *The Deerslayer, Satanstoe* is a novel dominated by the spirit of childhood. Although Corny differs in many significant ways from Natty Bumppo, his character is as essentially fixed. Like Leatherstocking, he remains childlike after his (formal) initiation. The effect of immutability is heightened by the first-person narration, for Corny's voice, even in the retrospective, adult position from which he tells his story, remains that of the innocent—a voice Cooper more than once treats with affectionate and humorous irony.

From every point of view, this is Corny's story. He narrates it himself, and in the fullest sense he is the "only child" of *Satanstoe* — the true center of the narrative.[9] The great public events of the novel take on importance primarily as they figure in his personal destiny. In *The Last of the Mohicans*, we saw how personal destinies

---

[9]Cooper had various thematic purposes in mind in killing off the attractive and amiable Guert Ten Eyck, but certainly one of them was to allow Corny to dominate the novel's conclusion totally. There is a hint of guilt in Corny's remark, "I could have called out to warn them [Guert and his companions] of the danger they ran; but it would have done no good, nor was there time for remonstrances" (464).

were overwhelmed by massive historical forces, but in *Satanstoe* such forces are contained, even organized to accommodate the hero's development. This contrast is most obvious in Cooper's use and treatment of the "great historical event" in these two novels. The massacre of Fort William Henry in *The Last of the Mohicans* is so violent that it breaks the narrative in half and turns its journey in an entirely new direction. Yet the comparable event in *Satanstoe*, the French defeat of the English at Fort Ticonderoga, has a very different function. Although Cooper vividly depicts its violence and suffering, the great battle is not a climactic turning point. Rather, the scene of war is just that, a "scene," one which diverts our attention only briefly from the major movement of the novel. Corny's and Guert's expedition to join the British forces, after they have located the Mooseridge estate, has the quality of an excursion. The military action serves primarily as a demonstration of these characters' valor; their personal victory in a skirmish with the enemy is given far more attention than the historically significant event of the British defeat.[10] In fact, the routing of the English troops prompts the impulsive Guert to disassociate himself (and Corny) from the whole effort, which he now sees as discredited: "'My advice is, t'at we get out of this army as we got into it—t'at is, py a one-sided movement'" (380). It is by just such a one-sided, or lateral, movement that the characters exit from the scene of the great historical event and return to their central pursuit, the securing of the Mooseridge and Ravensnest estates. After this exit, we hear no more about the French and Indian Wars; the battle becomes an experience which Corny may someday relate to his grandchildren.

Yet this is not to say that *Satanstoe* lacks historical meaning. Although Corny's personal destiny dominates our vision, this destiny intersects and symbolizes the nation's. The "journey to the north" is America's journey too, and the writer controls its progress just as carefully as he controls the hero's development.

The Littlepage and Mordaunt families represent the class of Americans upon whom Cooper centered his greatest hopes for social stability. Therefore, these families' acquisition of property in the unknown northern wilderness signifies a claim upon the future and the establishment of a substantial base for America's growth. But it is important to add that the wilderness explored by the *Satanstoe* characters is unknown in only a limited sense. This is not the geog-

---

[10]Cf. Harry B. Henderson, 3rd, *Versions of the Past,* p. 81.

raphy of the second journey of *The Last of the Mohicans,* a mythic
region beyond the demarcations of civilization. Corny Littlepage
and Herman Mordaunt do not probe the unknown; rather, they "discover" what they already (legally) possess, in the same way that
Corny "becomes" what he already is. The boundary lines of their
estates had been drawn long before the time period of the novel;
the purpose of the journey is to locate these lines, to lay claim to
what has already been recorded on the patent. Although it requires
the intuition of an Indian guide to find the Mooseridge estate,
Cooper's clear intention is to show that even here, in this apparently wild setting, boundaries exist. Wherever prior claims have been
made, possession is inviolate—except, of course, in the case of the
Indian, whose dispossession Cooper regarded as tragic but necessary (in this novel, the bitter voice of Susquesus reminds us of that
dispossession).

As the identifying landmark of the Mooseridge estate is first
seen, we experience the characteristic moment of appropriation
in Cooper's fiction, the moment when the eye gathers its possessions.
We suddenly know we have come to "the end of our journey" (343),
and the act of appropriation is confirmed by "the erection of a log-
house" (344). The site for this "hut" (347) is chosen because "water
was abundant and good, and because a small knoll was near the
spring" (345). These formations identify this place immediately as
the center of Cooper's imaginative geography, the generative site
from which a civilization can grow. Like Ben Boden's shanty in *The
Oak Openings,* or Captain Willoughby's first primitive dwelling in
Wyandotté, The Mooseridge hut will serve as a "citadel to retreat to"
(346), until more substantial structures can be raised.

While Mooseridge is being marked off as a site for future development (and, ultimately, sale), Herman Mordaunt vigorously and
quickly establishes a full-scale settlement at nearby Ravensnest. As
I suggested earlier, Mordaunt is the prototypal maker of civiliza-
tions in Cooper's fiction—strong, decisive, enterprising. Yet in
Satanstoe the writer shows toward this figure none of the ambivalence revealed in *The Pioneers.* Mordaunt is the paternal land-
holder whose protective attitude toward his settlers is convincingly
demonstrated during the Indian attack on Ravensnest.

The siege of Ravensnest reminds us of scenes in several of
Cooper's other novels. As in *The Wept of Wish-ton-Wish,* the Indians' most dangerous weapon is fire, but whereas fire totally de-

stroys the settlement in the earlier work, here it is extinguished before it can do harm. In fact, the defenders of Ravensnest control the flames from the beginning. They watch an Indian warrior set the fire, allow it to burn at the base of the fortress for a time because its light exposes the enemy to rifle fire, and then easily extinguish it with water. When we compare this image of easily contained fire with Cooper's characteristic depiction of a rapidly and totally consuming fire, we suspect that in *Satanstoe* the writer is "playing" with the element he feared most—further evidence of the book's pervasive authorial control. But the containment of fire also symbolizes the fact that the Indian is already an anachronistic force in the time and place of this setting (unlike the setting of *The Wept of Wish-ton-Wish,* in which he is an everpresent danger). Although Corny fears, in the confusion of night, that "we must be surrounded by hundreds of these ruthless foes" (456), the daylight reveals that this is but an isolated band which, once driven away, will never return. The victory of Corny and his friends is conclusive, and the narrator leaves no doubt that now the process of settlement will go on uninterrupted by Indian attack.

Later in history, Ravensnest will be "interrupted" again by far more dangerous "redskins." In *Satanstoe,* Cooper warns of this future danger, but as in *The Deerslayer,* he introduces the rapacious forces of the "outside" only in order to contain them. "Outside," in this case, is New England; the boundary between "the colony of New York and those that lie east of the Byram River" is characterized as "a broad moral line" (17). Cooper believed that Calvanism in New England had bred acquisitiveness, and many of the destructive figures in his fiction are of New England origin.[11] In *Satanstoe,* the invader from Connecticut is Jason Newcome, whose manners reveal how little he understands of "the fitness of things." Jason ignores, or tries to ignore, all distinctions between "rank, education, birth and experience" (326). His name identifies him as a trespasser (Newcome) and also as a thief (Jason) who would steal the Littlepage and Mordaunt "treasure"; he openly reveals his designs on Herman Mordaunt's property. But at this moment in history he is unable to enact his desire, for in *Satanstoe* the power is gathered on the side of the gentry. Later, in an America which Cooper saw endangered

[11]See McAleer, "Biblical Analogy in the Leatherstocking Tales," *passim.* [*Nineteenth-Century Fiction* 17 (December 1962), pp. 217-35.-Ed.] Also see Cooper's severe attack on Puritanism in *The Wept of Wish-ton-Wish.*

by the common man, legal distinctions would break down and
boundaries would be crossed with impunity. Jason's presence in this
novel represents the first intrusion of the "outside," and his own as
well as his descendants' influence will grow to dangerous proportions in later periods represented in *The Chainbearer* and *The Redskins* (in the latter novel, Jason's grandson attempts to burn the
Ravensnest estate). But in *Satanstoe,* Cooper contains these forces
just as he contains the Indians' fire; Jason is rendered ineffectual,
even laughable. Like Thomas Hutter in *The Deerslayer,* he represents the potential, rather than the reality, of spoliation and does
not immediately threaten Cooper's "island."

It is true that at points throughout the novel, and again on the
final pages, the "difficulties" of the future are predicted. But as in
The Deerslayer, the integrity of the island experience is never
violated, either by fictional marauders or by Cooper himself. Instead, the distant threat to the island adds a precariousness to the
moment of the novel without disturbing its idyllic quality. We know
that the world depicted in *Satanstoe* will not remain intact forever,
yet Cooper allows the narrative to close without introducing the
destruction brought by history. The Revolution and its accompany-
ing turbulence and dislocation are still almost two decades away.
The novel concludes not on a note of "difficulty" but with a sense
of secure possession. By marrying Anneke (who is, like Corny, an
only child and therefore the sole inheritor of her family's wealth),
the young hero takes possession of her estate as well as his own. Thus
the Littlepages and Mordaunts become "one family" (501), their
holdings consolidated.

Yet there is another consolidation at least as important as this.
For the journey into the wilderness has also joined Satanstoe to
Mooseridge and Lilacsbush to Ravensnest, which is to say that the
past has been linked to the future. Cooper believed that every historical advance must be related significantly to preexisting patterns and values. The joining of the old estates to the new, with an
established American family in control of the transition, symbolizes
the ideal of cultural continuity. Cooper's futuring, or westering, is
not that of the pioneer, but that of the settler, in the fullest sense of
the term.[12] It is entirely fitting, therefore, that the novel concludes

[12]See Sidney Mead's distinction between pioneers and settlers in "The American
People: Their Space, Time, and Religion," *The Lively Experiment.*

with a return to the world of Satanstoe and Lilacsbush; this is the significance of the title, which at first may appear inappropriate. For *Satanstoe* is a book about the value of "the old place" (494), and the "return to Satanstoe" (493) is, from this point of view, the most important journey of the novel. It enacts the rhythm of continuity, the full circle of return to the center and, significantly, to the mother: "My dear mother," Corny relates, "hugged me to her heart again and again, and seemed never to be satisfied with feasting her eyes on me" (491). Unlike *The Last of the Mohicans, Satanstoe* does not conclude with the characters stranded in a ruptured moment of history in the deepest of America's wilderness. Rather, Cooper dramatizes in this novel the full return that was aborted in the earlier work.

Furthermore, the "distance" between the world explored and the world returned to is not great. While *The Last of the Mohicans* describes an irreconcilable difference between its polar geographies, the imagery of *Satanstoe* suggests union rather than division. Like *The Oak Openings,* this novel works toward a complementary rather than an oppositional relationship between civilization and nature. Corny sees Anneke's Hudson River home as "a wilderness of shrubbery" (490). Correspondingly, the "canopied space" (408) of the real wilderness contains all those valued shapes and structures that make Cooper's forest a home. And, as we have seen, the wilderness of *Satanstoe* is not the undiscovered country of *The Last of the Mohicans* but is instead a region already plotted and appropriated by the human imagination.

The return to Satanstoe, "with all its endearing ties" (490), and to "the peace and security of Lilacsbush" (443), closes the circle of the novel's action and dramatizes the centripetal force of the writer's pastoralism. Cooper always gravitates imaginatively toward an island of space which contains his most valued possessions. Such an island of "eulogized space" is defined by what Bachelard calls "its protective value." It is the kind of space "that may be grasped, that may be defended against adverse forces, the space we love."[13] In *Satanstoe,* Cooper holds and protects this island by identifying it with his own and the nation's childhood. Cooper and the reader are returned to the landscape of home, even as the novel points toward

[13][Gaston Bachelard, *The Poetics of Space* (Boston: Beacon Press 1964), p. xxxi.-Ed.]

the promise (and danger) of the future. The journey draws a circle around the fictional experience of the book and serves the same function as the perimeter of the lake in *The Deerslayer.* This is a different kind of spatial boundary from that provided by the Glimmerglass, but it just as effectively excludes "the outer world."

The structure of *Satanstoe* also creates a temporal boundary. Begun in late winter and completed in midsummer, the novel's journey depicts the nation's springtime, a time when "the buds [were] just breaking into the first green of foliage" (332). Cooper's achievement is to make this springtime a permanent fact of the imagination by framing it in a timeless moment. Although *Satanstoe* dramatizes the first stage of America's journey into the future, its temporal quality is essentially ahistorical. Just as Corny does not develop as a character, the novel's circular motion encloses its action in a narrative framework that protects it from time. The form of the trilogy provides further protection, for the back cover of the book separates its fictional space from that of *The Chainbearer* and *The Redskins.* The world of *Satanstoe* is forfeited in the two later works, but it preserves itself in our imaginations through a convincing rendering of a state of permanence.

On the final pages, Corny defends "permanent principles" and attacks the New England "craving for change" (495). He is troubled, he says, by a tendency among figures like Jason Newcome to alter place names: "I love old names, such as my father knew the same places by.... So it is with Satanstoe; the name is homely...but it is strong and conveys an idea. It relates also the usages and notions of the country; and names ought always to be preserved" (494).[14] The real issue here is theft, for if Satanstoe's name were to be "frittered away" (495) by the likes of Jason Newcome, its essential identity would also be lost. The loss of the name is the first step in the loss of the thing itself, and Cooper's great fear was that social instability, brought about by "outsiders" such as Jason, would rob him of all the things he valued. This is why he felt compelled to conclude *Satanstoe* with a soliloquy by Corny on the importance of "permanent principles." Yet the speech is hardly necessary, for the novel itself has presented a far more convincing case for permanence. It describes a world of abundance, grace, and charm made secure by its location in the valued past.

[14]Cooper often complained of changes in place names. For example, see *The Sea Lions,* pp. 488-89. Also note his "veneration for...old names" in *L&J,* 5:367.

"The American Democrat"

by John P. McWilliams, Jr.

Cooper's treatise is not so much an exposition of political convictions as it is an attempt to deal with political dilemmas posed to the perpetuation of Cooper's ideal republic by national events and personal observations of recent years. The work cannot be viewed, as it often has been, as Cooper's definitive statement of his political feelings. Because it was designed as a formal textbook, a didactic guide to government, *The American Democrat* declares its truths with ringing finality. Yet it remains, in Cooper's canon, a transitional and unsure assessment of the national condition. In order to define these political dilemmas and to determine whether the years of absence and return had at all changed Cooper's political convictions, it is essential to compare *The American Democrat* to its forerunner, *Notions of the Americans*.

At the outset one must beware of oversimplifying the comparison. The two books were written to different audiences for different purposes. *Notions of the Americans* is designed to refute prejudicial European accounts of America—most particularly those of De Roos, Adam Hodgson, and the forthcoming *Travels* of Basil Hall.[1] *The American Democrat,* addressed to Cooper's countrymen, is a catechism in the first principles of republican politics. *Notions of the Americans* does not portray an unqualified utopia nor does *The American Democrat* resort to an easy despair. Nonetheless, there is

[1]R. E. Spiller, "Introduction" to *Notions of the Americans,* (New York: Frederick Unger, 1963), I, p. v, n. 1.

a decided change from eulogy to fault finding, a change that is as much the measure of altered intent as of darkening feelings.

The American Democrat outwardly denies none of the assertions and arguments made in *Notions of the Americans;* in fact, the later work reasserts nearly every tenet of Cooper's republican faith. Rather than contradicting or retracting statements of his earlier work, Cooper reaffirms them with crucial shifts in emphasis. Although the components and principles of Cooper's ideal republic remain unchanged, the purposes for which the principles are reaffirmed are markedly different. Cooper reacts to the thrust of recent political developments, not by altering his republicanism, but by arguing that old principles work toward more restrictive ends.

The most evident change between the two works is one of tone. An ecstatic hymn has been replaced by troubled praise. The view of America as a land of virtuous, productive farmers unhampered by the trammels of government has given way to a definition of all life as "a state of probation in which the trials exceed the enjoyments" (232).[2] The democratic republic, formerly the measure of political integrity and the seed of endless social progress, is by 1838 viewed as but the least imperfect of three alternative polities.

Cooper's familiar insistence upon maximizing individual liberty is nowhere more forthright than in *The American Democrat.* It is in 1838 that Cooper declares "The very object of the institution [democracy] is the utmost practicable personal liberty" (153). Furthermore, liberty continues to be associated with a republic of strictly delegated powers in which the majority rules through voting for representatives (111-118). In 1838, as in 1828, Cooper argues that "By leaving to the citizen as much freedom of action and of being, as comports with order and the rights of others, the institutions render him truly a freeman" (228).

In other passages of *The American Democrat,* however, we find Cooper emphasizing longstanding constitutional limitations on popular freedom, limitations which *Notions of the Americans* had scarcely acknowledged. By 1838, evidently, the troubles created by legislative usurpation, demagoguery, rotation in office, and leveling to mediocrity had, in Cooper's view, reached such a point that he longed to curb the exercise of individual liberty that he equally longed to maintain. Hence we find Cooper insisting that the Ameri-

[2][References for *The American Democrat* are from the Dekker and Johnston edition (Baltimore: Penguin Books, 1969).-Ed.]

can republic proceed along a narrow and difficult path between two principles neither of which he would relinquish:

> Liberty therefore may be defined to be a controlling authority that resides in the body of a nation, but so restrained as only to be exercised on certain general principles that shall do as little violence to natural justice, as is compatible with the peace and security of society. (118)

In this quotation, government according to natural justice continues to be, as always for Cooper, the ultimate good, because it approximates divine law. The means of obtaining natural justice, however, has become less clear. Majority rule is now conceived as a possible threat to natural justice rather than its civil precondition. A suspicion Cooper is reluctant to acknowledge underlies this statement —that the enactment of natural justice may necessitate strong restraints upon the majority rule of a free people. And so, faced with this difficulty, we find Cooper beginning to redefine the meaning of liberty: "Although it is true, that no genuine liberty can exist without being based on popular authority in the last resort, it is equally true that it can not exist when thus based, without many restraints on the power of the mass" (117).

True liberty, in short, exists only in the exercise of restraints. Insisting upon this maxim much more strongly than Judge Temple, Cooper sets the limits of the legal powers of the majority:

> The majority rules in prescribed cases, and in no other. It elects to office, it enacts ordinary laws, subject however to the restrictions of the constitution, and it decides most of the questions that arise in the primitive meetings of the people; questions that do not usually effect any of the principal interests of life.
>
> The majority does not rule in settling fundamental laws under the constitution; or when it does rule in such cases, it is with particular checks produced by time and new combinations; it does not pass judgment in trials at law, or under impeachment, and it is impotent in many matters touching vested rights. (113)

Here we find Cooper clinging to the utmost of liberty and to majority rule, yet desiring to confine the powers of the majority to "questions that do not usually effect any of the principal interests of life."

The second paragraph of the quotation reveals a meaningful shift in the purposes for which Cooper continues to praise the Constitution. In *Notions of the Americans,* the Constitution had been glorified because it guaranteed the natural right of the citizen against the remote possibility of oppressive government.[3] No problem of the changeability of the Constitution arose. In *The American Democrat,* however, Cooper is beginning to consider the Constitution as a bulwark of protection for the individual against the body of his own nation:

> The power of the people is limited by the fundamental laws, or the constitution, the rights and opinions of the minority, in all but those cases in which a decision becomes indispensable, being just as sacred as the rights and opinions of the majority; else would a democracy be, indeed, what its enemies term it, the worst species of tyranny. (155)

Thus minority rights, which are presently threatened, have become of greater concern to Cooper than majority rights, which are not. Both, however, are to be upheld. As a result, Cooper is often forced into the extremely delicate position of defending majority rule, yet simultaneously praising the Constitution, because its laws inhibit the threats of the majority.

Cooper's divided leanings concerning the merits of majority rule lead him into another dilemma. On the one hand, Cooper wishes to present the Constitution and all existing bodies of civil law as static and unchanging, as fixed and permanent defenses against those who would turn public opinion into law. At the same time, however, Cooper's devotion to and knowledge of the American polity lead him to acknowledge and to honor the changeability of law: "it is a requisite of liberty, that the body of a nation should retain the power to modify its institutions, as circumstances shall require" (111).

If the true republic is to be maintained, the Constitution cannot be changed, but unless change is permitted, the very meaning of American liberty is lost. This paradox underlies the change from ringing assertion to reluctant qualification in the statement quoted previously, "The majority does not rule in settling fundamental laws, under the constitution; or when it does rule in such cases, it is with particular checks produced by time and new combinations." The dilemma is apparent elsewhere: "The constitution contains the paramount laws of society. These laws are unchangeable, except as they are altered agreeably to prescribed forms, and until thus altered, no evasion of them is admissable" (163). Nearly ten more

[3]*Notions of the Americans,* II, 12-14.

years were to pass before Cooper was to acknowledge the full horror that this very problem posed to the perpetuity of his ideal republic. In Cooper's cataclysmic novel, *The Crater,* Mark Woolston decides to remain knowingly passive while demagogues, taking advantage of Mark's adherence to his Constitution's changeability, overthrow the hierarchical, landed republic that Mark and his creator had held so dear.

In *Notions of the Americans* the American republic had not been equated with perfection, but there had been no inherent or incurable flaws in its practices or ideology. *The American Democrat* announces a startling and significant change in Cooper's thinking: "the peculiar sins of a democracy must be sought for in the democratical character of the institutions" (143). The dangers to American democracy that Cooper had foreseen in 1828 had all been extrinsic limitations upon democracy: increased severity of civil law, limitations of the franchise, loss of the individual's natural and constitutional rights.[4] By 1838, however, the chief dangers are intrinsic: popular disregard for civil statutes, demagoguery, and loose construction of the Constitution.

Cooper's heady national faith had always been founded on confidence in the corrective power of the public will. In *The American Democrat,* however, Cooper begins to single out an uncontrollable and false public opinion as the flaw most deeply ingrained within the nation: "It is a besetting vice of democracies to substitute public opinion for law. This is the usual form in which masses of men exhibit their tyranny" (130). Recognizing, as he always had, that the constituency was the ultimate source of power in America, Cooper strikes out at the ease with which democratic institutions allow public opinion to become civil law:

> The condition of this country is peculiar, and requires greater exertions than common, in extricating the mind from prejudices. The intimate connexion between popular opinion and positive law is one reason, since under a union so close there is danger that the latter may be colored by motives that have no sufficient foundation in justice.
> (134)

Acutely aware that the virtues of the democratic polity are posited upon an enlightened populace, Cooper berates all those who would undermine popular intelligence: "In a democracy, misleading the

4*Notions of the Americans,* II, 335-336.

publick mind, as regards facts, characters, or principles, is corrupting all that is dear to society at its source, opinion being the fountain whence justice, honors, and the laws, equally flow" (177).

Fear that public opinion would override law gave rise to two problems with which Cooper's mind and writings would henceforth be preoccupied. The first is a problem of causation. Cooper was continually to alternate between two conjectures. Was public opinion being corrupted because self-seeking demagogues were deluding an intelligent constituency? Or had a debased, selfish constituency created its own demagogues in order to follow them to power? Not until Cooper was sure of the true quality of the constituency could he determine whether increased legal strictures might ever be necessary. Throughout *The American Democrat* Cooper vacilates between libertarian utterances that assume a practical, rational populace, and darker forebodings assuming that the people are credulous, selfish, and ignorant.

There also arose the problem of the method of demagoguery. If public opinion were manipulated until existing statutes were openly defied, those statutes could be invoked in a court of law, and the demagogue, assuming an honest judiciary, would be quelled. What, however, if the very forms and institutions of democracy were used by the demagogue to subvert the law? These questions, present in embryo in *The American Democrat,* were to become crucial to Cooper's later social fiction. *Home As Found* and the Littlepage trilogy deal with open defiance of the law, *The Crater* and *The Ways of the Hour* with the second, and far more troubling, question of subversion.

Either way Cooper viewed the dilemma, the demagogue had become the Achilles heel of democratic government: "The true theatre of a demagogue is a democracy, for the body of the community possessing the power, the master he pretends to serve is best able to reward his efforts" (154). Or, again, "the people are peculiarly exposed to become the dupes of demagogues and political schemers, most of the crimes of democracies arising from the faults and designs of men of this character" (128). The problem Cooper faced in assessing the constituency is clearly illustrated by these statements. The second quotation presumes a deluded but innocent populace; the first, however, implies a clever willingness to be deceived.

The demagogue was becoming a figure of such ominous import

to Cooper's view of America that he felt it desirable to insert into *The American Democrat* a sketch by which he could be identified:

> The demagogue is usually sly, a detractor of others, a professor of humility and disinterestedness, a great stickler for equality as respects all above him, a man who acts in corners, and avoids open and manly expositions of his course, calls blackguards gentlemen, and gentlemen folks, appeals to passion and prejudice rather than reason, and is in all respects, a man of intrigue and deception, of sly cunning and management, instead of manifesting the frank, fearless qualities of the democracy he so prodigally professes. (155-156)

It is both important and characteristic that Cooper's demagogue turns social distinctions and social prejudices to political advantage. Exactly the same methods are used by the long series of egalitarian demagogues who attempt to upset the order of the landed gentlemen in Cooper's later fiction: Steadfast Dodge, Aristabulus Bragg, Van Tassel, Jason Newcome, Seneky Newcome, and Williams. The demagogue, like the Whig, deliberately confuses social and political rights.

With the emergence of the demagogue, the vexing question posed by *The American Democrat* becomes sharply defined. Given Cooper's commitment to republican institutions, what measures will he advocate to cope with the threatening powers of the demagogue? Throughout the book Cooper suggests four methods of defense. The most obvious is control of the demagogue by swift recourse to all existing civil statutes relating to property, libel, and minority rights. This solution, advocated constantly, need not be belabored. To adopt it meant no sacrifice of any principle of Cooper's republican faith, only a shifting toward a more legalistic habit of mind.

The second method of defense is the landed gentleman, always Cooper's measure of manly virtue and social order, who, he contends, will have the intelligence and moral fibre to resist the incursions of the demagogue. Here, however, a new difficulty arises. Cooper realizes that the landed gentleman will provide a defense only if such men retain both social position and political power. By 1838 there were signs, which Cooper could not help but acknowledge, that his revered figure was losing the necessary influence.

In outline the gentleman remains the same figure whom Cooper had so highly valued in *Notions of the Americans,* yet how different the tone with which Cooper now describes him. Compare the following passages, the first from *Notions of the Americans,* the second from *The American Democrat:*

> The American who has the advantage of early association with men of breeding, and who possesses the advantages of fortune and education, occupies a station in society that the gentleman, or nobleman, of no country of different political institutions can ever fill. He sees, and knows that he exists without a superior. He has wealth, and manner, and education, and beyond this, neither he nor any of his countrymen can go.   (11, 293)
>
> There can be no question that the educated and affluent classes of a country, are more capable of coming to wise and intelligent decisions in affairs of state, than the mass of a population. Their wealth and leisure afford them opportunities for observation and comparison, while their general information and greater knowledge of character, enable them to judge more accurately of men and measures.   (113)

The earlier passage is deliberate overstatement designed to convince the European reader. The author's tone can be assured to the verge of truculence because the gentleman in America occupies the high place he merits. The later passage is equally overstated, but the cause of overstatement is special pleading. Cooper has been forced to urge that the landed class be allowed to retain the political and social preeminence which, in *Notions of the Americans,* had been assumed. A later passage in *The American Democrat* expresses Cooper's longing somewhat less delicately: "Power cannot be extended to a *caste,* without *caste's* reaping its principal benefit; but happy, indeed, is the nation, in which, power being the common property, there is sufficient discrimination and justice to admit the intelligent and refined to a just participation of its influence" (150).

Perhaps because Cooper suspects that the landed gentleman may prove an insufficient defense, he considers, with evident reluctance, two changes in his ideal polity: limitation of the franchise and repudiation of instruction—two further defenses against the demagogue.

Universal manhood suffrage, which had seemed to Cooper one of the glories of the American polity, comes under criticism. Cooper now finds dangerous what had once seemed a great benefit—the likelihood that universal suffrage makes a government more responsive to the needs of the citizenry.

The first sign of a changing attitude is Cooper's concern with defining the word "people." In *Notions of the Americans* the word had been used loosely to mean the general populace;[5] there had been no need for a more precise definition. *The American Democrat,* however, specifies the political meaning of the term:

> In a political sense, the people means those who are vested with political rights, and, in this particular instance, the people vested with political rights, were the constituencies of the several states, under their various laws, modifications and constitutions, which is but another name for the governments of the states themselves. "We the *people,"* as used in the preamble of the constitution, means merely, "We the *constituencies* of the several states." (85-86)

Cooper's insistence on a legalistic definition of the word, like his insistence on states' rights vis-à-vis federal powers, is another means of lessening the threat of a widening majority.

Although universal manhood suffrage had never been essential to Cooper's definition of American republicanism, he had always praised it. Now, however, unless Cooper were to support limitation of the franchise, he faced the prospect of condoning greater power in the hands of undesirables less fit to govern. Faced with these alternatives, Cooper reaches no conclusion. He presents the advantages of limiting manhood suffrage, but refuses to advocate their enactment:

> The laws which control the great and predominant interests, or those which give a complexion to society, emanate from the states, which may well enough possess a wide political base. But towns and villages regulating property chiefly, there is a peculiar propriety in excluding those from the suffrage who have no immediate local interests in them. An undue proportion of the dissolute, unsettled, vicious and disorganizing, collect in towns, and that balance of society, which, under other circumstances, might neutralize their influence, is destroyed, leaving, as a consequence, the power to control their governments, under a suffrage that is universal, in the hands of the worst part of the community. (193)

Those whom Cooper considers unworthy of the franchise are precisely the class that Cooper denigrated in works ranging from *The Pioneers* to *The Ways of the Hour,* the rootless "go-ahead" com-

[5]*Notions of the Americans,* II, 23-28.

moners (Cooper also called them "birds of passage") who thrived upon stirring up excitement in stable country villages. To deprive this class of the franchise, however, would achieve the same political effect as the direct representation of property. Because Cooper remains resolutely opposed to representing property, he stops short of approving limitation of the franchise.

Finally, Cooper considers curbing the demagogue by denying the legitimacy of instruction, a term of the age which referred to the obligation of an elected representative to vote the will of his constituency. In Cooper's discussion of this question, the same duality appears. On the one hand, Cooper's commitment to the polity he calls "confederated representative democracy" (160) leads him to affirm the doctrine of instruction:

> There is no doubt it is the intention of the American system, that the will of the constitutional majorities, to a certain extent, should be properly regarded by the representative; and that when the latter, who has been elected with the express understanding that he is to support a particular measure, or a particular set of principles, sees reason to change his opinion, he would act most in conformity with the spirit of the institutions, by resigning his trust.   (160-161)

In the succeeding paragraphs, however, Cooper so qualifies his initial approval of instruction that he seems to deny it altogether. He states that "no constituency has a right to violate the honest convictions of a representative" (161) and soon concludes that "there is no pretence that the obligation to regard the wishes of his constituents is more than implied, under any circumstances; the social compact, in a legal sense, leaving him the entire master of his own just convictions" (162). Exactly where Cooper stood upon the issue of instruction was probably not quite clear even to him. *Notions of the Americans,* however, had not even raised the question; the rectitude of the popular will had been assumed. Ten years later Cooper doubted the validity of instruction because he was hoping to find a means whereby those who govern need not be responsible to the errors of popular judgment. Thus, in *The American Democrat,* Cooper's fear of the congressional demagogue is complemented by his fear of the people. On the one hand, Cooper warns us against the legislator; on the other, against his constituency.

In *Notions of the Americans,* the American's individuality had been cause for glorifying political freedoms and predicting the greatness of the American future (I, 169-172). The term "individuality," considered in a national context, had implied both the American's right to be distinctive and the strength of his separate identity. Cooper's firm commitment to American individuality is reaffirmed in *The American Democrat,* but, as the treatise unfolds, the concept is redefined and applied to a different purpose:

> The principle of individuality, or to use a less winning term, of selfishness, lies at the root of all voluntary human exertion. We toil for food, for clothes, for houses, lands, and for property, in general. This is done, because we know that the fruits of our labor will belong to ourselves, or to those who are most dear to us. It follows, that all which society enjoys beyond the mere supply of its first necessities, is dependent upon the rights of property. (187)

The meaning of individuality has blended into the spirit of possession, and the spirit of possession has in turn been declared the basis for property rights. Extending the argument to its logical conclusion, Cooper argues that retention of property is as just a tenet of natural law as liberty of action: "we may infer that the rights of property, to a certain extent, are founded in nature. The food obtained by this toil cannot be taken from the mouth of man, or beast, without doing violence to one of the first of our natural rights" (187).

Leatherstocking had, of course, argued that, in a State of Nature, natural law dictated that use of God's bounty turned it into personal property. But Judge Temple had countered that, in a State of Civilization, the civil law is the only guarantor of one's natural right to the same property. Cooper had always believed that "the first great principle connected with the rights of property, is its inviolability in all cases in which the law leaves it in possession of the proprietor" (188). What is new in *The American Democrat* is not the argument for property, but the degree of insistence upon it. The protection of personal property rights by recourse to the civil law has become the most important test of the viability of the American republic. Republicanism in such later novels as *Home As Found,* the Littlepage trilogy and *The Crater* is measured, not by the constitutional political rights of the majority, but by the constitutional property rights of the minority. After 1837 Cooper seems to have agreed with

Locke that the primary function of contractual government is the preservation of property.[6] In *The Pioneers* and *The Prairie,* Cooper had openly debated questions of land ownership before resolving them in accord with the civil law. For the Effinghams and Little- pages, however, a gentleman's deed certifies unquestionable, al- most timeless ownership.

Cooper was at no time willing to extend the meaning of "all men are created equal" beyond the domain of political rights. His firmer insistence on social and moral inequality in *The American Demo- crat* must be attributed to the fact that by 1838 inequality was being challenged in a way that the author of *Notions of the Americans* had deemed impossible. In the earlier work, social inequality between gentry and yeoman did not need to be belabored because it was recognized and honored by all. Conversely, Cooper had argued that political equality allows each man those opportunities for self- betterment that would lead to a more enlightened and able con- stituency (II, 323). By 1838, however, Cooper's defense of political equality rests upon a significantly different basis:

> All men have essentially the same rights, an equality, which, so far from establishing that "one man is as good as another," in a social sense, is the very means of producing the inequality of condition that actually exists. By possessing the same rights to exercise their re- spective faculties, the active and frugal become more wealthy than the silly and ignorant; the polished and refined more respected and sought, than the rude and vulgar.   (137)

Whether equality of rights conforms to natural justice now seems secondary; the primary advantage of political equality is that it leads to social inequality. In Cooper's eyes, the republican polity no longer allows opportunities for the self-benefit of everyone; it separates the wheat from the chaff.

In addition to Cooper's uncompromising defense of political equality and property rights, there are other ways in which com-

---

[6]*Second Treatise on Civil Government,* p. 67. Although protection of property may have become Cooper's test for republican virtue, this narrowed criterion is not incompatible with Cooper's refusal to represent property. Confining the vote to the propertied has no connection with demanding that the republic protect property rights. Dekker misleads when he argues that, in *The American Democrat,* there is "always a powerful tension, verging on contradiction, between his [Cooper's] ab- solute commitments to the defense of property and his conviction that it ought not to rule" ("Introduction" to *The American Democrat,* p. 36).

ponents of his ideal polity are reaffirmed for shifting purposes. When Cooper praises his ideal of minimizing governmental legislation, the emphasis is no longer on the blessings accruing from a scarcity of statutes, but on the strict enforcement of those that presently exist. Checks and balances continue to be celebrated as the essence of limited government, yet their purpose seems no longer the checking of excess power so much as the balancing of powers to prevent change.[7] *The American Democrat* advocates restoring the constitutional balance of powers by use of the presidential veto against Congress, but Cooper's yearning for a strong executive does not quite square with his former ideal of a nearly invisible government.

The qualities of individuality, common sense and manly independence, qualities which the Bachelor so often had noted in the American character, have shaded almost imperceptibly into selfishness, gullibility, and license. Cooper may reassert his notion that "The principal advantage of a democracy, is a general elevation in the character of the people" (121), but, a few pages later, he admits that "the tendency of democracies is, in all things, to mediocrity" (129). Truth is no longer winnowed out by the clash of opinion; it is stifled by the majority disposition to defer to the wrong. Cooper's earlier faith in future laws that would result from the daily experience of American life[8] shifts to a reliance on the long-existing body of civil statutes. *Notions of the Americans* had decried the probability of political management because the enlightened constituency was vigilant (II, 226). In *The American Democrat,* however, the demagogue clearly takes his inevitable place as the most formidable threat to republican institutions.

The American Democrat, written as a "sort of higher school book"[9] for New York State, is the work in which Cooper defines what he had meant by his aphorism "Here, the democrat is the conservative."[10] As Cooper's faith in democratic man wavers, he praises strict enforcement of the civil laws and property rights of the old order. His reliance upon republican institutions grows as his faith

[7]Contrast Cooper's insistence on balance of powers with the thrust of the following passage from the *Letter to General Lafayette:* "Checks abounded in their [the Americans'] institutions; but a *balance* was avoided, as the certain means of a hazardous contest. In every instance, they placed the people as arbiters in the last resort" (39-40).

[8]*Notions of the Americans*, II, 162.

[9]*Letters and Journals*, III, 317.

[10]*A Letter to His Countrymen*, p. 99.

in republican man fails. Moreover, he sees advantages to limitation of the franchise, a stronger executive, repudiating instruction, and curbing majority rule. He does not, however, advocate any of these measures, nor does he argue for any laws repressive to the liberties or at variance with the institutions in which he has long believed. Cooper is not willing to condone the repressive actions that might save his ideal republic from the demagogue. *The American Democrat* arrives at no new political convictions; it only shows us Cooper's realization that, in 1838, the true democrat is he who wishes to conserve the republic. In this sense, and in this sense only, can we define Cooper's American as a conservative democrat.

The Later Landscapes

by Blake Nevius

What Cooper as a visual artist learned from his travels on the
continent is apparent in the later romances. His sharpened awareness of the pictorial values to be sought in the natural landscape and
of the means by which these values could be introduced into imagined landscape is most evident in such works as *The Pathfinder,*
The Deerslayer, Wyandotté, The Oak Openings, and the Littlepage trilogy—in other words, in the forest romances written after
his return. The opening chapters of the last two Leatherstocking
tales, for example, are unforgettable simply as pictures, and both
depend for their effect on a motif that Cooper exploited most vividly
in his later works: the natural clearing, such as glade, windrow, or
oak opening, whose value was both pictorial and psychological—
pictorial by virtue of the heightened contrasts between light and
shade, open space and interminable forest, and by virtue also of the
frame it provided within which the elements of the picture could be
composed and the action of the story arrested for a moment; psychological because it provided an exhilarating relief from the claus-
trophobic experience of the woods.

The first example is from the opening chapter of *The Pathfinder:*

> The particular wind-row of which we are writing lay on the brow of a
> gentle acclivity, and it opened the way to an extensive view to those
> who might occupy its upper margin, a rare occurrence for the traveller
> in the woods. . . . On the upper margin of the opening . . . the viewless
> influence had piled tree on tree, in such a manner as had not only
> enabled the two males of the party to ascend to an elevation of some

thirty feet above the level of the earth, but, with a little care and
encouragement, to induce their more timid companions to accompany
them. The vast trunks that had been broken and driven by the force
of the gust, lay blended like jackstraws.... One tree had been completely uprooted; and its lower end, filled with earth, had been cast
uppermost, in a way to supply a sort of staging for the four adventurers.

The scene, with its pile of storm-blasted and fallen trees in the foreground and the forest prospect stretching away to the horizon,
testifies to Cooper's power to enlist the sublime when the occasion
warranted in order to emphasize the dignity and grandeur of the
American wilderness. Dead or fallen trees speak eloquently to the
imagination, as in the landscapes of Salvator Rosa; they record, as
William Gilpin observed, "the history of some storm, some blast of
lightning, or other great event, which transfers its grand ideas to the
landscape, and in the representation of elevated subjects assists
the sublime."[1] Here is one instance, moreover, in which Cooper
has been able to unite the prospect view with a striking foreground
emphasis to achieve a landscape that a painter might reproduce.

The second example is from the magnificent opening chapter of
The Deerslayer. Following the general description of the forest, we
hear human voices calling from its depths and at length a shout
proclaiming success,

> ...and presently a man of gigantic mould broke out of the tangled
> labyrinth of a small swamp, emerging into an, opening that appeared
> to have been formed partly by the ravages of the wind, and partly by
> those of fire. This little area, which afforded a good view of the sky,
> although it was pretty well filled with dead trees, lay on the side of one
> of the high hills, or low mountains, into which nearly the whole sur-
> face of the adjacent country was broken.

An example of what Cooper calls those "oases in the solemn obscurity of the virgin forests of America," the clearing provides a
natural site for the reunion of Hurry Harry March and Deerslayer,
who have become separated in their journey toward Glimmerglass;
but the effect is theatrical, as if the curtain has gone up on an empty
stage and a moment later the principal actors emerge from the wings.
Reunited, the two woodsmen plunge again into the forest and min-

---

[1][William Gilpin, *Remarks on Forest Scenery* (London, T. Cadell and W. Davies,
1808), I:9.-Ed.]

utes later emerge on the shore of the lake. At this point Cooper has the opportunity to describe in both general and precise terms the setting which will accommodate all of the subsequent action, the fabled Glimmerglass, with its surface "so placid and limpid that it resembled a bed of the pure mountain atmosphere, compressed into a setting of hills and woods." This description, like many that occur later in the narrative, emphasizes the influence of picturesque theory on Cooper's visual imagination.

The general outline of the lake, which is about three leagues in length, meets the requirements of the picturesque; its margin is irregular, "being dented by bays and broken by many projecting points," and its banks are festooned with bushes and small overhanging trees. "The effect," writes Cooper, donning his landscape gardener's hat, "was precisely that at which the lover of the picturesque would have aimed, had the ordering of this glorious setting of forest been submitted to his control. The points and bays, too, were sufficiently numerous to render the outline broken and diversified." A quarter of a mile offshore stands Muskrat Castle, built on piles driven into a long narrow shoal submerged at a depth of six to eight feet below the surface. This is Tom Hutter's fortified dwelling, where he lives with his daughters, Hetty and Judith, and it is the central magnet around which, as with the standing rock in *The Prairie* and the fortified mound in *The Wept of Wish-ton-Wish*, the choreography of flight, capture, escape, and pursuit will be designed. Although the name "Muskrat Castle" is the facetious inspiration of a British officer, it lends itself to what I am persuaded is a serious strategy on Cooper's part. In one of many passages in his writings, similar in tone and burden, where he is citing the superiority of the old world over the new in the matter of picturesque features, his example is fortified structures:

> The necessity, in the middle ages, of building for defence, and the want of artillery before the invention of gunpowder, contributed to the construction of military works for the protection of the towns of Europe, that still remain, owing to their durable materials, often producing some of the finest effects that the imagination could invent to embellish a picture. Nothing of the sort, of course, is to be met with here, for we have no castles, have never felt the necessity of fortified towns, and had no existence at the period when works of this nature came within the ordinary appliances of society.... It is not to be denied that so far as the landscape is concerned, the customs of the

middle ages constructed much the most picturesque and striking collections of human habitations.[2]

With this emphasis in view, it seems clear that Cooper designed Muskrat Castle not simply as the central motif in a picturesque landscape but as a structure which might borrow its associations from the European past and, with the lapse of time, acquire an associational value of its own. Three separate passages encourage this inference. "As he approached the building of old Hutter," Cooper writes,

> Deerslayer thought, or rather *felt*, that its appearance was in singular harmony with all the rest of the scene. Although nothing had been consulted but strength and security, the rude, massive logs, covered with their rough bark, the projecting roof, and the form, would contribute to render the building picturesque in almost any situation, while its actual position added novelty and piquancy to its other points of interest.

Later in the narrative Tom Hutter and Hurry Harry are on board the Ark, at a distance from the Castle, as the dawn unfolds over Glimmerglass:

> Only one solitary object became visible in the returning light, that had received its form or uses from human taste or human desires, which as often deform as beautify a landscape. This was the castle; all the rest being native, and fresh from the hand of God. That singular residence, too, was in keeping with the natural objects of the view, starting out from the gloom, quaint, picturesque, and ornamental.

All the elements of the picturesque are present in these passages: the emphasis on roughness as opposed to smoothness, on the singularity (novelty) of the structure, on the contrast of the human artifact with the natural setting and, at the same time, its harmony with that setting. Fifteen years after the events of the romance are concluded, Deerslayer and Chingachgook return to the shores of Glimmerglass. "From the point," Cooper writes, "the canoe took its way toward the shoal, where the remains of the castle were still visible, a picturesque ruin." Time has done its work, and the epilogue evokes the same pleasing melancholy that the picturesque traveller derives from his experience of the more ancient and legitimate ruins

[2]*The Home Book of the Picturesque,* [(New York: G.P. Putnam, 1851), p. 66.-Ed.]

of Europe. (It is an effect Cooper will repeat in the epilogue of *Wyandotté*.) The events on Glimmerglass, exciting certainly, but of a deeper human significance that is usual in Cooper, have in retrospect conferred on the setting an associative value that, in kind if not in intensity is likewise present in Thomas Cole's Volney-like meditations on the ruin of empire when, seated on a fallen column at dusk in the Roman Campagna, he conceives his series of heroic canvases, *The Course of Empire*, and summons for his companions "a picture that found its parallel in the melancholy desolation by which, at that moment, they were surrounded."[3] Cooper had experienced his own vision on the identical site. His description of the Campagna in his Italian *Gleanings* not only echoes the thought and tone of Cole's meditation but reproduces with astonishing fidelity the scene as it appears in the painter's 1843 landscape of the Roman Campagna in the Wadsworth Atheneum:

> But that plain! Far and near it was a waste, treeless, almost shrubless, and with few buildings besides ruins. Long broken lines of arches, the remains of aqueducts, were visible in the distance; and here and there a tower rendered the solitude more eloquent, by irresistibly provoking a comparison between the days when they were built and tenanted, and the present hour.[4]

Another detail in Cooper's *Deerslayer* setting reinforces the impression that he is trying to fabricate, out of whatever materials lie at hand, associations which by attaching his American readers' imaginations to a particular place will enhance their attachment to the country as a whole, and also that, like Scott before him, he has more than one strategem for achieving this end. After Muskrat Castle, the most conspicuous feature in Cooper's survey of Glimmerglass is the so-called "rendezvous rock," shaped like a beehive or haycock and rising from the surface near the outlet of the lake at a short distance from the shore. Cooper as usual is scrupulous in fixing its appearance and location because, like the Castle, it provides a focal point for several incidents in the narrative. But unlike the Castle, the rock is an actual feature of Lake Otsego still to be seen at the northern end of the lake, standing about fifty feet from shore in water two feet deep. Like Glenns Falls in *The Last of the Mohicans*,

---

[3][Louis L. Noble, *The Course of Empire, Voyages of Life, and Other Pictures of Thomas Cole* (New York: Cornish, Lamport, and Co., 1853), p. 155.-Ed.]

[4]Cooper, *Gleanings in Europe: Italy*, II: 60.

or the "solitary and silent spring" in the same work, around which, as the reader is informed, will some day rise a fashionable spa, or the "Newport Ruin" of mysterious origin in *The Red Rover,* the rendezvous rock, in furnishing a real setting for imagined events, is translated into that realm where history and fiction become one and the "associations" which originate in the romancer's imagination survive as vividly as those established by actual history. It is only, one is tempted to claim, a matter of scale: what Scott in *The Heart of Midlothian* does for Arthur's Seat, Cooper does for a rock of more modest dimensions in his native lake. The device is so familiar as to be hardly worth noting except that Cooper, as we have seen, began his career at the moment when the question of what associations the American novelist might legitimately exploit was being aired most extensively. Cooper's forests and his strongholds, natural and man-made, his prehistoric mounds and Newport Ruins, his uprooted giants of the forest and beehive-shaped rendezvous rocks, which serve both the landscape artist and the romancer as picturesque elements and as sources of association, may be invoked to counter Cooper's lifelong complaint (as expressed in his 1850 preface to *The Red Rover*) that "the history of this country has very little to aid the writer of fiction, whether the scene be laid on the land or on the water."

In his last forest romance, *The Oak Openings* (1848), Cooper placed his action in the West beyond the frontier, as he had in *The Prairie,* in the "then unpeopled forest of Michigan," a region he had visited, though many years after 1812, when the events of the tale occur. "The American forest," he wrote, "has so often been described as to cause one to hesitate about reviving scenes that may possibly pall, and in retouching pictures that have been so frequently painted as to be familiar to every mind," but he promises that if the reader will bear with him he may discover in "the virgin forests of this widespread land...new subjects of admiration." This is not the wilderness of upper New York state; though wild, Michigan "[offers] a picture that [is] not without some of the strongest and most pleasing features of civilization." It is low and rolling country, and consequently lacking in those features readily available for picturesque representation, the mountain lakes and craggy rocks as well as the memorials of earlier habitation, the ruined forts and artificial mounds; and although wooded, "it [is] not as the American forest is wont to grow, with tall, straight trees towering towards the light, but with intervals between the low oaks that [are] scattered profusely over the view, and with much of that air of negligence that one is apt to see in grounds where art is made to assume the character of nature." In other words, the scenery is more park-like than wild, and this perception will govern Cooper's treatment of one of the central locales of the action, the Prairie Round, where the beehunter, Ben Boden, displays his skill to the Indians. The description of this "oak opening," it will be readily apparent, not only draws upon the vocabulary of the landscape gardener but presents a landscape which in its almost clipped and formal aspects would appeal more to the taste of a Capability Brown or Humphry Repton than to that of a Gilpin or Uvedale Price:

> This well-known area is of no great extent, possessing a surface about equal to that of one of the larger parks of Europe. Its name was derived from its form, which, without being absolutely regular, had so near an approach to a circle as to justify the use of this appelation. The face of this charming field was neither waving, nor what is called "rolling," nor a dead flat, as often occurs with river bottoms. It had just enough of undulation to prevent too much moisture, and to impart an agreeable variety to its plain. As a whole, it was clear of the forest; quite as much as if the axe had done its work there a thousand years before, though wood was not wanting. On the contrary, enough of the last was to be seen, in addition to that which formed the frame of this charming landscape, to relieve the view from all appearance of monotony, and to break it up into copses, thickets, trees in small clusters, and in most of the varieties that embellish local scenery. One who had been unexpectedly transferred to the spot might well have imagined that he was looking on the site of some old and long-established settlement, from which every appliance of human industry had been suddenly and simultaneously abstracted. Of houses, outbuildings, fences, stacks, and husbandry, there were no signs; unless the even and verdant sward, that was spread like a vast carpet, sprinkled with flowers, could have been deemed a sign of the last. There were the glades, vistas, irregular lawns, and woods, shaped with the pleasing outlines of the free hand of nature, as if consummate art had been endeavoring to imitate our great mistress in one of her most graceful moods.

Visually the scene lacks the high degree of definition we expect from Cooper, but this is mainly because he has relied too casually on a convention that will enable him to introduce his reader to an unfamiliar type of native landscape. The general analogy with the eighteenth-century English park, expressed in language associated with the depiction of nature in that century (the verdant swards sprinkled with flowers), hampers Cooper's intention as much as it assists it; he is more redundant that usual and to less effect.

The oak openings, of which Prairie Round is simply the most remarkable example, are another variety of those clearings that Cooper found so useful as a stage on which to mount many of his opening scenes. The theatrical metaphor that is only suggested in the opening scene of *The Deerslayer* is explicit in the parallel scene of *The Oak Openings.* One is aware from the beginning of Cooper's career of the theatrical quality of many of his episodes, a quality that lent itself so handily to the contemporary illustrator's emphasis on the foreground action—the scenes of death, partings, reunions, combat. But now, almost as if he were visualizing his episodes in terms of the early nineteenth-century American stage with its frequently elaborate scenic effects, Cooper drops easily into the theatrical analogy. The year is 1812, he tells us in the first chapter, the month July: "The sun was already approaching the western limits of a wooded view, when the actors in its [his legend's] opening scene must appear on a stage that is more worthy of a particular description."

The stage is one of the openings, and, as in the first chapter of *The Deerslayer,* the principal actors, nameless at first, are brought together in this open glade. Similarly, when in Chapter XVI Ben Boden and Corporal Flint make their nocturnal foray to spy on an Indian council, Cooper sets the stage with great care for the impressive and self-contained drama, complete with colorful dress, precisely timed entrances and exits among the characters, and oratorical set-pieces—a pageant by firelight enacted in a setting deliberately suggestive of the theater. "It [the council fire] was in the precise center of a bit of bottom land of about half an acre in extent, which was so formed and surrounded as to have something of the appearance of the arena of a large amphitheatre. There was one break in the encircling rise of ground, it is true, and that was at a spot directly opposite the station of Le Bourdon and his companion, where the rill which flowed from the spring found a passage out toward more open ground."[5] In other words, if we regard Le Bourdon (Ben Boden) and the corporal as occupying the vantage point of the audience in a theater, the single break in the amphitheater wall is at the rear center stage, and, appropriately, it is through this entrance that two of the principal actors in the drama, Scalping Peter and Parson Amen, make their appearance. How literally Cooper pursued the theatrical analogy is evident from the fact that, having concluded his "brief description of the natural accessories of this remarkable scene," he adds: "But it was from the human actors, and their aspects, occupations, movements, dress, and appearance generally, that the awe which came over both the bee-hunter and the corporal had its origin." As Henry and Margaret Ogden have noted, both Salvator Rosa and Gaspar Dughet (Poussin) often used landscape to evoke a mood "tense and somewhat theatrical in quality": "Their aim was to create a mood similar to that of the climactic moment in a stage play, and this purpose dominated their choice of figures and setting."[6] It is an effect that Hawthorne in "Ethan Brand," employing the same elements including the amphitheater and the vivid contrast between firelight (the kiln) and the surrounding darkness, can bring off without the stage manager commentary; and to recognize the difference between the two treatments is simply to emphasize Hawthorne's awareness in most of his fiction of the need, for the purposes of psychological drama, to exploit the possibilities of the close circumscription of space and of the conflict, mainly domestic, of individual wills and purposes. In *The Oak Openings* the drama is not psychological, except in the crudest terms; it moves in an opposite direction, towards melodrama, emphasizing pageant and decor. But in any case, the pictorial impulse, as in Hawthorne, is strongly and self-consciously active, and if Cooper, with his surveyor's passion for topographical accuracy, is in some respects the clumsier and less economical artist, he is, by the logic of his aims and materials, the

---

[5]The amphitheatral form provides the principle for a separate and recurrent type of ideal landscape, developed by Claude and his followers; and it can be assumed that Cooper, familiar with the tradition, is making use of the motif, not only in *The Oak Openings* but in such other works as *The Wept, Wyandotté*, and *The Crater*.

[6]Henry V. S. and Margaret Ogden, *English Taste in Landscape in the Seventeenth Century* (Ann Arbor: Univ. of Michigan Press, 1955), p. 148.

more ambitious. Except in works like *The Pioneers* and *Wyandotté*, and of course the so-called social novels, his landscapes, like the human actions with which they are associated, are by necessity greater in magnitude than Hawthorne's and more heroic than domestic.

Aside from the theatrical analogy, which Cooper could have derived as well from the theater as from the Italian tradition of landscape painting, the examples of landscape technique I have cited from the later forest romances seem to me to argue without question that Cooper's European experience not only sharpened his appreciation of landscape but gave him an aesthetic that enabled him to introduce a clarity of overall concept, composition, and detail that is lacking in his earlier generalized landscapes, whether real, ideal, or allegorical. The description of Prairie Round in *The Oak Openings* may be a lapse from his usual success, but even it suggests, to put the matter crudely, that he knows much better than he once did the kinds of pictures he is trying to compose. Glimmerglass in *The Deerslayer* is not the Glimmerglass of *The Pioneers,* and the difference is due less to the time settings than to the visual discipline that the author has acquired in the interval. And it is inconceivable that the opening chapters of *Wyandotté* could have been written prior to Cooper's European sojourn.

Chronology of Important Dates

1786   Father, William Cooper, established Cooperstown, New York.

1789   James Cooper born in Burlington, New Jersey, to William and Elizabeth (Fenimore) Cooper on September 15.

1790   Cooper family moved to Cooperstown.

1803   Entered Yale College.

1805   Dismissed from Yale for misconduct.

1806   Sailed as common sailor to England and the continent.

1808   Commissioned a midshipman in the United States Navy and stationed at Oswego on Lake Ontario. Served for three and a half years.

1809   Father died as result of blow received as he was leaving a political meeting.

1811   Married Susan Augusta DeLancey of Westchester County, New York. Lived on family land in Westchester and Otsego counties. Constructed home near Scarsdale in 1818.

1819   Last of his five older brothers died, leaving him responsible for family estates and debts.

1820   Published his first novel, *Precaution.*

1821   *The Spy.*

1822   Moved with family to New York City.

1823   *The Pioneers.*

1824   *The Pilot.*

1825   *Lionel Lincoln.*

1826   *The Last of the Mohicans;* added Fenimore to his name; sailed for Europe with his family. During the seven years abroad, his primary residence was in Paris, but he traveled widely through England, the Low Countries, Switzerland, Germany, and Italy. During this period he also developed a friendship with Lafayette.

1827   *The Prairie* and *The Red Rover.*

1828   *Notions of the Americans.*

1829   *The Wept of Wish-ton-Wish.*

1830   *The Water Witch.*

1831   Began his European trilogy with *The Bravo.*

1832   *The Heidenmauer.*

1833   *The Headsman.* Returned to the United States. Resided in New York for a time before moving his family permanently to Cooperstown.

1834   *A Letter to His Countrymen.*

1835   *The Monikins.*

1836   *Sketches of Switzerland.*

1837   *Gleanings in Europe: England.* Three Mile Point Controversy and the libel suits against the Whig press began. The suits continued through the rest of his life.

1838   *Gleanings in Europe: Italy; The American Democrat; Chronicles of Cooperstown.* Also published *Homeward Bound* and *Home as Found,* which intensified his struggles with the press.

1839   *The History of the Navy of the United States.*

1840   *The Pathfinder; Mercedes of Castile.*

1841   *The Deerslayer.*

1842   *The Two Admirals; The Wing-and-Wing.* Won judgment for libel against Horace Greeley and settlement from Thurlow Weed, but attacks continued in the press and so did Cooper's litigation.

1843   *The Autobiography of a Pocket Handkerchief; Wyandotté; Ned Myers.*

1844   *Afloat and Ashore; Miles Wallingford.*

1845   Began his defense of the landlord's position in the Anti-Rent Wars with the first two novels in the Littlepage trilogy, *Satanstoe* and *The Chainbearer.*

1846   Completed the trilogy with *The Redskins.*

1847   *The Crater.*

1848   *Jack Tier; The Oak Openings.*

1849   *The Sea Lions.*

1850   *The Ways of the Hour.*

1851   Died in Cooperstown on September 14.

Notes on the Editor and Contributors

WAYNE FIELDS, the editor of this volume, teaches at Washington University.

MARIUS BEWLEY is the author of *The Complex Fate* and *Maska and Mirrors,* as well as *The Eccentric Design.*

LESLIE A. FIEDLER, the author of *Love and Death in the American Novel,* is a novelist and literary critic who has surveyed America from a variety of perspectives. His works include *No! in Thunder* and *The Return of the Vanishing American.*

KAY SEYMOUR HOUSE is the author of *Cooper's Americans* and teaches at San Francisco State University.

ANNETTE KOLODNY, who teaches at the University of New Hampshire, is the author of *The Lay of the Land.*

D. H. LAWRENCE was not only a novelist and poet, but also a perceptive commentator on the various lands and peoples he visited. His *Studies in Classic American Literature* is a response as much to the United States as to its writers.

JOHN P. MCWILLIAMS, JR., teaches at Middlebury College, and is the author of *Political Justice in a Republic.* He is also coeditor (with George Dekker) of *Fenimore Cooper: The Critical Heritage.*

TERENCE MARTIN is the author of *The Instructed Vision: Scottish Common Sense Philosophy and the Origins of American Fiction* and teaches at Indiana University.

BLAKE NEVIUS has taught for many years at the University of California, Los Angeles. His works include, in addition to *Cooper's Landscapes,* studies of Edith Wharton, Ivy Compton-Burnett, and Robert Herrick.

VERNON LOUIS PARRINGTON made a monumental contribution to the study of American culture in his three-volume *Main Currents in American Thought.*

H. DANIEL PECK, who teaches at the University of California, Santa Barbara, is the author of *A World By Itself.*

THOMAS L. PHILBRICK is the author of *James Fenimore Cooper and the Development of American Sea Fiction.* He has also written *St. John de Crevècoeur* and teaches at the University of Pittsburgh.

DONALD A. RINGE is a member of the faculty at the University of Kentucky. His many contributions to Cooper studies include *James Fenimore Cooper* as well as *The Pictorial Mode.*

YVOR WINTERS had a remarkable career as both a teacher and a critic. The author of *The Function of Criticism, Maule's Curse,* and *In Defense of Reason,* he was also a poet.

Selected Bibliography

This bibliography is a very brief introduction to Cooper scholarship. For a more detailed examination see James Franklin Beard's chapter on Cooper in *Fifteen American Authors before 1900: Bibliographic Essays on Research and Criticism.* More recent criticism is surveyed annually in *American Literary Scholarship.*

Dekker, George. *James Fenimore Cooper: the Novelist.* London: Routledge & Kegan Paul, 1967.

Grossman, James. *James Fenimore Cooper.* New York: William Sloane Associates, 1949.

House, Kay Seymour. *Cooper's Americans.* Columbus, Ohio: Ohio State University Press, 1965.

McWilliams, John P., Jr. *Political Justice in a Republic: James Fenimore Cooper's America.* Berkeley, Calif.: University of California Press, 1972.

Nevius, Blake. *Cooper's Landscapes: An Essay on the Picturesque Vision.* Berkeley, Calif.: University of California Press, 1976.

Peck, H. Daniel. *A World by Itself: The Pastoral Moment in Cooper's Fiction.* New Haven, Conn.: Yale University Press, 1977.

Philbrick, Thomas. *James Fenimore Cooper and the Development of American Sea Fiction.* Cambridge, Mass.: Harvard University Press, 1961.

Railton, Stephen. *Fenimore Cooper: A Study of His Life and Imagination.* Princeton, N.J.: Princeton University Press, 1978.

Ringe, Donald A. *James Fenimore Cooper.* New Haven, Conn.: College and University Press, 1962.

—————. *The Pictorial Mode: Space and Time in the Art of Bryant, Irving, and Cooper.* Lexington, Ky.: University of Kentucky Press, 1971.

Spiller, Robert E. *Fenimore Cooper: Critic of His Times.* New York: Minton, Balch, and Company, 1931.

In addition to these book-length studies, there are a great many works on American literature that contain valuable sections on Cooper. Among these are Marius Bewley's *The Eccentric Design* (New York: Columbia University Press, 1963); Richard Chase's *The American Novel and Its Traditions* (Garden City, N.Y.: Doubleday, 1957); Leslie A. Fiedler's *Love and Death in the American Novel* (New York: Stein and Day, 1966); Harry B. Henderson's *Versions of the Past* (New York: Oxford University Press, 1974); A. N. Kaul's *The American Vision* (New Haven, Conn.: Yale University Press, 1963); Annette Kolodny's *The Lay of the Land* (Chapel Hill, N.C.: University of North Carolina Press, 1975); D. H. Lawrence's *Studies in Classic American Literature* (New York: The Viking Press, 1961); Marvin Meyer's *The Jacksonian Persuasion: Politics and Belief* (Stanford, Calif.: Stanford University Press, 1957); Vernon Louis Parrington's *The Romantic Revolution in America*, Main Currents in American Thought, vol. II, (New York: Harcourt, Brace and World, 1927); Joel Porte's *The Romance in America* (Middleton, Conn.: Wesleyan University Press, 1969); Richard Slotkin's *Regeneration through Violence* (Middleton, Conn.: Wesleyan University Press, 1973); and Henry Nash Smith's *The Virgin Land* (New York: Vintage Books, 1950).

Of special importance and value to any student of Cooper are the six volumes of *The Letters and Journals of James Fenimore Cooper*, edited by James Franklin Beard (Cambridge, Mass.: Harvard University Press, 1960, 1964, 1968).